1994

Handbook
for
Multilingual
Business
Writing

Second Edition
Revised and Updated

Handbook for Multilingual Business Writing

GERMAN • ENGLISH • SPANISH
FRENCH • ITALIAN

NTC Business Books
a division of National Textbook Company • Lincolnwood, Illinois U.S.A.

This edition first published in 1994 by NTC Business Books,
a division of NTC Publishing Group, 4255 West Touhy Avenue,
Lincolnwood (Chicago), Illinois 60646-1975 U.S.A.
Originally published by The Macmillan Press Ltd. © 1983, 1990
by Derrik Ferney, Paul Hartley, Angela Villa McLoughlin, and Gareth Thomas.

Manufactured in the United States of America.

3 4 5 6 7 8 9 0 VP 9 8 7 6 5 4 3 2 1

Inhalt, Contents, Materias, Table des matières, Sommario

DEUTSCH

Inhalt

Einleitung

Dieses Buch ist für jeden bestimmt, der englische, französische, deutsche, italienische oder spanische Geschäftsbriefe verstehen oder schreiben will. Es enthält wichtige Ausdrücke der Handelskorrespondenz in allen 5 Sprachen. Zusätzlich enthält das Buch die notwendigen Ausdrücke für Telefongespräche, das Bank- und Postwesen, und ein Städte- und Länderverzeichnis.

Das Buch ist nicht nur für diejenigen gedacht, die sich im Beruf mit Handelskorrespondenz zu befassen haben, sondern auch für Studenten und Lehrer. Die Verfasser haben dafür gesorgt, daß keine einzelne Sprache überrepräsentiert ist, und das Buch ist derart gestaltet, daß es sich sowohl für die französische Sekretärin eignet, die englische Geschäftsbriefe schreiben möchte, als auch für den italienischen Studenten, der deutsche Geschäftsbriefe verstehen will. Insgesamt sind zehn Sprachkombinationen möglich; deshalb ist das Buch eine unentbehrliche Hilfe für jede Firma, die im Import- oder Exporthandel tätig ist.

Benutzungshinweise

Das Buch besteht aus 5 verschiedenen Teilen (englisch, deutsch, französisch, italienisch, spanisch), wobei sich jeder Teil aus Abschnitten wie *Anfragen und Angebote, Bestellungen* usw. zusammensetzt. In allen Teilen ist jedem Ausdruck ein Buchstabe und eine Zahl (**A36, B39** usw.) zugeordnet, die auf den entsprechenden Ausdruck in den anderen Sprachen hinweisen. Nimmt man z.B. den englischen Ausdruck **B45** „the samples must be returned within 2 weeks", so findet man neben demselben Buchstaben und derselben Zahl in dem französischen Teil den Ausdruck „les échantillons doivent être renvoyés dans un délai de 2 semaines", in dem deutschen Teil den Ausdruck „die Muster müssen binnen 2 Wochen zurückgeschickt werden" usw.

Ist der gesuchte Ausdruck nicht zu finden dann empfiehlt sich die Verwendung eines Synonyms.

Um dem Benutzer die Auffindung eines bestimmten Wortes zu erleichtern, enthält das Buch einen Index für jede der fünf Sprachen. In jedem Index findet man neben dem Schlagwort den jeweiligen Buchstaben und die Zahl.

Ausdrücke, die in der amerikanischen Handelskorrespondenz üblich sind, sind in Klammern neben den entsprechenden englischen Ausdrücken angegeben.

A — Allgemeine Ausdrücke

A   1   Sehr geehrter Herr X
A   2   Sehr geehrte Herren
A   3   Sehr geehrter Herr X
A   4   Sehr geehrte Frau X
A   5   Sehr geehrtes Fräulein X
A   6   zu Händen von
A   7   vertraulich
A   8   Betr. (Betreff)
A   9   wir bestätigen den Empfang Ihres Schreibens
A 10   wir danken Ihnen für Ihr Schreiben
A 11   vom 3. dieses Monats (d.M.)
A 12   unter Bezugnahme auf Ihren Brief
A 13   Ihr Zeichen
A 14   unser Zeichen
A 15   Ihr Name wurde uns von Geschäftsfreunden gegeben
A 16   wir beantworten so schnell wie möglich Ihren Brief vom
A 17   wir haben keine Antwort auf unser Schreiben vom . . . erhalten
A 18   nach unserem Telefongespräch vom . . .
A 19   ich freue mich zu erfahren, daß
A 20   unser Vertreter hat uns mitgeteilt
A 21   auf Empfehlung unseres Vertreters
A 22   wir erfahren mit Bedauern, daß
A 23   Ihr Brief wurde uns von. . .weitergereicht
A 24   wir erfahren mit Interesse, daß
A 25   Ihr obenerwähnter Brief
A 26   Ihr weiter unten erwähntes Schreiben
A 27   wir werden Ihnen telefonisch mitteilen
A 28   wir werden Ihnen telegrafisch mitteilen
A 29   im Anschluß an unser Treffen am. . .
A 30   wir haben von. . .erfahren
A 31   wir bedauern, Ihnen mitzuteilen
A 32   wir freuen uns, Ihnen mitzuteilen
A 33   wir erfuhren mit Interesse
A 34   in der Anlage erhalten Sie unseren Katalog
A 35   wir bestätigen hiermit
A 36   bitte teilen Sie uns mit
A 37   bitte stellen Sie fest, warum

A 38   wir benötigen die Information für
A 39   sobald wie möglich
A 40   sobald wir . . . erhalten
A 41   unter Bezugnahme auf unser Schreiben
A 42   unter Bezugnahme auf unser Telefongespräch
A 43   zu unserem großen Bedauern
A 44   wir nehmen mit Überraschung zur Kenntnis, daß
A 45   wir wären Ihnen dankbar, wenn Sie uns . . . würden
       zukommen lassen
A 46   wir sind überzeugt, daß Sie diese Maßnahmen billigen
       werden
A 47   wir hoffen, daß es Ihnen möglich ist, . . . zu . . .
A 48   wir bedauern, nicht früher geantwortet zu haben
A 49   jetzt haben wir die Gelegenheit gehabt
A 50   wir legen . . . bei
A 51   separat
A 52   mit gleicher Post
A 53   postwendend
A 54   wir schicken Ihnen . . . zurück
A 55   die Sie uns zugeschickt haben
A 56   wir möchten Ihnen vorschlagen, daß
A 57   Sie können überzeugt sein, daß
A 58   bei Überprüfung unserer früheren Korrespondenz
A 59   es wird Sie nicht überraschen, daß
A 60   wir würden uns freuen, . . . zu . . .
A 61   wenn dies nicht möglich ist
A 62   wir haben gerade erfahren, daß
A 63   Sie werden sicher verstehen, daß
A 64   würden Sie bitte so freundlich sein
A 65   wie Sie bereits wissen
A 66   in Antwort auf Ihren Brief
A 67   unseren Akten zufolge
A 68   wir möchten Sie daran erinnern, daß
A 69   wir bedauern, Ihnen mitteilen zu müssen, daß
A 70   wie Sie in Ihrem Schreiben vom . . . gebeten haben
A 71   wir brauchen Einzelheiten über Ihre Produkte
A 72   wir würden gern Ihre Stellungnahme zu dieser
       Angelegenheit hören
A 73   wir glauben, daß es wichtig ist, daß sie
A 74   wir sorgen dafür, daß Ihnen . . . zugeschickt werden
A 75   im Anschluß an unser Gespräch mit Ihrem Vertreter
A 76   da wir Geschäftsverbindungen mit Ihnen aufnehmen
A 77   aus Ihrem Brief ersehen wir, daß

A 78 wir möchten darauf hinweisen, daß
A 79 ich hätte gern einen Termin mit Herrn X
A 80 unser Treffen am . . . muß leider ausfallen
A 81 zu Ihrer vollen Zufriedenheit
A 82 unsere Hauptstelle/Zentrale befindet sich in . . .
A 83 unsere Haupstelle/Zentrale hat ihren Sitz nach . . . verlegt
A 84 wir werden unser möglichstes tun, die Sache zu erledigen
A 85 Einzelheiten wie folgt
A 86 unser Leiter befindet sich zur Zeit auf einer Geschäftsreise
A 87 bitte teilen Sie uns möglichst bald mit
A 88 wir hoffen, daß Sie unsere Lage verstehen werden
A 89 wir bedauern sehr die Unannehmlichkeiten, die wir Ihnen bereitet haben
A 90 dies ist nicht genügend berücksichtigt worden
A 91 wir empfehlen Ihnen, das nochmals zu überlegen
A 92 wir waren von . . . beeindruckt
A 93 wir können . . . nicht annehmen
A 94 Einzelheiten über . . . finden Sie . . .
A 95 wenn wir Ihnen irgendwie dienen können
A 96 wir werden unser möglichstes tun
A 97 wir sind uns dessen bewußt, daß
A 98 wir haben Anweisungen gegeben, daß
A 99 sobald die Waren fertig sind
A 100 wenn falls Sie das Datum wissen
A 101 sobald Sie sich entscheiden, das zu machen
A 102 falls
A 103 wenn wir das gewußt hätten
A 104 in naher Zukunft
A 105 zu einem späteren Termin
A 106 wir würden uns freuen, diese Information zu erhalten
A 107 wir legen einen frankierten und adressierten Umschlag bei
A 108 anbei finden Sie einen internationalen Antwortschein
A 109 wenn nötig
A 110 rechtzeitig
A 111 Herr X hat uns an Sie verwiesen
A 112 wir haben bisher wenig Erfolg gehabt
A 113 mit gewöhnlicher Post
A 114 per Luftpost
A 115 per Einschreiben
A 116 wir bitten Sie, mit größter Umsicht vorzugehen
A 117 in zwei Wochen
A 118 deren Namen wir Ihnen gerne zuschicken würden
A 119 ihren Berichten nach zu urteilen

A 120	wir wären bereit
A 121	wir sind überzeugt, daß
A 122	wir wären an . . . interessiert
A 123	wir hoffen auf baldige Antwort
A 124	wir hoffen, Ihnen hiermit gedient zu haben
A 125	wir schätzen sehr
A 126	wir hoffen, daß Sie auch in Zukunft . . . werden
A 127	mit freundlichen Grüßen
A 128	mit freundlichen Grüßen
A 129	Anlage(n)
A 130	Unterschrift
A 131	im Auftrag (i.A.)

B—Anfragen und Angebote

B 1	wir hören, daß Sie . . . herstellen
B 2	wir sind auf die Herstellung von . . . spezialisiert
B 3	wir sind Eigentümer von
B 4	wir suchen einen zuverlässigen Lieferanten
B 5	bitte senden Sie uns vollständige Angaben über
B 6	wir interessieren uns hauptsächlich für die folgenden Artikel
B 7	bitte senden Sie mir alle Informationen, die mir helfen könnten
B 8	um die zweckdienlichste Wahl zu treffen
B 9	mehrere unserer Kunden haben Interesse an . . . geäußert
B 10	bitte senden Sie uns Prospekte über Ihre Waren
B 11	bitte senden Sie uns Ihren neuen Katalog
B 12	Ihre neueste Broschüre
B 13	Ihre neueste Preisliste
B 14	wir haben über Ihre Firma in den Handelszeitungen gelesen
B 15	wir sind seit vielen Jahren Kunden Ihrer Firma
B 16	Ihrer Anzeige entnehmen wir
B 17	unser Lagerbestand geht zu Ende
B 18	unser Lagerbestand ist erschöpft
B 19	können Sie ab Lager liefern?

B 20 wir haben auf Lager

B 21 Ihre Anfrage wegen unserer Produkte

B 22 wir benötigen die Ware bis spätestens 2. April

B 23 um uns zu helfen, Ihr Produkt auf den Markt zu bringen

B 24 wir sind bereit, Ihnen ein Sonderangebot zu machen

B 25 kürzlich, bei einem Besuch der Messe

B 26 ich sah ein Muster Ihrer Produkte

B 27 wir erlauben uns, Ihre besondere Aufmerksamkeit auf . . .
zu lenken/Sie besonders auf . . . aufmerksam zu machen

B 28 unter der Bedingung, daß

B 29 bitte senden Sie uns eine Auswahl von Artikeln aus Ihrem
Sortiment

B 30 wir haben vor, regelmäßige Bestellungen für diese Waren
aufzugeben

B 31 in großen Mengen

B 32 bitte teilen Sie uns mit, ob Sie mit einem Kauf auf Probe
einverstanden sind

B 33 wielange dürfen wir dieses Produkt zur Probe behalten?

B 34 wir sehen Ihrem Angebot mit Interesse entgegen

B 35 wir sind an Ihren Produkten interessiert

B 36 die Qualität der Waren ist von größter Bedeutung

B 37 vorausgesetzt, daß die Rohstoffpreise unverändert bleiben

B 38 unsere Waren werden sorgfältig geprüft, um Qualität zu
garantieren

B 39 auf all unsere Produkte geben wir 2 Jahre Garantie

B 40 mangelhafte Teile werden kostenlos ersetzt

B 41 auf Grund von Material—oder Arbeitsfehlern

B 42 bis 3 Monate nach Lieferung

B 43 wir nehmen Bestellungen für Mengen von mindestens . . .
entgegen

B 44 die Muster sind kostenlos

B 45 die Muster müssen binnen 2 Wochen zurückgeschickt
werden

B 46 wir werden Ihnen die Muster in Rechnung stellen

B 47 nebst Mustern

B 48 bitte senden Sie uns Muster Ihrer Produkte

B 49 von diesem Artikel können wir kein Probeexemplar
anbieten

B 50 in Kommission

B 51 zur Ansicht

B 52 wir möchten unser jetziges Sortiment erweitern

B 53 innerhalb von 4 Wochen nach Bestellung

B 54   bitte senden Sie uns ausführliche Angaben über Ihre Produkte

B 55   wir ersehen aus Ihrem Prospekt

B 56   wegen großer Nachfrage von unseren Kunden

B 57   die Artikel sind jetzt überholt

B 58   wir stellen diese Artikel nicht mehr serienmäßig her

B 59   wir schlagen vor, daß Sie sich mit . . . in Verbindung setzen

B 60   10 Motoren, Typ . . .

B 61   in folgenden Größen und Mengen

B 62   bitte geben Sie uns Ihren Preis für . . . an

B 63   wir möchten Ihre neuesten Modelle sehen

B 64   Angaben über Ihre neuesten Modelle

B 65   vorausgesetzt, daß Qualität und Preis zufriedenstellend sind

B 66   die Gewichte und Größen sind in dem illustrierten Katalog angegeben

B 67   für Bestellungen von mehr als . . .

B 68   für einen Auftrag von mindestens . . .

B 69   in den folgenden Farben

B 70   in den folgenden Mustern

B 71   nach der beiliegenden Zeichnung

B 72   ist Ihr Katalog in französischer Sprache verfügbar?

B 73   wir haben Ihr Werbematerial gesehen

B 74   bitte geben Sie uns Ihre Großhandelspreise an

B 75   Einzelhandelspreise

B 76   unsere Preise sind in der beiliegenden Liste angegeben

B 77   unsere Preise sind auf dem Muster angegeben

B 78   die angegebenen Preise sind ohne Rabatt

B 79   das sind unsere besten/niedrigsten Preise

B 80   wir können auf die Katalogpreise einen Rabatt von . . . % gewähren

B 81   wir können einen Einführungsrabatt von . . . % gewähren

B 82   können Sie uns einen Sonderrabatt gewähren?

B 83   Händlerrabatt

B 84   bitte geben Sie Ihre Zahlungsbedingungen an

B 85   unsere Preise sind gültig bis zum 8. Mai

B 86   bitte geben Sie die Preise einschließlich der Lieferung an die obengenannte Adresse an

B 87   bitte geben Sie die Preise in Pfund Sterling an

B 88   die Preise gelten zur Zeit der Lieferung

B 89   die in Ihrem Brief angegebenen Preise

B 90   Preise wie folgt

B 91	wenn Ihre Preise konkurrenzfähig sind
B 92	zum Preis von . . . das Stück
B 93	zum Sonderpreis von . . .
B 94	bitte geben Sie uns Angaben über Preise und Lieferzeiten/ Lieferfristen
B 95	das sind die niedrigsten Preise, die wir anbieten können
B 96	wir können einen Ausfuhrrabatt von . . . % gewähren
B 97	die Preise sind einschließlich Versicherung
B 98	unsere Preise sind niedriger als die der Konkurrenz
B 99	Preis pro Stück
B 100	ab Werk
B 101	ab Lager
B 102	unsere Preise verstehen sich fob London
B 103	einschließlich Verpackung
B 104	ausschließlich Verpackung
B 105	frachtfrei Madrid
B 106	frei Grenze
B 107	frachtfrei Grenze
B 108	c&f (Kosten und Fracht)
B 109	frei Waggon
B 110	cif (Kosten, Versicherung, Fracht)
B 111	fas (frei Längsseite Schiff)
B 112	frei Haus
B 113	frei Hafen
B 114	frei Lager
B 115	wir unterbreiten Ihnen gerne folgendes Angebot
B 116	können Sie uns für die Zahlung drei Wochen Ziel gewähren
B 117	wir arbeiten mit verringerter Gewinnspanne
B 118	für Großaufträge
B 119	das Angebot ist 5 Tage gültig
B 120	das Angebot ist fest bei Annahme bis zum 5. März
B 121	Zwischenverkauf vorbehalten
B 122	Preisänderungen behalten wir uns vor
B 123	wir danken Ihnen für Ihre Anfrage wegen unserer Produkte
B 124	wenn die Qualität der Waren unseren Erwartungen entspricht
B 125	wir werden Ihnen einen Probeauftrag erteilen
B 126	wenn die Waren zufriedenstellend sind
B 127	wir werden größere Aufträge erteilen
B 128	für Erstaufträge
B 129	für Nachbestellungen

B 130   solange der Vorrat reicht
B 131   Ihre Bestellung wird zu Ihrer vollen Zufriedenheit
        ausgeführt werden
B 132   unsere Verkaufsbedingungen lauten
B 133   die prompte und sorgfältige Ausführung Ihres Auftrags
B 134   wir bieten die von Ihnen genannten Waren wie folgt an
B 135   wenn Ihnen die Preise zusagen
B 136   zu den folgenden Bedingungen

C — Bestellungen

C 1   wir haben Ihr Angebot überprüft
C 2   wir haben Ihre Muster sorgfältig überprüft
C 3   die Artikel in Ihrem Katalog entsprechen unseren
        Bedürfnissen
C 4   wenn wir mit Ihrer ersten Sendung zufrieden sind
C 5   wir möchten auf Grund der uns zugeschickten Muster . . .
        bestellen
C 6   wir möchten Ihnen die folgende Bestellung erteilen
C 7   die bestellten Waren müssen sofort geliefert werden
C 8   wir sind bereit, einen Dauerauftrag aufzugeben
C 9   die Bestellung basiert auf Ihren Katalogpreisen
C 10   von den folgenden Artikeln möchten wir je 5 Stück
        bestellen
C 11   anbei finden Sie unsere Bestellung, Nummer 8765, auf . . .
C 12   bitte senden Sie uns sofort die folgenden Artikel
C 13   wir müssen darauf bestehen, daß die Waren ab Lager
        geliefert werden
C 14   wir benötigen die Waren innerhalb von zehn Tagen
C 15   wenn Sie innerhalb dieser Zeit nicht liefern können
C 16   wir beziehen uns auf unsere Bestellung vom 5. Mai
C 17   unter Bezugnahme auf unsere Bestellung Nummer 9675
C 18   wir finden Ihre Preise etwas hoch
C 19   wenn Sie Ihr Angebot um . . . % herabsetzen könnten
C 20   wir wären bereit, Ihnen die folgende Bestellung zu erteilen
C 21   Ihre Preise sind höher als die unseres früheren Lieferanten
C 22   wir können die Waren zu einem günstigeren Preis von
        einem anderen Lieferanten bekommen

C 23   wir sind einem anderen Lieferanten verpflichtet
C 24   wir haben unseren Bedarf schon gedeckt
C 25   wir haben Ihr Angebot zu spät erhalten
C 26   Ihr Muster war nicht von ausreichender Qualität
C 27   wenn Sie die Artikel in einer besseren Qualität liefern
        können
C 28   wenn Sie in kleineren Mengen liefern können
C 29   bitte teilen Sie uns die größte Menge mit, die Sie sofort
        liefern können
C 30   wir müssen Ihre Bestellung etwas ändern
C 31   wir hoffen, daß Sie diese Änderung annehmen können
C 32   Artikel Nummer 487 ist zur Zeit nicht verfügbar
C 33   wegen Probleme mit unserem Lieferanten
C 34   wegen eines Streiks
C 35   wegen eines Mangels an Rohstoffen
C 36   wegen eines Mangels an Arbeitskräften
C 37   wir sind mit unserer Produktion im Rückstand
C 38   deshalb können wir die Lieferung bis zum 4. März nicht
        garantieren
C 39   wir sind bereit, die Artikel umzutauschen
C 40   wir behalten uns das Recht vor, die Lieferung zu
        verweigern
C 41   wir möchten die Menge auf . . . erhöhen
C 42   wir können von Ihrem Angebot keinen Gebrauch machen
C 43   wir können Ihre Zahlungsbedingungen nicht annehmen
C 44   wir können Ihre Lieferungsbedingungen nicht annehmen
C 45   wir können Ihr Angebot nicht in Betracht ziehen
C 46   wir brauchen diese Artikel zur Zeit nicht
C 47   wir haben keinen Lagerraum vorhanden
C 48   zur Zeit können wir Ihre Bestellung nicht annehmen
C 49   wir sind zur Zeit mit Bestellungen überlastet
C 50   wir können erst im August mit der Herstellung beginnen
C 51   wir möchten unseren Auftrag widerrufen
C 52   wir haben unseren Auftrag telegrafisch widerrufen
C 53   bitte streichen Sie die folgenden Artikel von unserem
        Auftrag
C 54   wir behalten uns das Recht vor, den Auftrag zu widerrufen
C 55   wir haben Ihren Auftrag für unsere Waren heute erhalten
C 56   wir bestätigen Ihren Auftrag vom 12. Mai
C 57   wir werden Ihren Auftrag sobald wie möglich ausführen
C 58   Ihr Auftrag ist jetzt versandbereit
C 59   die von Ihnen bestellten Waren sind abholbereit
C 60   wir erwarten Ihre weiteren Anweisungen

C 61 bitte sorgen Sie dafür, daß die Waren abgeholt werden
C 62 wir haben mit der Herstellung der Waren begonnen
C 63 bitte bestätigen Sie den obenerwähnten Auftrag sobald wie möglich
C 64 wir benötigen ungefähr zehn Tage, um Ihren Auftrag auszuführen

D — Lieferung, Transport, Zoll

D   1 wir bestätigen den Liefertermin, den Sie in Ihrem Brief angegeben haben
D   2 wir erwarten Ihre Anweisungen bezüglich der Lieferung
D   3 wir müssen auf sofortiger Lieferung bestehen
D   4 die Lieferungsverzögerung ist auf . . . zurückzuführen
D   5 wir können die Waren sofort liefern
D   6 wir benötigen die Lieferung dringend
D   7 die Lieferungsverzögerung hat uns erhebliche Schwierigkeiten bereitet
D   8 bitte teilen Sie uns mit, wann die Lieferung erfolgen wird
D   9 unsere kürzeste Lieferzeit beträgt einen Monat
D 10 wir werden unser möglichstes tun, den Liefertermin einzuhalten
D 11 wir können die Waren früher als vereinbart liefern
D 12 unser Spediteur ist
D 13 wir werden die Waren bis Anfang Mai versandbereit haben
D 14 die Waren sind abholbereit
D 15 sobald wir Ihren Auftrag erhalten, werden wir die Waren abschicken
D 16 wir können die Waren in Containern liefern
D 17 die Lieferung erfolgt innerhalb von 4 Monaten
D 18 bitte teilen Sie uns mit, ob Sie die Waren bis zu diesem Termin liefern können
D 19 die Lieferzeit beträgt 4 Monate
D 20 die Waren müssen bis Ende nächsten Monats geliefert werden
D 21 die in unserem Brief angegebenen Liefertermine müssen eingehalten werden

D 22   die Lieferung muß rechtzeitig erfolgen

D 23   wir können die Waren nicht annehmen, wenn sie nicht rechtzeitig geliefert werden

D 24   es wird nicht möglich sein, die Waren innerhalb der vereinbarten Frist von 2 Monaten zu liefern

D 25   wir können spätestens am 5. August liefern

D 26   wir haben die Waren noch nicht erhalten

D 27   bitte teilen Sie uns den Grund für diese Verzögerung mit

D 28   Fracht bezahlt

D 29   die Sendung besteht aus

D 30   die Sendung wurde mit der 'Berlin' verschifft

D 31   das Schiff soll am 21. Juli in Dover eintreffen

D 32   wir hoffen, daß die Sendung in gutem Zustand bei Ihnen ankommt

D 33   wir haben die Sendung, die Sie am 15. März versandten, noch nicht erhalten

D 34   die Sendung, deren Lieferung Sie für den 13. Februar zugesagt hatten

D 35   wir werden alle Güter in einer einzelnen Sendung schicken

D 36   die Sendung besteht aus zwei Kisten, zu je 50 Kilo

D 37   die Verschiffung der Waren

D 38   die Waren wurden heute an Sie versandt

D 39   die Waren sind versandbereit

D 40   die Versanddokumente haben wir unserer Bank übergeben

D 41   die Waren werden am 9. Juni versandt

D 42   die Kisten sind von dem Spediteur abgeholt worden

D 43   sobald wir Ihre Anweisungen erhalten, werden wir Ihnen unsere Versandanzeige schicken

D 44   wir haben die von Ihnen bestellten Waren unserem Spediteur übergeben

D 45   in Ihrem Auftrag wird nicht angegeben, wie die Waren transportiert werden sollen

D 46   als Luftfracht

D 47   per Luftfracht

D 48   per Bahn

D 49   mit dem Flugzeug

D 50   mit dem Schiff

D 51   mit Lastkraftwagen

D 52   Transitwaren

D 53   Fracht bezahlt

D 54   ausschließlich Fracht

D 55   einschließlich Fracht

D 56 Frachtkosten
D 57 der Verschiffungshafen
D 58 der Bestimmungshafen
D 59 um Transportschäden möglichst zu beschränken
D 60 das Konnossement/die Frachtbrief
D 61 die Frachtrechnung
D 62 die Konsulatsfaktura
D 63 Verschiffungsdokumente
D 64 der Luftfrachtbrief
D 65 das Wertzeugnis
D 66 das Ursprungszeugnis war nicht in Ordnung
D 67 wir können die Waren nicht in der Weise verpacken, die
Sie angegeben haben
D 68 sorgfältige Verpackung der Waren ist erforderlich
D 69 die Verpackung muß fest sein
D 70 die Verpackung entspricht nicht unseren Anforderungen
D 71 bitte teilen Sie uns mit, ob Sie die Waren auf andere Weise
verpacken können
D 72 die Verpackung der Waren ist mangelhaft
D 73 bitte achten Sie sorgfältig auf die Verpackung
D 74 Ihre Beschwerden bezüglich der mangelhaften
Verpackung können wir nicht annehmen
D 75 Packkisten werden nicht zurückgenommen
D 76 Packkisten werden fortlaufend numeriert
D 77 Bitten um besondere Verpackung können wir leider nicht
entsprechen
D 78 wir müssen auf Verpackung der Waren in . . . bestehen
D 79 das Packpapier
D 80 die Wellpappe
D 81 die Holzwolle
D 82 innen ausgekleidet
D 83 Container
D 84 Trommeln
D 85 Ballen
D 86 Kisten
D 87 Kästen
D 88 Dosen
D 89 Gläser
D 90 Paletten
D 91 Fässer
D 92 Holzkisten
D 93 Säcke
D 94 die Kartons werden nicht zurückgenommen

D 95	die Kisten sind wie folgt zu beschriften
D 96	stoßfest
D 97	wasserdicht
D 98	gegen Schäden gesichert
D 99	vor Nässe schützen
D 100	kühl aufbewahren
D 101	hier oben
D 102	oben
D 103	unten
D 104	nicht werfen
D 105	hier öffnen
D 106	hier anheben
D 107	zerbrechlich
D 108	Vorsicht!
D 109	feuergefährlich
D 110	das Nettogewicht
D 111	das Bruttogewicht
D 112	das Eigengewicht/Leergewicht
D 113	die Verladung
D 114	die Ausladung
D 115	Gewichte und Ausmaße
D 116	das Bruttogewicht ist auf jeder Kiste angegeben
D 117	Zoll zu Lasten des Käufers
D 118	geliefert London verzollt
D 119	zollpflichtig
D 120	wir mußten einen Zoll von . . . auf die Artikel bezahlen
D 121	Sie werden einen Einfuhrzoll auf die Waren bezahlen müssen
D 122	Zoll zu Lasten des Empfängers
D 123	der Zollwert der Waren
D 124	die Zollerklärung
D 125	Zollgebühren
D 126	die Zollabfertigung
D 127	wir haben die Zollfaktura erhalten
D 128	das Zollamt in Aachen belegte die Sendung mit einer Zollstrafe
D 129	wir benötigen die Zollquittung
D 130	die Zollbehörde in Dover hat die Sendung beschlagnahmt
D 131	neue Zollbestimmungen sind in Kraft getreten
D 132	wir werden die Zollformalitäten erledigen
D 133	die Zollstrafe
D 134	das öffentliche Zollager
D 135	das private Zollager

D 136	unter Zollverschluß
D 137	die Lagerung
D 138	der Verderb
D 139	der Diebstahl
D 140	die Flughafensteuer
D 141	Hafengebühren
D 142	Umschlagsspesen
D 143	Zollgebühren
D 144	wir werden die Zollabfertigungsgebühren bezahlen

E — Rechnung, Zahlung, Mahnung

E	**1**	wir bestätigen den Empfang der Sendung
E	**2**	die Sendung ist gestern in unserer Fabrik eingetroffen
E	**3**	die Waren sind in gutem Zustand eingetroffen
E	**4**	die Sendung ist wohlbehalten bei uns eingetroffen
E	**5**	die am 4. April bestellten Waren sind rechtzeitig eingetroffen
E	**6**	als Anlage senden wir Ihnen unsere Rechnung Nr...
E	**7**	anbei finden Sie unsere Rechnung für die Ihnen am 3. Mai gelieferten Waren
E	**8**	die beiliegende Rechnung enthält die gegen Ihre Bestellung Nr. ... gelieferten Waren
E	**9**	wir bitten um baldige Begleichung der Rechnung
E	**10**	wir bitten Sie, die Rechnung bis zum 12. Mai zu begleichen
E	**11**	die Zahlung der Rechnung erbitten wir auf das Konto Nr ...
E	**12**	wir bitten um umgehende Begleichung der Rechnung
E	**13**	wir legen unseren Auszug bei
E	**14**	der zu zahlende Gesamtbetrag beläuft sich auf
E	**15**	der Rabatt ist schon in dieser Summe berechnet
E	**16**	der Rabatt ist schon abgezogen worden
E	**17**	nach Abzug von...%
E	**18**	wir haben die üblichen...% von Ihrer Rechnung abgezogen
E	**19**	wir müssen darauf hinweisen, daß Ihre Rechnung einen Fehler aufweist

E	20	Sie haben sich in Ihrer Rechnung Nr . . . verrechnet
E	21	bitte senden Sie uns eine berichtigte Rechnung
E	22	wir wären Ihnen dankbar, wenn Sie die Rechnung entsprechend berichtigen könnten
E	23	wir wären Ihnen dankbar, wenn Sie den Auszug berichtigen könnten
E	24	Ihre Rechnung gewährt einen Händlerrabatt von nur . . . %
E	25	wir haben . . . von der Rechnung abgezogen
E	26	der Fehler war auf einen Tippfehler zurückzuführen
E	27	ein Fehler in unserer Rechnungsabteilung
E	28	ein Versehen
E	29	wir bestätigen den berechtigten Saldo von . . .
E	30	wir legen eine Gutschriftsanzeige bei
E	31	die Belastungsanzeige
E	32	für Ihre baldige Begleichung wären wir dankbar
E	33	wir hoffen, Ihre Zahlung innerhalb der nächsten Woche zu erhalten
E	34	bitte senden Sie uns den fälligen Betrag in den nächsten Tagen
E	35	wir möchten Sie daran erinnern, daß unsere Zahlungsbedingungen. . . . sind
E	36	wir verweisen Sie auf unsere Zahlungsbedingungen
E	37	Dokumente gegen Akzept
E	38	per Nachnahme
E	39	Kasse gegen Dokumente
E	40	Zahlung im voraus
E	41	das Dokumentenakkreditiv
E	42	ein Dokumentenakkreditiv zu Ihren Gunsten
E	43	der dokumentäre Wechsel
E	44	widerruflich
E	45	unwiderruflich
E	46	bestätigt
E	47	unbestätigt
E	48	die Dokumententratte
E	49	der Sichtwechsel
E	50	der Nachsichtwechsel
E	51	der Datowechsel
E	52	Zahlung bei Erhalt der Ware
E	53	zum gegenwärtigen Wechselkurs
E	54	bar
E	55	Scheine
E	56	Münzen

E 57 gesetzliche Währung
E 58 Giroüberweisung
E 59 der Zahlungsempfänger
E 60 der Gläubiger
E 61 der Schuldner
E 62 der Solawechsel
E 63 der Handelskredit
E 64 zahlbar bei der . . . Bank
E 65 ein 60-Tage-Wechsel
E 66 ein Akkreditiv in Höhe von . . . , bei der . . . Bank zu eröffnen
E 67 wir haben unsere Bank angewiesen, Ihnen den fälligen Betrag zu zahlen
E 68 wir haben den Betrag von . . . auf Ihr Konto eingezahlt
E 69 wir haben diesen Betrag Ihrem Konto gutgeschrieben
E 70 wir haben unsere Bank angewiesen, den Betrag auf Ihr Konto zu überweisen
E 71 wir haben den Betrag von . . . auf Ihr Konto überwiesen
E 72 in Begleichung Ihres Kontos/Ihrer Rechnung
E 73 unser Konto bei . . . Bank
E 74 wir legen einen Scheck über . . . bei
E 75 ein gekreuzter Scheck/ein Verrechnungsscheck
E 76 ein Barscheck
E 77 eine Postanweisung
E 78 der Scheck ist eingelöst worden
E 79 ein Scheck auf Ihr Konto
E 80 beiliegend finden Sie einen Scheck über . . . zum Ausgleich Ihrer Rechnung
E 81 £600, abzüglich £45 für Verpackung
E 82 wir legen einen Scheck über die Hälfte des Betrags bei
E 83 die Banküberweisung
E 84 der Bankscheck
E 85 der Betrag ist Ihrem Konto gutgeschrieben worden
E 86 bitte senden Sie uns sobald wie möglich eine Quittung
E 87 wir bestätigen den Eingang Ihrer Zahlung
E 88 wir danken Ihnen für Ihre Zahlung
E 89 wir haben Ihre Tratte akzeptiert
E 90 Ihre Zahlung in Höhe von . . . ist bei unserer Bank eingegangen
E 91 wir danken Ihnen für Ihre prompte Begleichung unserer Rechnung
E 92 wir haben Ihre Zahlungsanzeige erhalten
E 93 Ihr Konto ist jetzt seit mehr als vier Wochen überfällig

E 94	Ihre Rechnung ist noch offenstehend
E 95	wir erwarten Ihre Zahlung
E 96	Ihr Konto weist noch einen Minusbetrag von . . . auf
E 97	die offenstehenden Rechnungen müssen bis Ende dieses Monats beglichen werden
E 98	wir haben noch nicht den Restbetrag unseres Septemberauszugs erhalten
E 99	da unser Auszug vielleicht verlorengegangen ist, legen wir eine Kopie bei
E 100	bitte teilen Sie uns den Grund für die Zahlungsverzögerung mit
E 101	da der fällige Betrag seit langer Zeit offensteht
E 102	bis jetzt haben wir auf unsere Bitte um Zahlung keine Antwort erhalten
E 103	wir bitten Sie, diese Angelegenheit sobald wie möglich zu erledigen
E 104	trotz unserer wiederholten Zahlungsaufforderungen
E 105	um den fälligen Betrag einzuziehen
E 106	Sie haben unsere Erinnerungsbriefe nicht beachtet
E 107	unsere Rechnungen müssen künftig sofort beglichen werden
E 108	Sie sind uns noch . . . schuldig
E 109	wir müssen Sie daran erinnern, daß wir bei Erstaufträgen nur zwei Wochen Ziel gewähren
E 110	wir möchten darauf hinweisen, daß die Zahlung am 4. Juli fällig war
E 111	dies ist unsere letzte Mahnung
E 112	wir müssen jetzt auf sofortiger Begleichung bestehen
E 113	wenn wir die Zahlung bis Anfang nächsten Monats nicht erhalten
E 114	Ihre Lieferungsverzögerung können wir nicht annehmen
E 115	die Rechnung ist verlorengegangen
E 116	wir werden gerichtliche Schritte unternehmen
E 117	der Betrag wird durch unseren Rechtsanwalt eingezogen
E 118	wir werden den fälligen Betrag durch unseren Rechtsanwalt einziehen lassen
E 119	wir müssen Schritte zur Einziehung des fälligen Betrags unternehmen
E 120	auf dem Klageweg
E 121	wir haben die Angelegenheit unserem Rechtsanwalt übergeben
E 122	wir werden Ihnen eine zusätzliche Zahlungsfrist von 12 Tagen einräumen

E 123	wir wären bereit, eine Teilzahlung anzunehmen
E 124	Sie haben um einen Zahlungsaufschub gebeten
E 125	wir hoffen, daß Sie Verständnis für unsere Lage haben
E 126	wir sind bereit, einen Zahlungsaufschub zu gewähren

F — Beschwerden

F 1	die am 3. dieses Monats gelieferten Artikel waren nicht die von uns bestellten
F 2	wir bedauern, uns über Ihre Sendung Nr . . . beschweren zu müssen
F 3	wir möchten auf einen Fehler in der Sendung hinweisen, die wir gestern erhalten haben
F 4	die Artikel waren in der falschen Farbe
F 5	sie waren in den falschen Größen
F 6	sie entsprachen nicht den Zeichnungen, die wir Ihnen zugeschickt hatten
F 7	die Qualität der Waren hat unsere Erwartungen nicht erfüllt
F 8	wir waren von der Qualität der Waren enttäuscht
F 9	aus diesen Gründen können wir die Waren nicht annehmen
F 10	die Artikel waren mangelhaft
F 11	Sie haben uns 500 . . . geschickt, statt der 250, die wir bestellt hatten
F 12	es hat einen Fehler in der Erledigung unserer Bestellung gegeben
F 13	der Inhalt der Kisten stimmt nicht mit der Versandanzeige überein
F 14	in der Sendung fehlte Artikel Nr . . .
F 15	die Waren entsprechen nicht den Mustern
F 16	die Artikel scheinen einer anderen Bauart zu sein
F 17	die Kisten waren zerbrochen
F 18	die Waren waren durch Feuer beschädigt
F 19	die Waren waren durch unsachgemäße Behandlung beschädigt
F 20	die Waren sind beschädigt angekommen
F 21	schwer beschädigt

F 22	einige Waren waren verkratzt
F 23	zerbrochen
F 24	leicht beschädigt
F 25	durch Hitze beschädigt
F 26	durch Wasser beschädigt
F 27	die Waren müssen während des Transports beschädigt worden sein
F 28	sie müssen schlecht verpackt worden sein
F 29	das Verpackungsmaterial entsprach nicht den üblichen Normen
F 30	die Kisten hätten mit Metallbändern befestigt werden sollen
F 31	die Kisten waren schlecht gebaut
F 32	die Artikel weisen Rost auf
F 33	die Schäden sind auf dem Transportweg zwischen dem britischen Zoll und unserer Fabrik eingetreten
F 34	die Schäden sind vor der Ankunft der Waren in Dover eingetreten
F 35	wir müssen Sie bitten, uns sobald wie möglich Ersatz zu schicken
F 36	das hat uns erhebliche Schwierigkeiten bereitet, da wir die Waren dringend brauchten
F 37	wir brauchen die übrigen Artikel dringend
F 38	wir bedauern, daß alle Artikel ersetzt werden müssen
F 39	wir sind bereit, die Waren zu behalten
F 40	zu einem ermäßigten Preis von ... das Stück
F 41	wir lassen die ganze Sendung an Sie zurückgehen
F 42	wir senden Ihnen einen Teil der Sendung zurück
F 43	wir senden Ihnen alle während des Transports beschädigten Artikel zurück
F 44	wir müssen jetzt die Bestellung widerrufen
F 45	wir sind bereit, die beschädigten Artikel abzunehmen, wenn Sie den Preis um . . . % herabsetzen
F 46	wir können die beschädigten Artikel nur zu einem erheblich reduzierten Preis verkaufen
F 47	alle Artikel müssen ersetzt werden
F 48	wir hoffen, daß Sie in Zukunft solche Fehler vermeiden werden
F 49	dies hat uns Schwierigkeiten mit einer Anzahl unserer Kunden bereitet
F 50	wir schlagen vor, daß Sie sich mit dem Spediteur in Verbindung setzen
F 51	die Schiffahrtsgesellschaft

F 52 die Eisenbahngesellschaft

F 53 die Fluggesellschaft

F 54 wir glauben daß es Ihnen obliegt, weitere Erkundigungen einzuholen

F 55 wir müssen um Entschädigung bitten, um unsere Verluste zu decken

F 56 wir müssen auf Entschädigung bestehen

F 57 wir müssen Sie bitten, uns den Wert der beschädigten Waren gutzuschreiben

F 58 wir werden unsere Lage hinsichtlich künftiger Bestellungen neu überlegen müssen

F 59 wir haben Ihre Beschwerde überprüft

F 60 da die Schäden während des Transports eingetreten sind

F 61 wir bitten Sie, die Sache mit . . . aufzunehmen

F 62 dies ist das erste Mal, daß wir mit diesem Spediteur zusammenarbeiten

F 63 unsere Versicherung deckt die Mängel, die Sie erwähnen

F 64 unsere Garantie deckt diese Schäden

F 65 nach den Bedingungen unserer Garantie

F 66 Sie dürfen Rückvergütung des schon bezahlten Betrags verlangen

F 67 wir bitten vielmals um Entschuldigung wegen dieses Fehlers

F 68 wir sind bereit, die Waren gegen solche gleicher Qualität umzutauschen

F 69 wir legen einen Scheck über . . . als Rückerstattung bei

F 70 wir werden die Waren auf unsere Kosten ersetzen

F 71 wir bedauern, daß die Sendung nicht zufriedenstellend war

F 72 wir sind bereit, Ihnen einen Rabatt von . . . % anzubieten

F 73 wir haben Ihre Rechnung um . . . % gekürzt

F 74 wir haben die Waren sehr sorgfältig überprüft

F 75 wir können keinen Mangel mit den Waren finden

F 76 wir können die Verantwortung für die Schäden nicht annehmen

F 77 wie Sie aus den Vertragsbedingungen ersehen werden

F 78 wir bedauern, daß wir die Waren nicht zurücknehmen können

F 79 wir schlagen vor, daß Sie die Angelegenheit der Versicherungsgesellschaft melden

F 80 wir müssen darauf hinweisen, daß die Garantiefrist abgelaufen ist

F 81 Sie müssen die Schiffahrtsgesellschaft bitten, die Schäden aufzunehmen

F 82 wir brauchen einen Bericht von dem Spediteur mit
Angabe der Schäden
F 83 unter diesen Umständen können wir Ihre Beschwerde
nicht annehmen

G — Vertretungen

G 1 wir suchen einen Vertreter für den Verkauf unserer
Waren im Ausland
G 2 wir brauchen einen Vertreter für den Verkauf unserer
Waren
G 3 wir suchen einen Vertreter für unsere Zweigstelle in . . .
G 4 der Vertreter muß ausschließlich für uns arbeiten
G 5 er muß sich dazu verpflichten, nicht für unsere
Konkurrenten zu arbeiten
G 6 und muß seine Tätigkeit auf dieses Gebiet beschränken
G 7 seine Hauptaufgabe würde darin bestehen, den Kunden
unsere Kataloge und Muster vorzuführen
G 8 für diese Stelle sind Fachkenntnisse erforderlich
G 9 wir brauchen einen Fachvertreter
G 10 Fachkenntnisse sind nicht erforderlich
G 11 wir bilden unsere Vertreter selbst aus
G 12 wir sind eine kleine Firma, die . . . herstellt
G 13 diese Artikel haben ausgezeichnete Absatzmöglichkeiten
G 14 wir erfahren, daß Sie beträchtliche Erfahrung in dem
Verkauf von Artikeln dieser Art besitzen
G 15 wären Sie in der Lage, diese Waren auf dem italienischen
Markt einzuführen?
G 16 wir möchten diesen Artikel auf dem deutschen Markt
einführen
G 17 wir glauben, daß im Ausland eine große Nachfrage nach
solchen Waren besteht
G 18 Sie vertreten schon mehrere britische Firmen
G 19 Ihre Aufgabe würde darin bestehen, diesen Markt für uns
auszuweiten
G 20 wir wären bereit, im Durchschnitt . . . pro Jahr für
Werbung auszugeben

G 21   wir erwarten, daß Sie in Ihren Ausstellungsräumen unser ganzes Warensortiment zeigen

G 22   der Vertreter wird Werbematerial kostenlos erhalten

G 23   wir sind die Alleinvertreter

G 24   die Alleinvertretung

G 25   wir sind Handelsvertreter/Komissionäre/ Kommissionsvertreter

G 26   wir brauchen Verkaufsbüros in Spanien

G 27   wir sind Vertragshändler

G 28   Verkaufsvertreter

G 29   hauptberufliche Vertreter

G 30   nebenberufliche Vertreter

G 31   der Zwischenhändler/die Mittlerfirma

G 32   der Konsignatar/Verkaufskommissionär

G 33   das Konsignationslager/Kommissionslager

G 34   Konsignationswaren

G 35   der Exportvertreter

G 36   der Einkaufsvertreter

G 37   der Auftraggeber

G 38   wir sind überzeugt, daß Ihre Waren hierzulande einen guten Absatz finden werden

G 39   wir haben erfahren, daß Sie einen Vertreter für Frankreich suchen

G 40   wir haben auf diesem Gebiet viel Erfahrung

G 41   wir möchten uns um die Vertretung bewerben

G 42   wir haben schon viele ähnliche Firmen mit Erfolg vertreten

G 43   wir haben gute Beziehungen zu den großen Warenhäusern in London

G 44   wir haben die Absicht, den deutschen Markt intensiv zu bearbeiten

G 45   wir sind bereit, den Kundendienst zu übernehmen

G 46   wir sind keiner anderen Firma in diesem Land verpflichtet

G 47   wir verpflichten uns, mit keinem Ihrer Konkurrenten zu arbeiten

G 48   wir wären auch bereit, Sie über den Verkauf und die Werbung der Waren zu beraten

G 49   wir haben ein weites Netz von Geschäftsbeziehungen in Frankreich

G 50   wir sind bereit, Ihnen die Vertretung zu übertragen

G 51   der Vertrag ist zunächst auf...Jahre beschränkt

G 52   der Vertrag kann um ein weiteres Jahr verlängert werden

G 53   jede Partei hat das Recht, den Vertrag zu widerrufen

G 54 mit einer Kündigungsfrist von . . . Monaten

G 55 es gibt eine Probezeit von . . . Monaten

G 56 Sie bekommen die Vertretung auf Probe

G 57 wir übertragen Ihnen das Alleinverkaufsrecht

G 58 wir können Ihnen einen Wagen zur Verfügung stellen

G 59 bitte teilen Sie uns binnen. . . Wochen mit, ob Sie diese Bedingungen annehmen können

G 60 wir haben schon einen Vertretervertrag mit einer anderen Firma abgeschlossen

G 61 wir können Ihnen die Vertretung unserer Erzeugnisse für Frankreich übertragen

G 62 wir werden Ihnen ausführliche Auskünfte über alle unsere Produkte zukommen lassen

G 63 unser Werbematerial muß ins Französische und ins Englische übersetzt werden

G 64 wir nehmen an, daß Sie diese Dokumente würden übersetzen lassen

G 65 wenn Sie es vorziehen, können wir die Übersetzung selbst veranlassen

G 66 wir werden Ihnen das Werbematerial zur Verfügung stellen

G 67 auf unsere Kosten

G 68 Spesen werden von unserer Firma erstattet

G 69 der Vertreter muß für seine Spesen selbst aufkommen

G 70 das Verkaufsgebiet des Vertreters

G 71 wir werden Werbematerial in französischer Sprache zur Verfügung stellen

G 72 wir werden eine intensive Werbekampagne durchführen

G 73 wir sind bereit, einen Teil der Kosten zu übernehmen

G 74 alle von dem Vertreter abgeschlossenen Geschäfte

G 75 Waren werden in Kommission verkauft

G 76 unsere Vertreter arbeiten auf Provisionsbasis

G 77 wir bieten ein Fixum von . . . , zuzüglich einer Provision von . . . %

G 78 es ist in unserer Firma nicht üblich, ein Fixum zu bezahlen

G 79 die gewöhnliche Provisionsrate für Auslandsvertreter beträgt . . . %

G 80 diese Provision wird auf alle Aufträge bezahlt, die durch Sie oder Ihre Zwischenhändler erteilt werden

G 81 auf alle Aufträge aus Ihrem Gebiet erteilen wir Provision

G 82 die Provision wird bei Erhalt des in der Rechnung angegebenen Betrags bezahlt

G 83 die Provision wird alle Ihre Spesen einschließen

G 84 unter der Bedingung, daß Sie uns eine ausführliche Spesenaufstellung schicken

G 85 wir werden Ihre Spesen gegen Vorlage der Quittungen rückvergüten

G 86 Spesen für die Bewirtung von Kunden werden zurückerstattet

G 87 die Provision beträgt . . . % des Umsatzes

G 88 wir bieten eine Provision von . . . % auf alle von Ihnen vermittelten Geschäfte

G 89 die Verkaufsprovision

G 90 die Provision wird vierteljährlich abgerechnet

G 91 die Provision ist auf alle Aufträge zahlbar

G 92 wir ziehen es vor, am Ende jedes Quartals abzurechnen

G 93 wir ziehen monatliche Abrechnungen vor

H — Referenzen

H 1 Herr . . . hat sich um die Stelle als . . . bei unserer Firma beworben

H 2 er hat Sie als Referenz angegeben

H 3 wir wären dankbar, wenn Sie uns Auskünfte über Herrn X geben könnten

H 4 Auskünfte über seinen Charakter und seine Fähigkeiten

H 5 seine Zuverlässigkeit

H 6 waren Sie mit seiner Arbeit zufrieden?

H 7 diese Stelle erfordert ein hohes Maß an Integrität

H 8 die Stelle stellt hohe Anforderungen

H 9 wir brauchen einen anpassungsfähigen Mitarbeiter

H 10 wir werden Ihre Auskunft mit größter Verschwiegenheit behandeln

H 11 er arbeitet seit 5 Jahren bei unserer Firma

H 12 er ist nur seit kurzer Zeit bei unserer Firma tätig

H 13 er arbeitet seit seinem Schulabschluß bei uns

H 14 er wurde von uns als . . . ausgebildet

H 15 er arbeitete für uns von Juni 19 . . . bis August 19 . . .

H 16 er verließ unsere Firma nach 3 Jahren, um im Ausland zu arbeiten

H 17	er wurde als . . . beschäftigt
H 18	ihm wurde vor 4 Jahren gekündigt
H 19	er wurde im April 19 . . . entlassen
H 20	er war ein leistungsfähiger Arbeiter/tüchtiger Mitarbeiter
H 21	er war völlig zuverläßig
H 22	ehrlich und fleißig
H 23	pünktlich
H 24	er wirkt sympathisch
H 25	er hat Fachkenntnisse auf dem Gebiet des/der
H 26	er ist ehrgeizig
H 27	er hat sich ohne Zweifel aus diesem Grund um diese Stelle beworben
H 28	in unserer Firma gibt es zur Zeit nur wenige Aufstiegsmöglichkeiten
H 29	er hat bei seiner Arbeit viel Initiative gezeigt
H 30	er war immer bei guter Gesundheit
H 31	er war nicht fleißig
H 32	er war nicht sehr zuverläßig
H 33	er fehlte oft bei der Arbeit
H 34	er kam oft spät zur Arbeit
H 35	er war nicht sehr pünktlich
H 36	er arbeitete oft nachlässig
H 37	aus gesundheitlichen Gründen
H 38	gesundheitlich hatte er gewisse Schwierigkeiten
H 39	und das hat seine Arbeit beeinflußt
H 40	ich kann ihn deshalb nicht ohne Bedenken empfehlen
H 41	er hat nur wenig Initiative gezeigt, und er arbeitet langsam
H 42	er ist sehr unzuverlässig
H 43	seine Arbeit war im allgemeinen zufriedenstellend
H 44	seine Arbeit war immer von sehr hoher Qualität
H 45	seine Arbeit war immer von höchster Qualität
H 46	er ist immer seinen Obliegenheiten/Verpflichtungen zu unserer vollsten Zufriedenheit nachgekommen
H 47	wir empfehlen ihn bedenkenlos
H 48	seine Arbeit war oft nicht zufriedenstellend
H 49	leider können wir Ihnen keine Auskunft über diesen Bewerber geben
H 50	wir kennen ihn erst seit kurzer Zeit
H 51	wir kennen ihn seit 10 Jahren
H 52	und wir freuen uns, daß er uns als Referenz angegeben hat
H 53	wir schlagen deshalb vor, daß Sie sich mit . . . in Verbindung setzen

H 54	sie müßten Ihnen ausführliche Auskunft über ihn geben können
H 55	die Firma . . . hat uns gerade einen großen Auftrag erteilt
H 56	sie hat uns gebeten, ihr einen Kredit einzuräumen
H 57	sie hat uns Ihren Namen als Referenz angegeben
H 58	da wir zum erstenmal mit dieser Firma geschäftlich tätig sind
H 59	wir wären für Auskünfte über ihre finanzielle Lage dankbar
H 60	und über ihre langfristigen Zukunftsaussichten
H 61	mittelfristig
H 62	kurzfristig
H 63	über ihre Konkurrenzfähigkeit auf dem Binnenmarkt
H 64	der Außenmarkt
H 65	wie ist ihr Ruf im Inland und im Ausland?
H 66	Auskunft über ihre Kreditwürdigkeit und Zuverlässigkeit
H 67	für jede Auskunft, die Sie uns über die Firma geben könnten, wären wir Ihnen dankbar
H 68	wir glauben, daß Sie die Firma seit einiger Zeit kennen
H 69	könnten wir, nach Ihrer Meinung, ihnen einen Kredit in Höhe von . . . einräumen?
H 70	ohne Stellung von Sicherheiten
H 71	in dieser Angelegenheit sichern wir Ihnen größte Verschwiegenheit zu
H 72	wir werden Ihre Auskunft streng vertraulich behandeln
H 73	zu Gegendiensten sind wir stets gern bereit
H 74	diese Firma ist uns seit 6 Jahren bekannt
H 75	wir sind seit 5 Jahren in Geschäftsbeziehungen mit der Firma
H 76	sie zählen zu unseren regelmäßigen Kunden
H 77	sie sind seit vielen Jahren Geschäftsfreunde von uns
H 78	die Firma genießt einen ausgezeichneten Ruf
H 79	ihre Vermögenslage ist gut
H 80	die Firma verfügt über beträchtliche finanzielle Mittel
H 81	diese Firma ist völlig zuverlässig
H 82	die Firma ist ihren Verpflichtungen immer pünktlich nachgekommen
H 83	wir sind sicher, daß Sie diesen Kredit ohne Bedenken einräumen können
H 84	in den letzten Monaten mußten wir mehrere Zahlungsaufforderungen an diese Firma schicken
H 85	sie sind uns noch . . . schuldig

H 86 sie haben unsere Rechnungen vom vergangenen Jahr noch nicht beglichen

H 87 sie befinden sich in einer schwierigen finanziellen Lage

H 88 ihr Kapital ist nicht ausreichend

H 89 es wäre nicht ratsam, dieser Firma Kredit zu gewähren

H 90 wir raten Ihnen zur Vorsicht

H 91 diese Auskunft wird ohne jede Haftung erteilt

H 92 diese Firma ist uns unbekannt

H 93 wir haben nur wenig Auskunft über diese Firma

H 94 wir glauben, daß die Firma erst vor kurzem gegründet wurde

H 95 wir sind leider nicht in der Lage, Sie in dieser Sache zu beraten

H 96 wir bedauern, daß wir die von Ihnen erbetene Auskunft nicht geben können

H 97 wir kennen die Firma nicht lang genug

H 98 wir müssen Sie deshalb an . . . verweisen

I — Stellenangebote und Bewerbungen

I 1 wir sind eine gut etablierte Firma mit Hauptsitz in Südengland

I 2 wir suchen . . .

I 3 wir brauchen . . .

I 4 wir haben Stellen für . . .

I 5 zum Eintritt am 8. Oktober

I 6 um einen unserer Vertreter zu ersetzen

I 7 um unseren Exportleiter zu ersetzen, der in den Ruhestand tritt

I 8 wir brauchen einen Mitarbeiter, der Erfahrung auf dem Gebiet der Exportverkäufe hat

I 9 wir brauchen einen erfahrenen Verkäufer

I 10 wir brauchen einen Mitarbeiter zwischen 25 und 35

I 11 er muß mindestens 5 Jahre Erfahrung auf dem Gebiet der/des . . . haben

I 12 englische Sprachkenntnisse wären erwünscht

I 13 Fremdsprachenkenntnisse sind erforderlich

I 14 der Bewerber/der gesuchte Kandidat muß zur Zusammenarbeit im Team fähig sein

I 15 er muß sich den Bedürfnissen verschiedener Kunden anpassen können

I 16 und anderen Mitarbeitern Verantwortung übertragen können

I 17 wir suchen einen sehr anpassungsfähigen Mitarbeiter

I 18 der unsere Exportabteilung leiten soll

I 19 mit dieser Stelle steht Ihnen ein Firmenwagen zur Verfügung

I 20 wir sind bereit, ein Gehalt von mindestens . . . zu zahlen

I 21 das Gehalt erfolgt nach Alter und Berufserfahrung

I 22 Gehalt nach besonderer Vereinbarung

I 23 das Jahresgehalt beträgt nicht weniger als . . . /das Gehalt beträgt nicht weniger als . . . jährlich

I 24 monatlich

I 25 das Nettogehalt beträgt . . .

I 26 das Bruttogehalt ist . . .

I 27 eine Prämie wird bezahlt

I 28 ungefähr . . . % werden für Steuer abgezogen

I 29 für soziale Sicherung/Krankenversicherung

I 30 das Gehalt ist steuerfrei

I 31 Unterkunft wird von der Firma kostenlos zur Verfügung gestellt

I 32 6 Wochen Urlaub pro Jahr

I 33 der bezahlte Urlaub

I 34 eine 35-Stunden-Woche

I 35 eine 6-Tage-Woche

I 36 in unserer Firma gilt eine Gleitzeitregelung

I 37 Bewerber müssen bereit sein, Überstunden zu leisten

I 38 die Firma hat ihre eigene Pensionskasse

I 39 bitte geben Sie die Namen von zwei Personen, die bereit sind, Auskunft über Sie zu geben

I 40 eine Referenz muß von Ihrem jetzigen Arbeitgeber sein

I 41 wir brauchen auch eine Referenz von Ihrem Bankdirektor

I 42 Ihrer Anzeige in der/dem . . . entnehme ich

I 43 ich habe von Geschäftsfreunden erfahren

I 44 ich habe Ihre Anzeige letzte Woche im/in der . . . gelesen

I 45 ich möchte mich um diese Stelle bewerben

I 46 bitte schicken Sie mir nähere Angaben über diese Stelle

I 47 mit einem Bewerbungsformular

I 48 wie Sie aus dem beiliegenden Lebenslauf ersehen werden

I 49 ich bin mit dieser Arbeit sehr vertraut

I 50 ich habe auch an mehreren Konferenzen über dieses Thema teilgenommen

I 51 ich glaube, daß ich die Anforderungen dieser Stelle erfüllen kann

I 52 ich bin gegenwärtig bei einer Exportfirma beschäftigt

I 53 ich suche eine ähnliche Stelle

I 54 ich möchte jetzt meine Stelle wechseln

I 55 ich möchte für ein größeres Unternehmen arbeiten

I 56 mit internationalen Beziehungen

I 57 um meine Berufschancen zu verbessern

I 58 aus persönlichen Gründen

I 59 ich suche eine Stelle mit mehr Verantwortung

I 60 ich möchte im Ausland arbeiten

I 61 ich möchte meine Beförderungschancen verbessern

I 62 ich suche eine Stelle mit besseren Aufstiegschancen

I 63 ich möchte meine Fremdsprachenkenntnisse anwenden

I 64 ich spreche fließend Deutsch und Französisch

I 65 in Englisch habe ich Grundkenntnisse

I 66 ich bin in . . . qualifiziert

I 67 ich habe ein Diplom in . . .

I 68 ich habe einen akademischen Grad in . . . erworben

I 69 . . . Worte/Anschläge pro Minute schreibe ich auf der Maschine

I 70 in Kurzschrift schreibe ich . . . Worte/Silben pro Minute

I 71 ich habe mit Mikrocomputern gearbeitet

I 72 ich habe an einer Textverarbeitungsmaschine gearbeitet

I 73 ich bin in . . . geboren

I 74 ich besuchte die Schule in . . .

I 75 wo ich die folgenden Prüfungen bestand

I 76 in den folgenden Fächern

I 77 ich studierte an der Universität in . . .

I 78 wo ich . . . als Hauptfach studierte

I 79 mit . . . als Nebenfach

I 80 ich habe das Abschlußexamen in den folgenden Fächern bestanden

I 81 ich habe das Staatsexamen bestanden

I 82 mit Auszeichnung

I 83 ich bin in den folgenden Prüfungen durchgefallen

I 84 dann war ich 4 Jahre bei einer Exportfirma tätig

I 85 ich verbrachte 3 Jahre im Ausland

I 86 ich wurde 19 . . . zum Abteilungsleiter befördert

I 87 ich wurde 19 . . . entlassen

I 88 ich bin seitdem arbeitslos
I 89 ich nahm an Abendkursen in . . . teil
I 90 ich wurde als zweisprachige Sekretärin/
Fremdsprachenkorrespondentin ausgebildet
I 91 falls Sie mich zu einem Vorstellungsgespräch einladen
möchten
I 92 ich könnte jederzeit bei Ihnen vorsprechen
I 93 ich kann mich nur freitags vorstellen
I 94 könnte ich mich zu einem späteren Termin vorstellen?
I 95 ich könnte mich ab dem 16. Juni vorstellen
I 96 ich bitte Sie, meine Bewerbung wohlwollend zu
prüfen/berücksichtigen
I 97 ich sende Ihnen anbei ein Dienstzeugnis von meinem
früheren Arbeitgeber
I 98 beiliegend finden Sie Kopien von Dienstzeugnissen von
meinen letzten zwei Arbeitgebern
I 99 und Kopien meiner Diplomzeugnisse
I 100 in der Anlage gebe ich die Namen von zwei Personen, die
bereit sind, jede gewünschte Auskunft über mich zu geben
I 101 die folgenden haben sich bereit erklärt, Auskunft über
mich zu erteilen
I 102 ich wäre Ihnen dankbar, wenn Sie sich mit meinem
gegenwärtigen Arbeitgeber nicht in Verbindung setzen
würden
I 103 vor dem Vorstellungsgespräch
I 104 ohne meine vorherige Zustimmung
I 105 ich lege einen frankierten und adressierten Umschlag bei
I 106 ich lege einen internationalen Antwortschein bei
I 107 ich gebe Ihnen gerne nähere/weitere Auskünfte
I 108 ich habe mich um die Stelle als. . . beworben
I 109 und ich wäre dankbar, wenn Sie bereit wären, Referenzen
für mich zu geben

J — Anschriftenänderung usw.

J 1 unser Hauptsitz ist nicht mehr in London
J 2 unsere Zentrale ist nach Frankfurt verlegt worden
J 3 wir haben eine neue Zweigstelle in Madrid eröffnet

J	4	wegen der ständigen Ausweitung unserer Firma
J	5	wir sind in ein neues und größeres Gebäude in Bordeaux umgezogen
J	6	das bedeutet, daß wir all unseren Kunden besser dienen können
J	7	wir versichern Ihnen, daß die Qualität unserer Dienstleistungen unverändert bleibt
J	8	unsere Anschrift hat sich geändert
J	9	und lautet jetzt wie folgt
J	10	bitte schicken Sie alle Post an diese Adresse
J	11	bitte teilen Sie Ihrer Versandabteilung diese Anschriftenänderung mit
J	12	unsere Telefonnummer hat sich geändert
J	13	unsere Telefonnummer ist jetzt . . .
J	14	wir haben den Namen unserer Firma geändert
J	15	der Name er Firma ist jetzt . . .
J	16	wir haben mit der Firma . . . fusioniert
J	17	ab dem 14. Mai ist unser neuer Name . . .
J	18	wir sind nicht mehr in diesem Geschäftszweig tätig
J	19	wir stellen diese Artikel nicht mehr her
J	20	wir haben die Herstellung dieser Artikel vor drei Jahren eingestellt
J	21	wir sind jetzt nur auf die Herstellung von . . . spezialisiert
J	22	Firma . . . & Co hat die Herstellung dieser Artikel übernommen
J	23	unsere Fabrik in Turin wird im März abgebaut/abgerissen
J	24	und wir verlegen unsere Produktion nach Zürich
J	25	wir haben unsere Fabrik in Birmingham stillegen müssen
J	26	wir haben unsere Exportabteilung geschlossen
J	27	wir schlagen vor, daß Sie sich mit unserer Dachorganisation in Verbindung setzen
J	28	unsere befreundete Firma in Paris
J	29	wir sind von . . . übernommen worden
J	30	. . . haben . . . % der Aktien unserer Firma erworben
J	31	die Firma wurde liquidiert
J	32	wir haben vor 6 Monaten das Geschäft aufgelöst
J	33	die Firma hat Konkurs gemacht
J	34	der Konkursverwalter ist eingesetzt worden
J	35	Herr . . . ist zum . . . befördert worden
J	36	er ist jetzt stellvertretender Direktor
J	37	er ist Leiter unserer neuen Exportabteilung in Wien
J	38	er ist Mitglied des Vorstandes geworden
J	39	er ist in eine andere Zweigstelle versetzt worden

J	40	Herr...ist nicht mehr bei dieser Firma tätig
J	41	er ist in eine andere Firma eingetreten
J	42	er ist im August in den Ruhestand getreten
J	43	unser Direktor, Herr..., ist vor sechs Monaten gestorben
J	44	er ist durch Herrn...ersetzt worden
J	45	sein Aufgabenbereich ist von Herrn...übernommen worden

K — Reisen und Hotelreservierungen

K	1	ich möchte einen Platz im Zug von Paris nach Heidelberg reservieren
K	2	Abfahrt Paris 13.45, Ankunft Heidelberg 19.55
K	3	der Schnellzug
K	4	der TEE
K	5	ist in diesem Zug eine Platzreservierung erforderlich?
K	6	Platzreservierung ist in allen Schnellzügen erforderlich
K	7	dieser Zug fährt nicht an Staatlichen Feiertagen
K	8	der Zug fährt nur an Werktagen
K	9	der Nahverkehrszug
K	10	der Sonderzug
K	11	der Entlastungszug
K	12	der Zug fährt ab Gleis 6
K	13	ein Fensterplatz
K	14	in einem Nichtraucherabteil
K	15	der Liegewagen
K	16	der Schlafwagen
K	17	der Speisewagen
K	18	der Büffetwagen
K	19	Paßkontrolle im Zug
K	20	möchten Sie erster Klasse fahren?
K	21	ein Platz in einem Abteil erster Klasse
K	22	wann kommt der Zug in . . . an?
K	23	in der Anlage sende ich Ihnen eine Kopie meiner beabsichtigten Route

K 24	eine einfache Fahrkarte
K 25	eine Tagesrückfahrkarte
K 26	eine Rückfahrkarte
K 27	eine Bahnsteigkarte
K 28	ist dieser Zug zuschlagpflichtig?
K 29	gibt es eine Gepäckaufbewahrung auf dem Bahnhof?
K 30	wo sind die Schließfächer?
K 31	wo ist das Fundbüro?
K 32	ist diese Fahrkarte für alle Buslinien gültig?
K 33	der Fahrschein ist nicht übertragbar
K 34	kann ich für die Buslinien eine Monatskarte kaufen?
K 35	eine Mehrfahrtenkarte
K 36	wann fährt das Schiff von Calais ab?
K 37	die Autofähre
K 38	bitte senden Sie mir Informationen über Ihre Autofährdienste
K 39	das Luftkissenboot/das Hovercraft
K 40	eine Zweibettkabine
K 41	eine Kabine erster Klasse
K 42	ich möchte Plätze für einen Wagen und 2 Passagiere reservieren lassen
K 43	können Sie für eine Gruppe von 20 Personen eine Fahrpreisermäßigung anbieten?
K 44	auf der Fähre von Dover nach Calais
K 45	um wieviel Uhr ist Flug Nr . . . nach . . . ?
K 46	der Charterflug
K 47	der Linienflug
K 48	ich möchte 3 Plätze im erstmöglichen Flug nach . . . reservieren
K 49	ab welchem Terminal fliegt die Maschine?
K 50	werden während des Flugs Mahlzeiten serviert?
K 51	Economy Class
K 52	Club Class
K 53	bitte bestätigen Sie Ihre Reservierung 24 Stunden vor dem Abflug
K 54	sind die Flughafensteuern in dem Preis eingeschlossen?
K 55	das Handgepäck
K 56	die Stewardeß
K 57	der Steward
K 58	Getränke werden während des Flugs serviert
K 59	Passagiere müssen sich mindestens 45 Minuten vor dem Abflug am Terminal melden
K 60	ich suche ein Zimmer in der mittleren Preislage

K 61	ich möchte ein Einzelzimmer mit Bad reservieren
K 62	ein Doppelzimmer
K 63	ein Zweibettzimmer
K 64	mit Dusche
K 65	mit WC und Dusche
K 66	bitte teilen Sie mir den Preis eines Einzelzimmers mit
K 67	in der Hochsaison
K 68	in der Vorsaison
K 69	in der Nachsaison
K 70	vom 19. bis zum 30. April
K 71	nehmen Sie Gruppen an/sind Gruppen bei Ihnen willkommen?
K 72	ich möchte im Oktober eine Konferenz unserer Verkaufsvertreter organisieren
K 73	und ich suche ein passendes Hotel in der Nähe des Flughafens
K 74	wir möchten mit dem Bus vom Flughafen abgeholt werden
K 75	wir möchten mit dem Bus zum Hotel gebracht werden
K 76	der Preis eines Doppelzimmers für 3 Übernachtungen ist . . .
K 77	das sind Inklusivpreise
K 78	einschließlich Frühstück
K 79	die Halbpension
K 80	die Vollpension
K 81	einschließlich Bedienung und Mehrwertsteuer
K 82	das Trinkgeld
K 83	bitte geben Sie den Inklusivpreis an
K 84	alle Zimmer haben Zentralheizung
K 85	alle Zimmer mit fließendem Kalt- und Warmwasser
K 86	das Frühstück kann bis 10 Uhr eingenommen werden
K 87	das Hotel hat seinen eigenen Parkplatz
K 88	die Tiefgarage
K 89	das Parkhaus
K 90	es gibt einen Parkplatz in unmittelbarer Nähe
K 91	das Hotel liegt sehr ruhig
K 92	es hat Konferenzeinrichtungen/Konferenzräume
K 93	es hat einen Konferenzraum für 100 Personen
K 94	es ist nicht weit vom Stadtzentrum
K 95	wie weit ist das Hotel vom Flughafen?
K 96	fahren die Linienbusse zum Flughafen?
K 97	es ist nur wenige Minuten vom Stadtzentrum
K 98	es ist in einem ruhigen Vorort
K 99	neben dem Fluß

K 100	es hat einen Fahrstuhl
K 101	der Nachtportier
K 102	es hat eine Wechselstube
K 103	ich schreibe, um meine Reservierung zu bestätigen
K 104	bitte senden Sie mir ein Menü und eine Weinkarte
K 105	bitte teilen Sie mir mit, ob eine Anzahlung erforderlich ist
K 106	bitte schicken Sie die Rechnung an meine Firma...
K 107	ich muß leider meinen Abreisetag ändern
K 108	und ich werde erst am 21. Juli in ... ankommen
K 109	ich muß meine Reservierung in Ihrem Hotel rückgängig machen/stornieren

L — Immobilienmarket: Verkauf und Vermieten

L 1	Haus zu verkaufen
L 2	Haus zu vermieten
L 3	die Wohnung
L 4	das Appartement
L 5	die Luxuswohnung/das Penthouse
L 6	die Villa
L 7	das Einzelhaus
L 8	der Bungalow
L 9	das Doppelhaus
L 10	das Reihenhaus
L 11	zwei Schlafzimmer, Wohnzimmer, Küche, Badezimmer, Garage, Garten
L 12	wir möchten ein Haus für ungefähr 18 Monate mieten
L 13	bitte teilen Sie uns die Miete für eine solche Wohnung mit
L 14	die Miete beträgt ... monatlich
L 15	jährlich
L 16	wenn Sie bereit sind, die Wohnung für 2 Jahre zu mieten
L 17	wir können Ihnen eine Ermäßigung von ... % bieten
L 18	wir suchen Büroräume im Stadtzentrum
L 19	wir möchten ein Haus im Stadtzentrum kaufen
L 20	wir sind bereit, höchstens ... zu bezahlen
L 21	in bester Nachbarschaft

L 22 im Vorort
L 23 im Grünen/inmitten von Grünanlagen
L 24 weitere Auskunft erhalten Sie von . . .
L 25 Hypotheken stehen zur Verfügung
L 26 Anleihen stehen zur Verfügung
L 27 zu einem Zinssatz von . . . %
L 28 zinslos
L 29 zu einer Miete von . . . monatlich
L 30 zum Preis von . . . pro Quadratmeter
L 31 wir können eine Hypothek arrangieren/vermitteln/ besorgen
L 32 ein Darlehen kann durch unsere Versicherungsgesellschaft arrangiert werden
L 33 wir haben mehrere Ferienhäuser in Südfrankreich zu verkaufen
L 34 kostenlose Besichtigungsflüge
L 35 das Time-Sharing

M — Geschäftsberichte

M 1 die Versammlung wird im Hauptsitz der Gesellschaft stattfinden
M 2 die jährliche Hauptversammlung
M 3 unsere diesjährige Hauptversammlung findet am 3. Juli statt
M 4 die ordentliche Hauptversammlung
M 5 eine außerordentliche Versammlung ist einberufen worden
M 6 die Tagesordnung für die jährliche Hauptversammlung
M 7 Besprechungspunkte
M 8 Diverses
M 9 die folgenden nahmen an der Versammlung teil:
M 10 der Generaldirektor
M 11 der Vorsitzende
M 12 der Verkaufsleiter
M 13 der Exportleiter
M 14 der Auslandsvertreter
M 15 der Personalleiter

M	16	die Vertreter der Arbeiter
M	17	die Gewerkschaftsmitglieder
M	18	die Aktieninhaber
M	19	der Vorstand
M	20	Protokollführung . . . /für die Protokollführung war . . . verantwortlich
M	21	der Vorsitzende hieß die Aktieninhaber willkommen
M	22	und legte den Bericht für das letzte Geschäftsjahr vor
M	23	und legte das Protokoll der letzten Versammlung vor
M	24	wir haben die Produktion gesteigert
M	25	die Produktion ist gestiegen
M	26	wir haben unsere Produktion um . . . % gegenüber dem Vorjahr gesteigert
M	27	und wir haben neue Arbeitsplätze geschaffen
M	28	unser Umsatz erhöhte sich um . . . %
M	29	die Umsatzzunahme/Umsatzsteigerung
M	30	unseren Export erhöhten wir um . . . %
M	31	wegen eines Anstiegs der Investitionen/wegen erhöhter Investitionen
M	32	wir haben beträchtliche Mittel in unseren Fabriken investiert
M	33	wir haben unseren Marktanteil erhöht
M	34	unsere Waren fanden einen guten Absatz in anderen europäischen Ländern
M	35	um unsere Marktposition zu festigen
M	36	wir müssen unsere Marktposition ausbauen
M	37	der Außenmarkt
M	38	der Binnenmarkt
M	39	unsere größten Absatzmärkte sind Frankreich und Italien
M	40	unsere Verkäufe in Deutschland haben sich günstig entwickelt
M	41	mit einem Inlandsabsatz von . . .
M	42	unser Gesamtabsatz stieg von . . . auf . . .
M	43	unser Gesamtabsatz sank von . . . auf . . .
M	44	auf längere Sicht erwarten wir günstige Absatzmöglichkeiten
M	45	wir haben unsere vorhandenen Kapazitäten voll ausgeschöpft
M	46	wir müssen unseren Vorsprung in diesem Bereich behaupten
M	47	unser langfristiges Investitionsprogramm

M 48   wird uns ermöglichen, die Qualität unserer Erzeugnisse
       zu verbessern

M 49   unser Entwicklungsprogramm

M 50   kurzfristig

M 51   mittelfristig

M 52   wir erwarten eine Steigerung unseres Geschäftsvolumens

M 53   unser Anlagevermögen stieg um . . . %

M 54   das Fremdkapital

M 55   unser Umlaufvermögen nahm um . . . % zu

M 56   das Unternehmen hat sein Stammkapital auf . . . erhöht

M 57   eine erhöhte Dividende von . . . je Aktie wurde gezahlt

M 58   der Ertrag

M 59   der Gewinn

M 60   der Nettogewinn

M 61   der Gewinn nach Abzug der Steuern

M 62   das Unternehmen erhöhte seinen Gewinn um . . . % im
       ersten Quartal

M 63   die Zuwachsrate

M 64   der allgemeine Konjunkturabschwung

M 65   hat die Nachfrage beeinträchtigt

M 66   im zweiten Halbjahr schwächte sich die Nachfrage ab

M 67   und wir sind auf Absatzschwierigkeiten gestoßen

M 68   es hat einen Rückgang der Produktion gegeben

M 69   wir müssen mit einem leichten Rückgang der Produktion
       rechnen

M 70   unser Export/Exportvolumen ist gesunken/
       zurückgegangen

M 71   und das hat unsere Wachstumschancen verringert

M 72   die Verteuerung der Energie und anderer Rohstoffe

M 73   hat sich nachteilig ausgewirkt

M 74   die Konkurrenz hat sich auch verschärft

M 75   wegen Konkurrenz von anderen Firmen in dieser
       Branche/diesem Bereich

M 76   unsere Konkurrenzfähigkeit ist geschwächt worden

M 77   Personalkosten waren auch sehr hoch

M 78   letztes Jahr verzeichnete das Unternehmen einen Verlust
       von . . .

M 79   unsere Verluste in bestimmten Bereichen waren
       besonders schwer

N — Bedienung des Telefons

N   1   ich möchte mit Herrn . . . sprechen
N   2   bleiben Sie bitte am Apparat
N   3   der Anschluß ist besetzt
N   4   ich verbinde gleich/jetzt
N   5   hier . . . / . . . am Apparat
N   6   auf Wiederhören
N   7   Herr . . . ist im Augenblick nicht da
N   8   möchten Sie eine Nachricht für ihn hinterlassen?
N   9   können Sie ihm die folgende Nachricht geben?
N 10   hier automatischer Anrufbeantworter
N 11   können Sie mich bitte mit . . . verbinden?
N 12   ich rufe von einer Fernsprechkabine an
N 13   bitte hängen Sie den Hörer ein und wählen Sie noch
         einmal
N 14   das Ortsgespräch
N 15   das Ferngespräch
N 16   das Auslandsgespräch
N 17   das R-Gespräch
N 18   ich möchte ein R-Gespräch nach . . . anmelden
N 19   ich möchte ein Gespräch mit Voranmeldung
N 20   das Telefonbuch
N 21   Sie müssen die Nummer im Telefonbuch nachschlagen
N 22   die Auskunft
N 23   ich hätte gern die Rufnummer der Firma . . .
N 24   können Sie mir die Vorwahl für Manchester geben?
N 25   ich habe eine schlechte Verbindung
N 26   ich muß einhängen
N 27   Sie können die Nummer selbst wählen
N 28   ich muß die Nummer nochmals wählen
N 29   ich habe die falsche Nummer gewählt/habe mich verwählt
N 30   es ist jemand in unserer Leitung
N 31   das Gespräch wurde unterbrochen
N 32   der Freiton/das Freizeichen
N 33   der Besetzton/das Besetztzeichen
N 34   Sie müssen beim Wählen die '0' weglassen
N 35   Ich rufe aus England an
N 36   Ich rufe später zurück

O — Bank und Postamt

O 1   ich möchte ein Sparkonto eröffnen
O 2   ein laufendes Konto
O 3   ein Sparkonto
O 4   ein gemeinsames Konto
O 5   ein Konto ist in Ihrem Namen eröffnet worden
O 6   wie ist der gegenwärtige Zinskurs?
O 7   wie hoch sind die Bankgebühren?
O 8   das Scheckbuch
O 9   der Dauerauftrag
O 10   mein Konto ist bei der . . . Bank
O 11   meine Kontonummer ist...
O 12   ich habe ein Postscheckkonto
O 13   ich möchte . . . auf mein Konto überweisen
O 14   ich möchte mein Konto auflösen
O 15   ich möchte . . . abheben
O 16   Abhebungen in dieser Höhe sind nicht sofort verfügbar
O 17   ich möchte...auf mein laufendes Konto einzahlen
O 18   Ihr Konto ist überzogen
O 19   und Ihr Überziehungskredit ist auf...begrenzt
O 20   Sie haben diesen Kredit jetzt überschritten
O 21   ich möchte diesen Scheck einlösen
O 22   kann ich diese Reiseschecks hier einlösen?
O 23   ich möchte diesen Scheck auf mein Konto einzahlen
O 24   ich möchte einen Tagesauszug
O 25   Auszüge werden monatlich an Sie geschickt
O 26   wie (hoch) ist mein Saldo im Augenblick?
O 27   (das) Haben
O 28   (der) Soll
O 29   ein langfristiges Darlehen
O 30   kurzfristig
O 31   der Zahlungsempfänger
O 32   die Sparkasse
O 33   die Bausparkasse
O 34   die Kreditkarte
O 35   die Euroscheck-Karte
O 36   fünf Briefmarken zu . . . , bitte
O 37   ich möchte dieses Paket nach Frankreich schicken
O 38   per Luftpost
O 39   mit gewöhnlicher Post

O	40	mit Paketpost
O	41	per Einschreibepost/Einschreiben
O	42	als Eilzustellung
O	43	Sie müssen eine Zollerklärung ausfüllen
O	44	ich möchte ein Telegramm nach . . . schicken
O	45	per Telex
O	46	postlagernd
O	47	ich möchte eine Postüberweisung in Höhe von . . . aufgeben
O	48	Postfach Nummer . . .
O	49	die Postleitzahl

P — Versicherung

P	1	ich möchte eine Versicherung abschließen
P	2	die Personenversicherung
P	3	die Sachversicherung
P	4	die Versicherungsgesellschaft
P	5	der Versicherte, Herr . . . , hat uns gebeten, . . . zu . . .
P	6	ich habe Ihren Brief an die Schadensabteilung weitergeleitet
P	7	in der Anlage erhalten Sie eine Deckungsbestätigung
P	8	ich brauche einen Versicherungsantrag
P	9	die Police werden Sie bald erhalten
P	10	die Police muß von unserem Hauptsitz ausgestellt werden
P	11	wir legen die Bedingungen der Police bei
P	12	die Policenummer ist . . .
P	13	Sie müssen uns den Namen des Versicherungsnehmers geben
P	14	die Police hat eine Laufzeit von . . .
P	15	ich möchte meine Police erneuern
P	16	ich habe meine Police gekündigt
P	17	die Versicherungssumme beträgt . . .
P	18	die monatliche Prämie beträgt . . .
P	19	die Versicherung deckt . . .
P	20	der Versicherungsanspruch
P	21	der Schaden
P	22	die höhere Gewalt/Force Majeure

P 23   die Feuerversicherung
P 24   die Kraftfahrzeugversicherung
P 25   die Haftpflichtversicherung
P 26   die Vollkaskoversicherung
P 27   die Reiseversicherung
P 28   Sie müssen eine grüne Versicherungskarte besitzen
P 29   Sie müssen den Unfall bei unserem Hauptsitz/Stammhaus
        melden
P 30   Sie müssen die Namen der Zeugen feststellen
P 31   die Unfallversicherung
P 32   die Reisegepäckversicherung
P 33   die Krankenversicherung
P 34   der Versicherungsmakler

Q — Büroeinrichtungen und Informationstechnologie

Q   1   der Aktenschrank
Q   2   die Kartei
Q   3   das Diktiergerät
Q   4   der Schreibtisch
Q   5   der Telexapparat
Q   6   die programmierbare Schreibmaschine/elektronische
        Schreibmaschine
Q   7   der Mikrocomputer
Q   8   der Bildschirm/Datenbildschirm
Q   9   die Textverarbeitungsmaschine/der Textautomat
Q 10   die Tastatur
Q 11   die Taste
Q 12   der Computer-Terminal
Q 13   die Diskette/die Floppy-Disk
Q 14   das Diskettenlaufwerk
Q 15   der Datenspeicher
Q 16   der Speicher
Q 17   der Silikon-Chip
Q 18   der Mikroprozessor
Q 19   der Taschenrechner
Q 20   der Korrekturlack/die Korrekturflüssigkeit

Q 21 der Datumsstempel
Q 22 die Büroklammer
Q 23 die Heftklammer
Q 24 die Heftmaschine
Q 25 der Bleistiftspitzer
Q 26 die Frankiermaschine
Q 27 der Notizblock
Q 28 die Sammelmappe
Q 29 der Drucker
Q 30 die Photokopiermaschine
Q 31 die Informationstechnologie
Q 32 der Bildschirmtext/Viewdata
Q 33 das System entspricht den Normen der internationalen Telekommunikationen
Q 34 es kann von einem Telefon in Ihrem Büro angesprochen werden
Q 35 das elektronische Telefonverzeichnis kann vom Terminal abgefragt werden
Q 36 ein Modem bildet die Schnittstelle mit dem Telekommunikationsnetz
Q 37 der Zwei-Wege-Kommunikation zwischen Computern
Q 38 das System verfügt über elektronische Post und Mailbox
Q 39 mit diesem Modell kann man in einem Brief verschiedene Textblöcke aus anderen Dateien aufrufen
Q 40 der Teletex
Q 41 der Telekopierer/der Fernkopierer/das Telefaxgerät
Q 42 dieses System erlaubt Ihnen, einen Computer an das Telexnetz anzuschließen
Q 43 es hat eine automatische Rückruffunktion
Q 44 es schickt Mitteilungen außerhalb der Hauptgeschäftszeiten
Q 45 die Telekonferenz/Videokonferenz
Q 46 online/Direktverbindung
Q 47 die Echtzeit/der Echtzeitbetrieb
Q 48 CAD/das computer-gestützte Konstruieren
Q 49 CAM/das computer-gestützte Fertigen
Q 50 CAL/das computer-gestützte Lernen
Q 51 Desktop Publishing/das DTP
Q 52 das Expertensystem
Q 53 die Datenbank/das Datenbanksystem
Q 54 das relationale Datenbanksystem
Q 55 die Information wird jeden Tag aktualisiert
Q 56 die Tabellenkalkulation

Q	57	Daten sind in Dateien abgelegt, die vom System verwaltet werden
Q	58	die gespeicherte Information ist in numerierten Seiten abgelegt
Q	59	die Diskette kann von jedem kompatiblen Computer gelesen werden
Q	60	dieses Modell ist IBM-kompatibel
Q	61	das Betriebssystem dieses Modells läuft mit MS-DOS und ist nicht PC-DOS-kompatibel
Q	62	der Clone
Q	63	das Betriebssystem
Q	64	Fehlermeldungen
Q	65	das Byte
Q	66	das Kilobyte
Q	67	das Megabyte
Q	68	dieses Modell hat einen Hauptspeicher mit 512 KB
Q	69	die Speicherkapazität der Diskette ist 1000 KB/das Laufwerk hat eine Speicherkapazität von 1000 KB
Q	70	die Software
Q	71	das Software-Paket
Q	72	dieses Paket ist auf Diskette angeboten
Q	73	die Konfiguration kann Ihren Bedürfnissen angepaßt werden
Q	74	und eine italienische Version ist erhältlich
Q	75	das Programm hat ein Kursorbewegungsmenü
Q	76	der Kursor kann durch die Maus bewegt werden
Q	77	der Lesestift
Q	78	die Systemdiskette
Q	79	die Arbeitsdiskette
Q	80	double-sided/doppelseitig
Q	81	double density/doppelte Spurdichte
Q	82	die Diskette muß formatiert werden
Q	83	eine $3\frac{1}{2}''$ Diskette
Q	84	das Diskettenverzeichnis
Q	85	das Nebenverzeichnis
Q	86	die Quellendiskette
Q	87	die Zieldiskette
Q	88	die (zurück)kopierte Diskette
Q	89	die Datei kann von Diskette A zu Diskette B kopiert werden
Q	90	das Programm ist kopiergeschützt
Q	91	Text verschieben
Q	92	Text löschen

Q 93	Text hinzufügen
Q 94	es gibt ein Wörterbuch zur Kontrolle der Rechtschreibung
Q 95	Dateien verbinden
Q 96	Text kann direkt an den Drucker gesandt werden
Q 97	die Hardware
Q 98	der Personalcomputer
Q 99	der Minicomputer
Q 100	der Großrechner/der Mainframe
Q 101	die (Floppy-)Diskette
Q 102	die Festplatte
Q 103	der CD ROM
Q 104	die Bildplatte
Q 105	Peripheriegeräte
Q 106	der Schwarz-Weiß-Monitor (Bildschirm)/der monochrome Monitor
Q 107	der Farbmonitor
Q 108	der LCD-Monitor
Q 109	der Plasma-Monitor/Plasmabildschirm
Q 110	der Bildschirm verfügt über 25 Zeilen mit je 80 Zeichen
Q 111	der Drucker mit paralleler Schnittstelle
Q 112	der Drucker mit serieller Schnittstelle
Q 113	der Matrixdrucker
Q 114	der Typenraddrucker
Q 115	der Laserdrucker
Q 116	die Schriftart
Q 117	der Druckkopf
Q 118	der Formulartraktor/die (Einzel)Blattzuführung
Q 119	die Lärmschutzhaube (für den Drucker)
Q 120	der Plotter
Q 121	der Scanner
Q 122	die Korrespondenzqualität
Q 123	das Druckband kann leicht ausgewechselt werden
Q 124	ein niedriger Lärmpegel
Q 125	der Wartungsvertrag
Q 126	die laufende Wartung
Q 127	jedes abgenutzte oder fehlerhafte Teil wird kostenlos ersetzt
Q 128	die Einstellung
Q 129	unter der Voraussetzung/Bedingung, daß die Maschine regelmäßig überprüft/inspiziert wird
Q 130	die Hardware kann nicht am Ort repariert werden
Q 131	die Festplatte ist beschädigt

Q 132	der Fehler war auf eine Reduzierung der Stromleistung zurückführen
Q 133	der Ausfall wurde von einem Softwarefehler verursacht
Q 134	die Stromversorgung
Q 135	das Benutzerhandbuch
Q 136	die Komponente
Q 137	das Gehäuse
Q 138	der Cassettenrekorder war nicht mit dem Computer verbunden
Q 139	die Funktionstaste funktionierte nicht
Q 140	Sie hätten den Inhalt der Diskette aufführen sollen
Q 141	dieses Faxgerät sendet gewöhnlich eine A4-Seite in weniger als 12 Sekunden
Q 142	das Terminal ist außer Betrieb
Q 143	der Fehler liegt bei dem 16-Bit-Prozessor
Q 144	der Prozessor sollte bis zu 8 Terminale bedienen
Q 145	der Benutzer wußte nicht, daß die Wartung nicht kostenlos war
Q 146	die Paketvermittlung

R — Städte- und Länderverzeichnis

R	**1**	Aachen
R	**2**	Afrika
R	**3**	Alexandria
R	**4**	Algerien
R	**5**	Algier
R	**6**	Amsterdam
R	**7**	Antwerpen
R	**8**	Argentinien
R	**9**	Arnheim
R	**10**	Asien
R	**11**	Athen
R	**12**	Australien
R	**13**	Österreich
R	**14**	Avignon

R	**15**	Baden-Baden
R	**16**	Bagdad
R	**17**	Bahrain
R	**18**	Barcelona
R	**19**	Basel
R	**20**	Bayreuth
R	**21**	Beirut
R	**22**	Belfast
R	**23**	Belgien
R	**24**	Belgrad
R	**25**	Berlin
R	**26**	Bern
R	**27**	Bilbao
R	**28**	Bochum
R	**29**	Bolivien
R	**30**	Bombay
R	**31**	Bonn
R	**32**	Bordeaux
R	**33**	Brasilia
R	**34**	Brasilien
R	**35**	Bregenz
R	**36**	Bremen
R	**37**	Bremerhaven
R	**38**	Braunschweig
R	**39**	Brüssel
R	**40**	Bukarest
R	**41**	Budapest
R	**42**	Bulgarien
R	**43**	Buenos Aires
R	**44**	Cadiz
R	**45**	Kairo
R	**46**	Kanada
R	**47**	Kanarische Inseln
R	**48**	Kapstadt
R	**49**	Tschad
R	**50**	Chile
R	**51**	China
R	**52**	Köln
R	**53**	Kolumbien
R	**54**	Konstanz
R	**55**	Kopenhagen
R	**56**	Cordoba
R	**57**	Korinth

R 58	Costa Rica
R 59	Kuba
R 60	die Tschechoslowakei
R 61	Damaskus
R 62	Delhi
R 63	Dänemark
R 64	Dijon
R 65	Djakarta
R 66	Dortmund
R 67	Dresden
R 68	Dubai
R 69	Dublin
R 70	Dünkirchen
R 71	Düsseldorf
R 72	Ekuador
R 73	Edinburgh
R 74	die EWG/EG
R 75	Ägypten
R 76	Eindhoven
R 77	Europa
R 78	England
R 79	Erfurt
R 80	Äthiopien
R 81	Falklandinseln
R 82	Finnland
R 83	Florenz
R 84	Frankreich
R 85	Frankfurt
R 86	Freiburg
R 87	Gdansk
R 88	Genf
R 89	Genua
R 90	Ghana
R 91	Gießen
R 92	Gotha
R 93	Göttingen
R 94	Graz
R 95	Großbritannien
R 96	Griechenland
R 97	Groningen
R 98	Guyana
R 99	Den Haag
R 100	Halle

R 101	Hamburg
R 102	Hannover
R 103	Havanna
R 104	Heidelberg
R 105	Helsinki
R 106	Holland
R 107	Honduras
R 108	Ungarn
R 109	Island
R 110	Indien
R 111	Indonesien
R 112	Innsbruck
R 113	Interlaken
R 114	Iran
R 115	Irak
R 116	Irland
R 117	Israel
R 118	Istanbul
R 119	Italien
R 120	Elfenbeinküste
R 121	Jamaika
R 122	Japan
R 123	Jena
R 124	Jerusalem
R 125	Jordanien
R 126	Kaiserslautern
R 127	Karl Marx Stadt (Chemnitz)
R 128	Karlsruhe
R 129	Kassel
R 130	Kiel
R 131	Kitzbühel
R 132	Klagenfurt
R 133	Koblenz
R 134	Krakow
R 135	Lausanne
R 136	Libanon
R 137	Leipzig
R 138	Libyen
R 139	Lille
R 140	Lima
R 141	Linz
R 142	Lissabon
R 143	Laibach/Ljubljana

R 144	London
R 145	Lübeck
R 146	Luzern
R 147	Lugano
R 148	Luxemburg
R 149	Lyon
R 150	Maastricht
R 151	Magdeburg
R 152	Mainz
R 153	Malaysia
R 154	Malta
R 155	Mannheim
R 156	Marseille
R 157	Mekka
R 158	Mexiko
R 159	Mexico City
R 160	Mailand
R 161	Monaco
R 162	Montevideo
R 163	Montreux
R 164	Marokko
R 165	Moskau
R 166	München
R 167	Münster
R 168	Neapel
R 169	Niederlande
R 170	Neu-Delhi
R 171	New York
R 172	Neuseeland
R 173	Nikaragua
R 174	Nizza
R 175	Nordirland
R 176	Norwegen
R 177	Nürnberg
R 178	Oslo
R 179	Ostende
R 180	Padua
R 181	Panama
R 182	Paraguay
R 183	Paris
R 184	Passau
R 185	Peking
R 186	Peru

R 187	Philippinen
R 188	Piräus
R 189	Polen
R 190	Portugal
R 191	Prag
R 192	Katar
R 193	Recife
R 194	Reykjavik
R 195	Riad
R 196	Rio de Janeiro
R 197	Rom
R 198	Rostock
R 199	Rotterdam
R 200	Rumänien
R 201	Rußland
R 202	Saarbrücken
R 203	St. Petersburg (Leningrad)
R 204	Salzburg
R 205	Sardinien
R 206	Saudi-Arabien
R 207	Schottland
R 208	Sevilla
R 209	Sizilien
R 210	Singapur
R 211	Südafrika
R 212	Südamerika
R 213	Südkorea
R 214	Spanien
R 215	Split
R 216	Steyr
R 217	Stockholm
R 218	Straßburg
R 219	Stuttgart
R 220	Schweden
R 221	die Schweiz
R 222	Syrien
R 223	Tanger
R 224	Teheran
R 225	Tel Aviv
R 226	Thailand
R 227	Den Haag
R 228	Saloniki
R 229	Tokio

R 230	Toronto
R 231	Toulon
R 232	Toulouse
R 233	Trier
R 234	Tripoli/Tripolis
R 235	Tunis
R 236	Tunesien
R 237	Turin
R 238	die Türkei
R 239	Ulm
R 240	die Vereinigten Arabischen Emirate
R 241	das Vereinigte Königreich
R 242	die Vereinigten Staaten
R 243	Utrecht
R 244	Vancouver
R 245	Venezuela
R 246	Venedig
R 247	Wien
R 248	Wales
R 249	Warschau
R 250	Weimar
R 251	Westindien
R 252	Wismar
R 253	Wolfsburg
R 254	Jugoslawien
R 255	Zagreb/Agram
R 256	Zaragoza/Saragossa
R 257	Zürich
R 258	Zwickau

S — Abkürzungen

S 1 Rechnung
S 2 Gebr.
S 3 Gesellschaft
S 4 bei
S 5 Dtz.
S 6 Ausgabe
S 7 EG
S 8 z.B.
S 9 Anl.
S 10 usw.
S 11 d.h.
S 12 d.M.
S 13 GmbH
S 14 pp./i.A.
S 15 MwSt

Index

ENGLISH

Contents

Introduction

This book is intended for anyone who has to produce, or understand, commercial correspondence in English, French, German, Italian or Spanish. It contains important expressions in each of the five languages, in sections designed to facilitate easy usage. In addition to these expressions, the book also contains the necessary vocabulary for making telephone calls, for bank and post office transactions, and lists of countries and cities in each of the various languages.

The book is intended to be of use not only to those who deal with commercial correspondence as a necessary part of their job, but also to students and teachers of the subject. The authors have also sought to avoid any bias toward any particular language, and the book is thus arranged in such a way as to be equally useful to the French secretary wishing to produce letters in English as to the Italian student who wishes to understand letters in German. Altogether, ten such language combinations are possible, which makes the book an invaluable aid to any firm dealing with imports or exports.

How to use the book
There are five separate language sections, each of which is subdivided into sections such as *Enquiries and offers*, *Orders*, etc. Within each section, every expression has a key letter and number (**A36, B39** etc.), Which corresponds exactly to the appropriate expression in each of the other languages. If we take for example, English expression **B45** 'the samples must be returned within 2 weeks', we find under the same letter and number in the French section the expression 'les échantillons doivent être renvoyés dans un délai de 2 semaines', in German 'die Muster müssen binnen 2 Wochen zurückgeschickt werden' etc.

If the expression you are looking for is not listed, remember to check whether a synonym could be used instead.

To enable the user to locate a particular word or expression quickly and easily, an index is included for each language, which refers directly to the relevant key letter and number.

Words and expressions in square brackets in the English section are in American English.

A — General expressions

A	1	Dear Sir
A	2	Dear Sirs
A	3	Dear Mr X
A	4	Dear Madam
A	5	Dear Miss
A	6	for the attention of
A	7	confidential
A	8	re
A	9	we acknowledge receipt of your letter
A	10	we thank you for your letter
A	11	of the 3rd of this month
A	12	with reference to your letter
A	13	your reference
A	14	our reference
A	15	your name was given to us by business associates
A	16	**we hasten [wish] to reply to your letter of**
A	17	we have not received a reply to our letter of
A	18	following our telephone conversation of
A	19	I am pleased to hear that
A	20	our representative has informed us
A	21	on the recommendation of our representative
A	22	we are sorry to learn that
A	23	your letter was passed on to us by
A	24	we are interested to hear that
A	25	**your above-mentioned [aforementioned] letter**
A	26	your letter mentioned below
A	27	we shall let you know by telephone
A	28	we shall let you know by telegram
A	29	following our meeting on
A	30	we have learned from
A	31	we regret to inform you
A	32	we are pleased to inform you
A	33	we were interested to hear that
A	34	please find enclosed our catalogue
A	35	we hereby confirm
A	36	please inform us
A	37	please find out the reason
A	38	the information is required for

A 39	as soon as you can
A 40	as soon as we receive
A 41	further [pursuant] to our letter
A 42	further [pursuant] to our telephone call
A 43	we deeply regret that
A 44	we note with surprise that
A 45	we would be grateful if you would send us
A 46	we trust you will approve of these measures
A 47	we hope you will find it possible to
A 48	we are sorry not to have replied sooner
A 49	we have now had the opportunity to
A 50	we are enclosing
A 51	under separate cover
A 52	by the same post [mail]
A 53	by return of post [mail]
A 54	we are returning to you
A 55	which you sent to us
A 56	may we suggest that
A 57	you may rest assured that
A 58	on referring to earlier correspondence
A 59	it will come as no surprise to you
A 60	we shall be very happy to
A 61	if this is not possible
A 62	we have just learned that
A 63	we are sure you will understand that
A 64	please be good enough to
A 65	as you are aware
A 66	in reply to your letter
A 67	according to our records
A 68	we would remind you that
A 69	we regret to have to remind you that
A 70	as requested in your letter of
A 71	we shall require details of your products
A 72	we would welcome your views on this matter
A 73	we feel it is important for you to
A 74	we are arranging to send you
A 75	following our discussion with your representative
A 76	as we are entering into business relations with you
A 77	we see from your letter that
A 78	we wish to point out that
A 79	I should like an appointment to see X
A 80	we shall have to cancel our meeting of
A 81	to your full satisfaction

A 82	our head [home] office is in
A 83	our head [home] office has moved to
A 84	we shall do our best to settle the matter
A 85	details as follows
A 86	our manager is currently on a business trip
A 87	let us know as soon as possible
A 88	we hope you will understand our position
A 89	we are sorry for the trouble we have caused you
A 90	this has not been properly taken into account
A 91	we recommend you to reconsider
A 92	we were impressed by
A 93	we cannot accept
A 94	you will find particulars of
A 95	if we can be of service in any way
A 96	we shall do our utmost
A 97	we realize that
A 98	we have given instructions that
A 99	as soon as the goods are ready
A 100	when you know the date
A 101	should you decide to do this
A 102	in the event that
A 103	if we had known this
A 104	in the near future
A 105	at a later date
A 106	we should be glad to receive this information
A 107	we enclose a stamped addressed envelope
A 108	we enclose an international reply coupon
A 109	should the need arise
A 110	on time
A 111	Mr X has referred us to you
A 112	we have not so far had much success
A 113	by surface mail
A 114	by airmail
A 115	by registered post [mail]
A 116	we would ask you to exercise special care
A 117	in two weeks time
A 118	whose names we would be glad to send you
A 119	to judge by their reports
A 120	we would be prepared to
A 121	we are convinced that
A 122	we should be interested in
A 123	we hope for an early reply

A 124   we hope we have been of help to you
A 125   we appreciate very much
A 126   we hope you will continue to
A 127   Yours sincerely
A 128   Yours faithfully [Very truly yours]
A 129   enc(s)
A 130   signed
A 131   pp. / on behalf of .

B — Enquiries [Queries] and offers

B   1   we understand you are manufacturers of
B   2   we specialise [specialize] in the manufacture of
B   3   we are proprietors of
B   4   we are looking for a reliable supplier
B   5   please send us full information on
B   6   we are mainly interested in the following items:
B   7   please send me any information which may help me
B   8   in order to make the best choice for my purpose
B   9   several of our customers have expressed interest in
B 10   please send us brochures about your goods
B 11   please send us your latest catalogue
B 12   your new brochure
B 13   your latest price list
B 14   we have read about your firm in the trade press
B 15   we have been customers of your firm for many years
B 16   we see from your advertisement
B 17   our stock of goods is running out
B 18   our stock has run out
B 19   can you supply from stock?
B 20   we have in stock
B 21   your enquiry [query] concerning our products
B 22   we require the goods by April 2 at the latest
B 23   to help us to introduce your product onto the market
B 24   we are prepared to make you a special offer
B 25   during a recent visit to the trade fair
B 26   I saw a sample of your products
B 27   allow us to draw your special attention to
B 28   on condition that

B	29	please send us a selection of items from your range
B	30	we expect to place regular orders for these goods
B	31	in large quantities
B	32	please let us know if you allow a trial purchase
B	33	how long may we keep this product on a trial basis?
B	34	we await your offer with interest
B	35	we are interested in your products
B	36	the quality of the goods is of prime importance
B	37	provided prices of raw materials do not change
B	38	our products are carefully tested to ensure quality
B	39	all our products carry a two-year guarantee
B	40	we replace defective parts free of charge
B	41	due to faulty materials or workmanship
B	42	up to three months after delivery
B	43	we accept orders for minimum quantities of
B	44	no charge will be made for samples
B	45	the samples must be returned within 2 weeks
B	46	we shall invoice you for the samples
B	47	together with the samples
B	48	please send us samples of your products
B	49	we cannot offer this item on a trial basis
B	50	on a sale or return basis
B	51	on approval
B	52	we wish to extend our present range
B	53	within four weeks of order
B	54	please send us precise details of your products
B	55	we have seen from your brochure
B	56	because of heavy demand from our customers
B	57	the items are now obsolete
B	58	we no longer mass-produce these articles
B	59	we suggest you contact
B	60	10 motors, type . . .
B	61	in the following sizes and quantities
B	62	please give us a quotation for
B	63	we should like to see your latest models
B	64	details of your latest models
B	65	provided quality and price are satisfactory
B	66	the weights and measures are indicated in the illustrated catalogue
B	67	for quantities of more than
B	68	for a minimum order of
B	69	in the following colours [colors]
B	70	in the following designs

B 71	in accordance with the enclosed drawing
B 72	is your catalogue available in French?
B 73	we have seen your advertising material
B 74	please give us your wholesale prices
B 75	retail prices
B 76	our prices are quoted in the enclosed list
B 77	our prices are marked on the sample
B 78	the prices quoted are without discount
B 79	these are our lowest prices
B 80	we grant a discount of . . . % on the catalogue prices
B 81	we can offer an introductory discount of . . . %
B 82	can you allow us a special discount?
B 83	trade discount
B 84	please state terms of payment
B 85	our prices are binding until 8 May
B 86	the prices quoted should include delivery to the above address
B 87	please quote prices in pounds sterling
B 88	prices current at time of shipment
B 89	the prices quoted in your letter
B 90	prices as follows
B 91	if your prices are competitive
B 92	at a price of . . . each
B 93	at a special price of
B 94	please give details of prices and delivery times
B 95	these are the lowest prices we can offer
B 96	we can give an export rebate of . . . %
B 97	our prices include insurance
B 98	our prices are lower than those of our competitors
B 99	price per item
B 100	ex works
B 101	ex warehouse
B 102	our prices are FOB London
B 103	packing included
B 104	packing not included
B 105	carriage [freight] paid to Madrid
B 106	franco frontier
B 107	carriage [freight] paid to frontier
B 108	C & F. (cost and freight)
B 109	F.O.R. (free on rail)
B 110	C.I.F. (cost, insurance, freight)
B 111	F.A.S. (free alongside ship)
B 112	franco domicile

B 113	free harbour [harbor]
B 114	free warehouse
B 115	we are pleased to submit the following quotation:
B 116	can you allow us a credit term of 3 weeks?
B 117	we are working at a reduced profit margin
B 118	for bulk orders
B 119	the offer is firm for 5 days
B 120	the offer is firm subject to acceptance by March 5
B 121	subject to the goods being unsold
B 122	we reserve the right to alter prices
B 123	we thank you for your enquiry [inquiry] [query] about our goods
B 124	if the quality of the goods meets our expectations
B 125	we shall place a trial order with you
B 126	if the goods are satisfactory
B 127	we shall place larger orders
B 128	for first orders
B 129	for subsequent orders
B 130	as long as supplies last
B 131	your order will be carried out to your complete satisfaction
B 132	our conditions of sale are:
B 133	the prompt and careful execution [filling] of your order
B 134	we offer you the goods you specified as follows:
B 135	if the prices are acceptable to you
B 136	on the following terms

C — Orders

C	**1**	we have examined your offer
C	**2**	we have carefully examined your samples
C	**3**	the items in your catalogue meet our requirements
C	**4**	if we are satisfied with your first consignment
C	**5**	we wish to order, on the basis of the samples sent to us
C	**6**	we wish to place the following order with you
C	**7**	the order must be delivered immediately
C	**8**	we are prepared to place a standing order
C	**9**	the order is based on your catalogue prices
C	**10**	we wish to order 5 each of the following items
C	**11**	please find our enclosed order, number 8765, for . . .
C	**12**	please send us the following items immediately

C	13	we must insist that the goods be supplied from stock
C	14	we require the goods within ten days
C	15	if you cannot deliver within this period
C	16	we refer to our order of May 5
C	17	with reference to our order number 9675
C	18	we find your prices rather high
C	19	if you could reduce your offer by . . . %
C	20	we would be prepared to place the following order with you
C	21	your prices are higher than those of our previous supplier
C	22	we can obtain the goods at a more favorable price from another supplier
C	23	we are committed to another supplier
C	24	we have already covered our needs
C	25	we received your offer too late
C	26	your sample was not of a sufficiently high quality
C	27	if you can supply the items in a better quality
C	28	if you can supply in smaller quantities
C	29	please let us know the maximum quantity you can supply immediately
C	30	we must modify your order slightly
C	31	we hope that this modification is acceptable to you
C	32	item number 487 is not available at the moment
C	33	because of problems with our supplier
C	34	because of a strike
C	35	because of shortage of raw materials
C	36	due to a shortage of staff
C	37	we are behind with production
C	38	we cannot therefore guarantee delivery by March 4
C	39	we are prepared to exchange the articles
C	40	we reserve the right to refuse delivery
C	41	we wish to increase the quantity to . . .
C	42	we cannot make use of your offer
C	43	we cannot accept your conditions of payment
C	44	we cannot accept your conditions of delivery
C	45	we cannot take your offer into consideration
C	46	we do not need these items at present
C	47	we have no storage space available
C	48	we cannot accept your order at this time
C	49	our order book is full
C	50	we cannot start manufacture until August
C	51	we wish to cancel our order
C	52	we have cancelled our order by telegram

C 53 please delete the following items from our order
C 54 we reserve the right to cancel the order
C 55 we received your order for our goods today
C 56 we confirm your order of May 12
C 57 we shall execute [fill] your order as soon as possible
C 58 your order is now ready for delivery
C 59 your order is now awaiting collection
C 60 we await your further instructions
C 61 please arrange to collect the goods
C 62 we have started manufacture of the goods
C 63 please confirm the above order as soon as possible
C 64 we require approximately ten days to complete your order

D — Delivery, transport, customs

D 1   we confirm the delivery date you stipulated in your letter
D 2   we await instructions with regard to delivery
D 3   we must insist on immediate delivery
D 4   the delay in delivery is due to
D 5   we can deliver the goods immediately
D 6   we require delivery urgently
D 7   the delay in delivery has caused us considerable problems
D 8   please let us know when delivery will be made
D 9   our earliest delivery time would be one month
D 10 we will do our utmost to keep to the delivery date
D 11 we can deliver the goods earlier than agreed
D 12 our forwarding agents are
D 13 we shall have the goods ready for shipment by the beginning of May
D 14 the goods await collection
D 15 as soon as we receive your order we will ship the goods
D 16 we can deliver the goods in containers
D 17 delivery will take place within 4 months
D 18 please let us know whether you can deliver the goods by this date
D 19 the delivery time is 4 months
D 20 the goods must be delivered by the end of next month
D 21 the delivery dates given in our letter must be adhered to
D 22 delivery must be made on time

D 23 we cannot accept the goods if they are not delivered on time

D 24 it will not be possible to deliver the goods within the agreed period of 2 months

D 25 we can deliver by August 5

D 26 we have not yet received the goods

D 27 please let us know the reason for this delay

D 28 carriage [freight] paid

D 29 the consignment consists of

D 30 the consignment was shipped on the SS Berlin

D 31 the ship should arrive in Dover on July 21

D 32 we hope that the consignment will reach you in good condition

D 33 we have not yet received the consignment which you despatched [sent] on March 15

D 34 the consignment you promised to deliver on February 13

D 35 we shall send all the goods in a single consignment

D 36 the consignment consists of two cases, each weighing 50 kilos

D 37 the shipment of the goods

D 38 the goods were despatched [sent] to you today

D 39 the goods are ready for despatch [shipment]

D 40 we have given the despatch [shipment] documents to our bank

D 41 the goods will be despatched [sent] on June 9

D 42 the cases have been collected by the carriers

D 43 as soon as we receive instructions, we shall send you our advice of despatch [shipment notice]

D 44 we have given the goods you ordered to our transporter

D 45 your order does not state how the goods are to be transported

D 46 as air freight

D 47 by air freight

D 48 by rail

D 49 by air

D 50 by ship

D 51 by lorry [truck]

D 52 goods in transit

D 53 freight paid

D 54 exclusive of freight

D 55 inclusive of freight

D 56 freight charges

D 57 port of despatch [shipment]

D 58	port of destination
D 59	in order to reduce damage in transit to a minimum
D 60	bill of lading
D 61	freight note
D 62	consular invoice
D 63	shipping documents
D 64	air consignment note
D 65	certificate of value
D 66	the certificate of origin was not in order
D 67	we cannot pack the goods in the way you requested
D 68	careful packing of the goods is essential
D 69	the packing must be strong
D 70	the packing does not meet our standard
D 71	please let us know if you have an alternative form of packing
D 72	the packing of your goods is poor
D 73	please pay careful attention to packing
D 74	we cannot accept your comments concerning faulty packing
D 75	packing cases may not be returned
D 76	packing cases will bear consecutive numbers
D 77	we cannot accept requests for special packing
D 78	we must insist on packing of goods in
D 79	wrapping paper
D 80	corrugated cardboard
D 81	wood wool
D 82	lined with
D 83	containers
D 84	drums
D 85	bales
D 86	crates
D 87	cases
D 88	tins [cans]
D 89	jars
D 90	palettes
D 91	barrels
D 92	wooden crates
D 93	sacks
D 94	the cartons are non-returnable
D 95	the crates are to be marked as follows
D 96	shockproof
D 97	waterproof
D 98	damage-proof

D 99	keep dry
D 100	keep cool
D 101	this way up
D 102	top
D 103	bottom
D 104	handle with care
D 105	open here
D 106	lift here
D 107	fragile
D 108	caution!
D 109	flammable
D 110	net weight
D 111	gross weight
D 112	dead weight
D 113	loading
D 114	unloading
D 115	weights and dimensions
D 116	the gross weight is given on each crate
D 117	duty to be paid by purchaser
D 118	delivered to London, duty paid
D 119	liable to duty
D 120	we have had to pay a duty of . . . on the items
D 121	you will have to pay import duty on the goods
D 122	duty to be paid by consignee
D 123	the dutiable value of the goods
D 124	customs declaration
D 125	customs charges
D 126	customs clearance
D 127	we have received the customs invoice
D 128	the customs office in Aachen imposed a fine on the consignment
D 129	we require the customs receipt
D 130	the customs authorities in Dover have seized the consignment
D 131	new customs regulations have come into force
D 132	we shall attend to the customs formalities
D 133	customs fine
D 134	customs warehouse
D 135	bonded warehouse
D 136	under bond
D 137	storage
D 138	spoilage
D 139	pilferage

D 140 airport tax
D 141 harbour [harbor] dues
D 142 handling charges
D 143 customs tariffs
D 144 we shall pay the clearance charges

E — Invoices, payments and reminders

E 1 we acknowledge receipt of the consignment
E 2 the consignment arrived at our factory yesterday
E 3 the goods arrived in good condition
E 4 the consignment reached us safely
E 5 the goods we ordered on April 4 arrived on time
E 6 please find enclosed our invoice no. . . . .
E 7 we enclose our invoice for the goods delivered to you on May 3
E 8 the enclosed invoice covers the goods delivered against your order number . . .
E 9 we ask for early settlement of our invoice
E 10 we ask you to settle the invoice by May 12
E 11 we request payment of the invoice to account number . . .
E 12 we ask you to settle the invoice by return
E 13 we enclose our statement
E 14 the total amount payable is . . .
E 15 the discount is already included in the figure
E 16 the discount has already been deducted
E 17 after deduction of . . . %
E 18 we have deducted the customary . . . % from your invoice
E 19 we must point out that there is an error in your invoice
E 20 you have made an error in totalling your invoice number . . .
E 21 please send us an amended invoice
E 22 we should be grateful if you could adjust the invoice accordingly
E 23 we should be grateful if you could correct the statement
E 24 your invoice allows a trade discount of only . . . %

E 25   we have deducted . . . from the invoice
E 26   the mistake was due to a typing error
E 27   an error in our accounts department
E 28   an oversight
E 29   we confirm the adjusted balance of . . .
E 30   we enclose a credit note
E 31   debit note
E 32   we should appreciate your prompt payment
E 33   we expect receipt of your payment within the next week
E 34   please let us have the amount due within the next few days
E 35   we wish to remind you that our conditions of payment are
E 36   we refer you to our conditions of payment
E 37   documents against acceptance
E 38   C.O.D. (cash on delivery)
E 39   documents against payment
E 40   payment in advance
E 41   documentary letter of credit
E 42   a documentary letter of credit in your favour [favor]
E 43   documentary bill of exchange
E 44   revocable
E 45   irrevocable
E 46   confirmed
E 47   unconfirmed
E 48   documentary draft
E 49   sight bill [draft]
E 50   term sight bill [draft at . . . days sight]
E 51   date bill
E 52   payment on receipt of goods
E 53   at the current rate of exchange
E 54   in cash
E 55   notes
E 56   coins
E 57   legal tender
E 58   giro [bank] transfer
E 59   payee
E 60   creditor
E 61   debtor
E 62   promissory note
E 63   commercial credit
E 64   payable at the . . . bank
E 65   a 60 days draft
E 66   a credit of . . . to be opened with the . . . bank
E 67   we have instructed our bank to pay you the sum owed

E 68	we have paid the sum of . . . to your account
E 69	we have credited this amount to your account
E 70	we have instructed our bank to pay the sum to your account
E 71	we have transferred the sum of . . . to your account
E 72	in settlement of your account
E 73	our account at . . . bank
E 74	we enclose a cheque [check] for . . .
E 75	a crossed cheque [check]
E 76	an open cheque [check]
E 77	a postal order [money order]
E 78	the cheque [check] has been cashed
E 79	a cheque [check] on your account
E 80	we enclose a cheque [check] for . . . in settlement of your invoice
E 81	£600, less £45 for packing
E 82	we enclose a cheque [check] for half the amount
E 83	bank transfer
E 84	bank draft
E 85	the amount has been credited to your account
E 86	please send us a receipt as soon as possible
E 87	we confirm receipt of your payment
E 88	we thank you for your payment
E 89	we have accepted your draft
E 90	your payment to the amount of . . . has been received by our bank
E 91	we thank you for your prompt payment of our invoice
E 92	we have received your remittance advice
E 93	your account is now more than four weeks overdue
E 94	our invoice is still unpaid
E 95	we await your remittance
E 96	your account still shows a debit balance of . . .
E 97	the outstanding invoices must be paid by the end of this month
E 98	we have not received the balance of our September statement
E 99	as our statement may have gone astray [gotten lost], we enclose a copy
E 100	please let us know the reason for the delay in payment
E 101	as the amount owing [owed] is considerably overdue
E 102	we have as yet had no reply to our request for payment
E 103	please attend to this matter without delay
E 104	despite our repeated requests for payment

E 105	in order to recover the amount due
E 106	you have ignored our reminders
E 107	in [the] future, our invoices must be settled immediately
E 108	you still owe us . . .
E 109	we must remind you that we only allow two weeks' credit for first orders
E 110	we wish to point out that the payment was due on July 4
E 111	this is our last request for payment
E 112	we must now insist on immediate payment
E 113	if we do not receive payment by the beginning of next month
E 114	your delay in payment is quite unacceptable
E 115	the invoice was mislaid
E 116	we shall take legal steps
E 117	the amount will be collected by our lawyer
E 118	we shall have the amount owed collected by our lawyer
E 119	we must take steps to collect the amount due
E 120	by legal means
E 121	we have placed the matter in the hands of our lawyers
E 122	we shall allow you an additional period of 12 days to make payment
E 123	you may make a part [partial] payment
E 124	you asked for a postponement of payment
E 125	we hope you will understand our position
E 126	we are prepared to grant an extension

F — Complaints

F 1	the goods delivered on the 3rd of this month were not the ones we had ordered
F 2	we regret to have to complain about your consignment number . . .
F 3	we wish to point out an error in the consignment we received yesterday
F 4	the items were in the wrong colour [color]
F 5	they were in the wrong sizes
F 6	they did not comply with the drawings we sent you
F 7	the quality of the goods did not meet our expectations
F 8	we were disappointed with the quality of the goods
F 9	for these reasons we cannot accept the goods

F	10	the items were faulty
F	11	you sent us 500 . . . instead of the 250 which we had ordered
F	12	there has been an error in the execution of our order
F	13	the contents of the crates do not agree with the delivery note
F	14	article number . . . was missing from the consignment
F	15	the goods are not in accordance with the samples
F	16	the items appear to be of different construction
F	17	the crates were broken
F	18	the goods were damaged by fire
F	19	the goods were damaged by rough handling
F	20	the goods arrived damaged
F	21	badly damaged
F	22	several of the items were scratched
F	23	broken
F	24	slightly damaged
F	25	damaged by heat
F	26	damaged by water
F	27	the goods must have been damaged in transit
F	28	they must have been badly packed
F	29	the packaging materials were substandard
F	30	the crates should have been bound with metal bands
F	31	the crates were badly constructed
F	32	the items are rusty
F	33	the damage occurred between British customs and our factory
F	34	the damage occurred before the arrival of the goods at Dover
F	35	we must ask you to send us a replacement as soon as possible
F	36	this has caused us considerable difficulties, as we needed the goods urgently
F	37	we need the remaining items urgently
F	38	we regret that all of the items will have to be replaced
F	39	we are prepared to retain the goods
F	40	at a reduced price of . . . per article
F	41	we are returning the whole consignment
F	42	we are returning part of the consignment
F	43	we are returning all of the articles damaged en route
F	44	we must now cancel the order
F	45	we are prepared to accept the damaged goods if you reduce the price by . . . %

F 46   we can only sell the damaged goods at a considerably reduced price

F 47   all of the items will have to be replaced

F 48   we hope that you will avoid similar errors in future

F 49   this has caused us considerable difficulties with a number of clients

F 50   we suggest that you contact the forwarding agents

F 51   the shipping company

F 52   the railway company

F 53   the airline

F 54   we feel that it is your responsibility to make further enquiries [queries]

F 55   we must ask for compensation to cover our losses

F 56   we must insist on compensation

F 57   we must ask you to credit us with the value of the damaged goods

F 58   we shall have to reconsider our position with a view to future orders

F 59   we have checked your complaint

F 60   as the damage happened in transit

F 61   we ask you to refer the matter to . . .

F 62   this is the first time we have dealt with this haulage [freight] company

F 63   our insurance covers the faults [damage] you mention

F 64   our guarantee covers this damage

F 65   according to the terms of our guarantee

F 66   you may claim reimbursement of the money already paid

F 67   we offer you our sincere apologies for this error

F 68   we are prepared to exchange the goods for those of a similar quality

F 69   we enclose a cheque [check] for . . . as a refund

F 70   we shall replace the goods at our expense

F 71   we are sorry that our consignment was unsatisfactory

F 72   we are prepared to offer you a discount of . . . %

F 73   we have reduced your bill by . . . %

F 74   we have checked the goods very carefully

F 75   we can find no fault with the goods

F 76   we cannot accept responsibility for the damage

F 77   as you will see from the terms of the contract

F 78   we regret that we cannot take the goods back

F 79   we suggest that you report the matter to the insurance company

F 80   we must point out that the period of guarantee has expired

F 81   you must ask the shipping company to certify the damage
F 82   we require a report from the forwarding agents listing the damage
F 83   under the circumstances, we cannot accept your complaint

G — Agencies

G 1   we are looking for an agent to sell our goods abroad
G 2   we require a representative for the sale of our products
G 3   we are looking for a representative for our branch in . . .
G 4   the agent must work exclusively for us
G 5   he must undertake not to work for our competitors
G 6   and must confine his activities to this area
G 7   his main task would be to present our catalogues and samples to customers
G 8   the post requires specialist knowledge
G 9   we require a specialist representative
G 10   no specialist knowledge is required
G 11   we train our representatives ourselves
G 12   we are a small firm manufacturing . . .
G 13   these articles have excellent sales potential
G 14   we hear that you have considerable experience of selling this type of article
G 15   would you be able to introduce these goods onto the Italian market?
G 16   we wish to launch this product onto the German market
G 17   we feel that there is considerable demand abroad for such goods
G 18   you already represent a number of British firms
G 19   it would be your job to develop this market for us
G 20   we should be prepared to spend an average of . . . per year on advertising
G 21   we expect you to display a full range of our products in your showrooms
G 22   the representative will receive advertising material free of charge
G 23   we are the sole agents
G 24   sole agency

G	25	we are commission agents
G	26	we require sales offices in Spain
G	27	we are franchised dealers
G	28	selling agents
G	29	full-time agents
G	30	part-time agents
G	31	middleman
G	32	consignee
G	33	consignment stock
G	34	goods on consignment
G	35	export agent
G	36	buying agent
G	37	principal
G	38	we are sure that your goods will find a ready market in this country
G	39	we understand that you are looking for a representative in France
G	40	we are very experienced in this type of work
G	41	we wish to apply for the agency
G	42	we have successfully represented many similar firms
G	43	we have good connections with the large stores in London
G	44	we intend to work the German market intensively
G	45	we are prepared to take over the after-sales service
G	46	we have no commitments to any other firms in this country
G	47	we agree not to represent any of your competitors
G	48	we would also be prepared to advise on marketing and advertising of the goods
G	49	we have a large network of contacts in France
G	50	we are prepared to grant you the agency
G	51	the contract is limited initially to . . . years
G	52	the contract may be renewed for a further year
G	53	the contract may be cancelled by either party
G	54	with . . . months notice
G	55	there is a trial period of . . . months
G	56	the agency is on a trial basis
G	57	we shall grant you the sole selling rights
G	58	we can place a car at your disposal
G	59	please let us know within . . . weeks if these terms are acceptable
G	60	we have already concluded an agency agreement with another company
G	61	we can grant you the French agency for our products
G	62	we shall send you full details of all our products

G	63	our brochures will have to be translated into French and English
G	64	we trust that you can arrange translation of these documents
G	65	we can arrange translation ourselves, if you prefer
G	66	publicity material will be provided by us
G	67	at our expense
G	68	expenses will be paid by our company
G	69	expenses must be paid by the agent
G	70	agent's territory
G	71	we shall provide brochures in French
G	72	we shall carry out an intensive advertising campaign
G	73	we are prepared to take on part of the cost
G	74	all business concluded by the agent . . .
G	75	goods are sold on a commission basis
G	76	our representatives work on a commission basis
G	77	we offer a fixed salary of . . . plus commission of . . . %
G	78	it is not our practice to offer a fixed salary
G	79	our normal rate of commission for overseas representatives is . . . %
G	80	this commission is payable on all orders placed through you or your intermediaries
G	81	the commission is payable on all orders coming from your area
G	82	the commission is paid on receipt of the amount invoiced
G	83	the commission is to include any expenses which you incur
G	84	provided you send us full details of your expenses
G	85	we shall pay your expenses upon presentation of receipts
G	86	expenses for entertaining customers will be reimbursed
G	87	the commission will be . . . % of the turnover
G	88	we offer a commission of . . . % on all business negotiated by you
G	89	selling commission
G	90	the commission will be paid quarterly
G	91	commission is payable on all orders
G	92	we prefer to settle at the end of every quarter
G	93	we prefer monthly statements

H — References

H	1	Mr X has applied for the post of . . . with our company
H	2	he has given your name as referee [a reference]
H	3	we should be grateful if you could give us information about Mr X
H	4	information on his character and ability
H	5	his reliability
H	6	have you been satisfied with his services?
H	7	the post demands a high degree of integrity
H	8	the post is a demanding one
H	9	we require someone adaptable
H	10	your information will be treated in the strictest confidence
H	11	he has worked for our company for 5 years
H	12	he has been with us for only a short time
H	13	he has been with us since leaving school [graduating]
H	14	he was trained by us as a . . .
H	15	he worked for us from June 19 . . . to August 19 . . .
H	16	he left our company after 3 years to work abroad
H	17	he was employed as a . . .
H	18	he was dismissed 4 years ago
H	19	he was made redundant [laid off] on April 19 . . .
H	20	he was an efficient worker
H	21	he was totally reliable
H	22	honest and hardworking
H	23	punctual
H	24	he has a pleasant disposition
H	25	he has specialist knowledge of . . .
H	26	he is ambitious
H	27	it is no doubt for this reason that he has applied for this post
H	28	promotion opportunities are limited in our company at present
H	29	he has shown considerable initiative in his work
H	30	he was always in good health
H	31	he was not a very good worker
H	32	he was not very reliable
H	33	he was frequently absent from work
H	34	he was often late for work
H	35	he was not very punctual
H	36	he was often rather slipshod in his work

H	37	for health reasons
H	38	his health was poor
H	39	and this has affected his work
H	40	I therefore have some hesitation about recommending him to you
H	41	he has shown little initiative and he works slowly
H	42	he is very unreliable
H	43	his work was generally satisfactory
H	44	his work was always of a very high quality
H	45	his work was always of the highest quality
H	46	he carried out his duties to our complete satisfaction
H	47	we have no hesitation in recommending him
H	48	his work was often unsatisfactory
H	49	we feel that we cannot give you any information on this applicant
H	50	we have known him only a short time
H	51	we have known him for ten years
H	52	and we are pleased to act as referees on his behalf [to act as a reference for him]
H	53	we therefore suggest that you contact . . .
H	54	they should be able to give you more detailed information on him
H	55	the company . . . has just placed a large order with us
H	56	they have asked for credit
H	57	you were quoted as referees [a reference]
H	58	as this is the first time we have done business with this company
H	59	we should be grateful for information on their financial position
H	60	and on their long-term prospects
H	61	middle-term
H	62	short-term
H	63	on their competitiveness with regard to the domestic market
H	64	the overseas market
H	65	what is their reputation both at home and overseas?
H	66	information on their credit status and reliability
H	67	we should be grateful for any information you could give us about the company
H	68	we believe you have known the firm for some time
H	69	could we, in your opinion, allow them a credit of . . . ?
H	70	without security
H	71	we assure you of our complete confidence in this matter

H 72   we shall treat your information with the greatest discretion
H 73   we shall always be pleased to reciprocate
H 74   we have known this company for 6 years
H 75   we have done business with the firm for 5 years
H 76   they are regular customers of ours
H 77   they have been business associates of ours for many years
H 78   the firm has a excellent reputation
H 79   it is in a good financial position
H 80   the company has considerable financial resources
H 81   this company is completely reliable
H 82   the company has always fulfilled its obligations promptly
H 83   we feel sure that you can allow this credit without hesitation
H 84   we have had to send several reminders to this firm in recent months
H 85   they still owe us . . .
H 86   they have still not settled our invoices from last year
H 87   they are in a difficult financial position
H 88   they have insufficient capital
H 89   it would not be advisable to grant this firm credit
H 90   we advise you to be cautious
H 91   we can accept no responsibility for this information
H 92   as we do not know this firm
H 93   we have little information on this company
H 94   we believe that the company was founded only recently
H 95   we feel that we are not in a position to advise you in this matter
H 96   we regret that we are unable to give the information which you request
H 97   we have not known the company long enough
H 98   we must therefore refer you to . . .

I — Job applications and advertisements

I 1   we are a well-established firm based in the south of England

I	2	we are looking for . . .
I	3	we require . . .
I	4	we have vacancies for . . .
I	5	to commence duties on October 8
I	6	to replace one of our representatives
I	7	to replace our retiring export manager
I	8	we require someone experienced in the field of export sales
I	9	we require an experienced salesman
I	10	the person we are looking for will be in the age range 25-35
I	11	and will have at least 5 years experience in the field of . . .
I	12	a knowledge of English is desirable
I	13	a knowledge of foreign languages is essential
I	14	the person appointed must be capable of working within a team
I	15	he must be able to adapt to the needs of different clients
I	16	and to delegate responsibility
I	17	we are looking for a very adaptable person
I	18	to lead our export department
I	19	the position includes a company car
I	20	we are prepared to pay a salary of at least . . .
I	21	salary according to age and experience
I	22	salary negotiable
I	23	salary of not less than . . . per annum
I	24	per month
I	25	the salary is . . . net
I	26	the gross salary is . . .
I	27	a bonus is payable
I	28	approximately . . . % is deducted for tax
I	29	for social security [national health insurance]
I	30	the salary is tax-free
I	31	accommodation will be provided free of charge by the company
I	32	6 weeks holiday [vacation] per year
I	33	paid holiday [vacation]
I	34	a 35-hour week
I	35	a 6-day week
I	36	a flexible time scheme [schedule] is in operation
I	37	applicants must be prepared to work overtime
I	38	there is a company pension scheme [plan]
I	39	please give the names of two people who would be prepared to act as referees [references]
I	40	one of your referees [references] should be your present employer
I	41	we also require a reference from your bank manager

I 42   I see from your advertisement in the . . .
I 43   I have learned from business associates
I 44   I have read your advertisement in last week's edition of the
       . . .
I 45   I wish to apply for this post
I 46   please send me further details of the post
I 47   together with an application form
I 48   as you will see from the enclosed curriculum vitae [resume]
I 49   I have considerable experience of this kind of work
I 50   I have also attended several conferences on this subject
I 51   I feel that I can meet the requirements of this post
I 52   I am currently working for an export firm
I 53   I am looking for a similar post
I 54   I now wish to change my job
I 55   I wish to work for a larger organization
I 56   with international connections
I 57   to improve my career prospects
I 58   for personal reasons
I 59   I am looking for a position with more responsibility
I 60   I wish to work abroad
I 61   I wish to improve my chances of promotion
I 62   I am looking for a post with better prospects
I 63   I wish to make use of my knowledge of languages
I 64   I speak fluent French and German
I 65   I have a basic knowledge of English
I 66   I have qualifications in . . .
I 67   I have a diploma in . . .
I 68   I have a degree in . . .
I 69   my typing speed is . . . per minute
I 70   my shorthand speed is . . . per minute
I 71   I have experience of work with microcomputers
I 72   I have used a word processor
I 73   I was born in . . .
I 74   I went to school in . . .
I 75   where I passed the following examinations
I 76   in the following subjects
I 77   I went to university in . . .
I 78   where I studied . . . as my main subject [my major]
I 79   and . . . as my subsidiary subject [my minor]
I 80   I graduated in the following subjects
I 81   I passed the state exam
I 82   with distinction
I 83   I failed in the following subjects

I **84**   I then worked for 4 years for an export firm
I **85**   I spent 3 years abroad
I **86**   I was promoted to department manager in 19 . . .
I **87**   I was made redundant [laid off] in 19 . . .
I **88**   I have been unemployed since then
I **89**   at night school, I followed [took] courses in . . .
I **90**   I was trained as a bilingual secretary
I **91**   should you wish to invite me for [an] interview
I **92**   I can come to interview [to be interviewed] at any time
I **93**   I can only come to interview [to be interviewed] on Fridays
I **94**   could I come to interview [to be interviewed] at a later date?
I **95**   I shall be available from June 16 onwards
I **96**   I hope that you will consider my application favorably
I **97**   I enclose a testimonial [reference] from my previous employer
I **98**   I enclose copies of testimonials [references] from my last two employers
I **99**   and copies of my diplomas/certificates
I **100**   the names of two referees [references] are given below
I **101**   the following have agreed to act as referees [references] on my behalf
I **102**   I should be grateful if you would not approach my present employers
I **103**   prior to the interview
I **104**   without my prior consent
I **105**   I enclose a stamped addressed envelope
I **106**   I enclose an international reply coupon [envelope]
I **107**   I should be pleased to provide you with any further information you may require
I **108**   I have applied for the post [position] of
I **109**   and I should be grateful if you would be prepared to act as referee [a reference] on my behalf

J — Change of address, etc.

J **1**   our head [home] office is no longer in London
J **2**   our head [home] office has moved to Frankfurt
J **3**   we have now opened a new branch in Madrid
J **4**   because of the steady growth in our business
J **5**   we have moved to new and larger premises in Bordeaux

J	6	this means that we shall be able to give better service to all our customers
J	7	we assure you that we shall maintain our former high standard of service
J	8	our address has changed
J	9	and is now as follows
J	10	please forward any correspondence to this address
J	11	please inform your despatch [shipping] department of this change of address
J	12	our telephone number has changed
J	13	our telephone number is now...
J	14	we have changed the company's name
J	15	the company's name is now...
J	16	we have merged with...
J	17	as of May 14 we shall be known under the new name of...
J	18	we are no longer in this line of business
J	19	we no longer manufacture these goods
J	20	we ceased production of these articles three years ago
J	21	we now specialize only in the manufacture of . . .
J	22	production of these articles has been taken over by Messrs...& Co
J	23	our factory in Turin is being demolished in March
J	24	and we are switching production to Zürich
J	25	we have had to close our factory in Birmingham
J	26	we have closed our export department
J	27	we suggest that you contact our parent company
J	28	our associated company in Paris
J	29	we have been taken over by...
J	30	...have acquired...% of our company's shares
J	31	the company has gone out of business
J	32	we ceased trading six months ago
J	33	the company has gone bankrupt
J	34	the receiver has been called in
J	35	Mr...has been promoted to the position of...
J	36	he is now deputy director
J	37	he is manager of our new export department in Vienna
J	38	he has been appointed to the board of directors
J	39	he has been transferred to another branch
J	40	Mr...no longer works for this company
J	41	he has moved to another company
J	42	he retired in August
J	43	our managing director, Mr..., died six months ago
J	44	he has been replaced by Mr...

J 45 his duties have been taken over by Mr...

K — Travel and hotel reservations

K	**1**	I should like to reserve a seat on the Paris–Heidelberg train
K	**2**	departing Paris at 13:45, arriving Heidelberg at 19:55
K	**3**	express train
K	**4**	TEE (Trans-Europe Express)
K	**5**	is it necessary to reserve a seat on this train?
K	**6**	seat reservation is necessary on all express trains
K	**7**	this train does run on public holidays
K	**8**	the train runs only on working days
K	**9**	local train
K	**10**	special train
K	**11**	relief train
K	**12**	the train leaves from platform 6
K	**13**	a window seat
K	**14**	in a non-smoking compartment
K	**15**	couchette [bed in a sleeper]
K	**16**	sleeper
K	**17**	dining-car
K	**18**	buffet car
K	**19**	passport control on the train
K	**20**	do you want to travel first class?
K	**21**	a seat in a first-class compartment
K	**22**	what time does the train arrive in...?
K	**23**	I enclose a copy of my intended itinerary
K	**24**	a single ticket
K	**25**	a day return
K	**26**	a return ticket
K	**27**	platform ticket
K	**28**	is a supplement payable for this train?
K	**29**	is there a left-luggage office on the station?
K	**30**	where are the luggage lockers?
K	**31**	where is the lost-property [lost and found] office?
K	**32**	is this ticket valid for all bus routes?
K	**33**	the ticket is not transferable

K	**34**	can I get a monthly ticket for the bus?
K	**35**	a multi-journey [multi-ride] ticket
K	**36**	what time does the boat leave Calais?
K	**37**	car ferry
K	**38**	please send me details of your car ferry services
K	**39**	hovercraft
K	**40**	a cabin for 2
K	**41**	a first class cabin
K	**42**	I wish to reserve a place for a car and two passengers
K	**43**	can you offer a discount for a group of 20?
K	**44**	on the Dover-Calais ferry
K	**45**	what time is flight no. . . . to . . .?
K	**46**	charter flight
K	**47**	scheduled flight
K	**48**	I wish to book 3 seats on the first available flight to...
K	**49**	which terminal does the plane leave from?
K	**50**	are meals served during the flight?
K	**51**	economy class
K	**52**	club class
K	**53**	please confirm your booking 24 hours before departure
K	**54**	are the airport taxes included in the price?
K	**55**	hand luggage
K	**56**	air hostess
K	**57**	steward
K	**58**	drinks are served during the flight
K	**59**	passengers must check in at least 45 minutes before departure
K	**60**	I am looking for a medium-priced room
K	**61**	I wish to reserve a single room with bath
K	**62**	a double room
K	**63**	a twin-bedded room
K	**64**	with shower
K	**65**	with toilet and shower
K	**66**	please let me know your price for a single room
K	**67**	during the high season
K	**68**	in the early season
K	**69**	the late season
K	**70**	from the 19th to the 30th of April
K	**71**	do you accept group bookings?
K	**72**	I wish to organize a conference of our sales representatives in October
K	**73**	and I am looking for a suitable hotel near to the airport
K	**74**	we wish to be picked up from the airport by coach

K 75   we wish to be taken to the hotel by coach
K 76   the price of a double room for three nights is...
K 77   these are inclusive prices
K 78   including breakfast
K 79   half board
K 80   full board
K 81   including service and V.A.T. [Value Added Tax—similar to sales tax]
K 82   tip
K 83   please quote the inclusive price
K 84   all rooms have central heating
K 85   all rooms have hot and cold running water
K 86   breakfast is served until 10 o'clock
K 87   the hotel has its own car park
K 88   underground car park
K 89   multi-storey [story] car park
K 90   there is a car park nearby
K 91   the hotel is in a quiet position
K 92   it has conference facilities
K 93   it has a conference room for 100 people
K 94   it is close to the city centre [center]
K 95   how far is it from the hotel to the airport?
K 96   is there a bus service to the airport?
K 97   it is only a few minutes from the city centre [center]
K 98   it is in a quiet suburb
K 99   by the river
K 100   it has a lift [elevator]
K 101   night porter
K 102   it has a bureau de change [foreign-currency exchange]
K 103   I am writing to confirm my reservation
K 104   please send me a menu and wine list
K 105   please let me know if you require a deposit
K 106   please send the bill to my company, Messrs...
K 107   unfortunately, I have to change my date of departure
K 108   and will not arrive in...until July 21
K 109   I have to cancel my reservation at your hotel

L — Property: sales and rentals

L	1	house for sale
L	2	house to let [rent]
L	3	flat
L	4	appartment [apartment]
L	5	penthouse
L	6	villa
L	7	detached house [one-family house]
L	8	bungalow
L	9	semi-detached house [two-family house]
L	10	town house
L	11	2 bedrooms, living room, kitchen, bathroom, garage, garden
L	12	we wish to rent a house for approximately 18 months
L	13	please let us know the rent for such a flat [an apartment]
L	14	the rent is...per month
L	15	per annum
L	16	if you are prepared to rent the flat for two years
L	17	we can offer you a discount of...%
L	18	we are looking for office accommodation in the town centre [center]
L	19	we wish to purchase a property in the centre [center] of town
L	20	we are prepared to pay a maximum of...
L	21	in a desirable position
L	22	in a residential area
L	23	in the green belt
L	24	further details available from...
L	25	mortgages available
L	26	loans available
L	27	at...% interest
L	28	interest-free
L	29	at a rent of...per month
L	30	at a price of...per square metre [meter]
L	31	we can arrange a mortgage
L	32	a loan can be arranged through our insurance company
L	33	we have a number of holiday [vacation] properties for sale in the South of France
L	34	free inspection flights
L	35	time-sharing

M — Financial reports

M	1	the meeting will be held at the head [home] office of the company
M	2	the annual general [shareholders'] meeting
M	3	our a.g.m. will take place this year on July 3
M	4	the ordinary general meeting
M	5	an extraordinary meeting has been called
M	6	the agenda for the a.g.m.
M	7	matters arising
M	8	a.o.b. (any other business)
M	9	the following took part in the meeting:
M	10	general manager
M	11	chairman
M	12	sales manager
M	13	export manager
M	14	overseas representative
M	15	personnel manager
M	16	workers' representatives
M	17	trade [labor] union members
M	18	shareholders
M	19	the executive board
M	20	the minutes were taken by…
M	21	the chairman welcomed the shareholders to the meeting
M	22	and presented the report for the last financial year
M	23	and presented the minutes of the last meeting
M	24	we have increased production
M	25	production has increased
M	26	we have increased our production by…% in comparison with last year
M	27	and created new jobs
M	28	our turnover increased by…%
M	29	increase in turnover
M	30	we increased our exports by . . . %
M	31	because of an increase in investments
M	32	we have invested considerable resources in our factories
M	33	we have increased our share of the market
M	34	our goods found a ready market in other European countries
M	35	in order to consolidate our position in the market
M	36	we must develop our position in the market

M	37	the foreign market
M	38	the domestic market
M	39	our largest markets are France and Italy
M	40	there has been a favourable development in our sales in Germany
M	41	with domestic sales of . . .
M	42	our total sales increased from . . . to . . .
M	43	our total sales decreased from . . . to . . .
M	44	in the long term we expect good sales possibilities
M	45	we have used our available capacity to the full
M	46	we must maintain our lead in this sector
M	47	our long-term investment programme
M	48	will allow us to improve the quality of our products
M	49	our development programme
M	50	short-term
M	51	medium-term
M	52	we expect an increase in our total business
M	53	our capital assets increased by . . . %
M	54	borrowed capital
M	55	our liquid assets rose by . . . %
M	56	the company increased its share capital to . . .
M	57	an increased dividend of . . . per share was paid
M	58	returns
M	59	profit
M	60	net profit
M	61	profit after tax
M	62	the company increased its profits by . . . % in the first quarter of the year
M	63	growth rate
M	64	the general economic recession
M	65	has reduced demand
M	66	in the second half of the year demand declined
M	67	and we have met difficulties with sales
M	68	there has been a decline in production
M	69	we must reckon with a slight decrease in production
M	70	and exports have decreased
M	71	this has reduced our growth possibilities
M	72	the increase in energy and other raw material prices
M	73	has had a detrimental effect
M	74	competition has also increased
M	75	because of competition from other firms in this sector
M	76	our competitiveness has been weakened
M	77	staffing costs were also very high

M 78 the company made a total loss last year of £ . . .
M 79 our losses in certain areas were particularly heavy

N — Use of the telephone

N 1 I should like to speak to Mr . . .
N 2 hold the line
N 3 the line is engaged [busy]
N 4 I'm connecting you now
N 5 hello
N 6 goodbye
N 7 Mr . . . isn't here at the moment
N 8 would you like to leave a message?
N 9 can you give him the following message?
N 10 this is a recorded message
N 11 can you give me extension . . . please?
N 12 I'm ringing from a call-box [pay-phone]
N 13 replace the receiver and dial again
N 14 local call
N 15 long-distance call
N 16 international call
N 17 reverse charges [collect] call
N 18 I'd like a reverse charges [collect] call to . . .
N 19 I'd like to make a person to person call
N 20 telephone directory
N 21 you'll have to look up the number in the directory
N 22 directory enquiries
N 23 can you give me the number of Messrs . . . ?
N 24 can you give me the STD [area] code for Manchester?
N 25 I've got a bad connection
N 26 I'll have to hang up
N 27 you can dial the number yourself
N 28 I'll have to dial the number again
N 29 I dialled the wrong number
N 30 I've got a crossed line
N 31 I was cut off
N 32 dialling tone [dial tone]
N 33 engaged tone [busy signal]

N 34 you have to omit the '0' when dialling the number
N 35 I'm phoning from England
N 36 I'll call back

O — Bank and post office

O 1 I'd like to open a savings account
O 2 a current [checking] account
O 3 a deposit [savings] account
O 4 a joint account
O 5 an account has been opened in your name
O 6 what is the present rate of interest?
O 7 what are the bank charges?
O 8 cheque [check] book
O 9 standing order
O 10 my account is with the . . . bank
O 11 my account number is . . .
O 12 I have a Post Office account
O 13 I want to transfer . . . to my account
O 14 I wish to close my account
O 15 I want to draw [withdraw] . . .
O 16 withdrawals of that amount are subject to a short delay
O 17 I want to pay in . . . to [deposit . . . in] my current [checking] account
O 18 your account is in the red
O 19 and your overdraft limit is . . .
O 20 you have now exceeded this amount
O 21 I want to cash this cheque [check]
O 22 can I cash these travellers' cheques [travelers' checks] here?
O 23 I should like to pay this cheque into [deposit this check in] my account
O 24 I'd like a statement
O 25 statements are sent to you monthly
O 26 what is my balance at the moment?
O 27 credit
O 28 debit
O 29 a long-term loan
O 30 short-term
O 31 payee
O 32 savings bank

O	33	building society [savings and loan]
O	34	credit card
O	35	Eurocheque card
O	36	five . . . p stamps, please
O	37	I want to send this parcel to France
O	38	by air mail
O	39	by surface post [mail]
O	40	by parcel post
O	41	by registered post [mail]
O	42	by express delivery
O	43	you must fill in a customs declaration
O	44	I'd like to send a telegram to . . .
O	45	by telex
O	46	poste restante
O	47	I'd like a money order for . . .
O	48	PO box number . . .
O	49	address code/routing code [zip code]

P — Insurance

P	1	I wish to take out insurance
P	2	personal insurance
P	3	property insurance
P	4	insurance company
P	5	the insured, Mr . . . , has asked us to . . .
P	6	I have passed your letter to the claims department
P	7	I enclose a cover note
P	8	I require a proposal form
P	9	you will receive the policy shortly
P	10	the policy has to be issued by our head [home] office
P	11	the terms of the policy are enclosed
P	12	the policy number is . . .
P	13	you must give us the name of the policy holder
P	14	the period of the policy is . . .
P	15	I wish to renew my policy
P	16	I have cancelled the policy
P	17	the sum assured is . . .
P	18	the monthly premium is . . .
P	19	the insurance covers . . .

P	20	claim
P	21	damage
P	22	act of God
P	23	fire insurance
P	24	motor [car] insurance
P	25	third party insurance
P	26	comprehensive insurance
P	27	travel insurance
P	28	you must be in possession of a Green Card
P	29	you must report the accident to our head [home] office
P	30	you must secure [get] the names of witnesses
P	31	accident insurance
P	32	luggage insurance
P	33	sickness insurance
P	34	insurance broker

Q — Office terminology and technology

Q	1	filing-cabinet
Q	2	card-index
Q	3	dictaphone
Q	4	desk
Q	5	telex
Q	6	memory typewriter
Q	7	microcomputer
Q	8	v.d.u.
Q	9	word processor
Q	10	keyboard
Q	11	key
Q	12	computer terminal
Q	13	floppy disc
Q	14	disc drive unit
Q	15	data bank
Q	16	memory
Q	17	silicon chip
Q	18	microprocessor

Q 19 pocket calculator
Q 20 correction fluid
Q 21 date stamp
Q 22 paper clip
Q 23 staple
Q 24 stapler
Q 25 pencil sharpener
Q 26 franking [stamp] machine
Q 27 memo pad
Q 28 loose-leaf binder
Q 29 printer
Q 30 photocopier
Q 31 information technology
Q 32 viewdata
Q 33 the system conforms with international telecommunications norms
Q 34 it can be accessed by telephone from your office
Q 35 the electronic telephone directory can be accessed from the terminal
Q 36 a modem provides the interface with the telecoms network
Q 37 two-way communication between computers
Q 38 the system has electronic message and mail facilities
Q 39 this model provides mail merge facilities
Q 40 teletex
Q 41 fax (facsimile machine)
Q 42 this system allows you to link a computer to the Telex network
Q 43 it has an automatic call-back facility
Q 44 it sends messages at off-peak times
Q 45 teleconferencing
Q 46 online
Q 47 real time
Q 48 Computer Aided Design (CAD)
Q 49 Computer Aided Manufacture (CAM)
Q 50 Computer Aided Learning (CAL)
Q 51 Desktop Publishing
Q 52 expert system
Q 53 database
Q 54 relational database
Q 55 the information is updated every day
Q 56 spreadsheet
Q 57 data is stored as files, which are managed by the system
Q 58 the stored information is organized into numbered pages

Q 59   the disk can be read by any compatible computer
Q 60   this model is IBM compatible
Q 61   this model runs on MS-DOS and is not PC-DOS compatible
Q 62   clone
Q 63   operating system
Q 64   error messages
Q 65   byte
Q 66   kilobyte (K)
Q 67   megabyte
Q 68   this model has 512 K of RAM
Q 69   disk capacity is 1000 K
Q 70   software
Q 71   software package
Q 72   this package is supplied on disk
Q 73   the configuration can be adapted to suit your needs
Q 74   and an Italian version is available
Q 75   the program has a cursor-driven menu
Q 76   the cursor can be moved by using the mouse
Q 77   light pen
Q 78   system disk
Q 79   working disk
Q 80   double-sided
Q 81   double-density
Q 82   it is necessary to format the disk
Q 83   a 3.5″ disk
Q 84   disk directory
Q 85   sub-directory
Q 86   source disk
Q 87   target disk
Q 88   backup copy
Q 89   the file can be copied from disk A to disk B
Q 90   the programme is protected
Q 91   move text
Q 92   delete text
Q 93   add text
Q 94   there is a dictionary to check and correct spelling
Q 95   merge files
Q 96   text can be sent direct to the printer
Q 97   hardware
Q 98   personal computer
Q 99   mini−computer
Q 100   mainframe

Q 101	floppy disk
Q 102	hard disk
Q 103	CD ROM
Q 104	videodisk
Q 105	peripherals
Q 106	monochrome monitor
Q 107	colour monitor
Q 108	liquid crystal monitor
Q 109	plasma monitor
Q 110	the screen displays 25 lines of 80 characters
Q 111	parallel printer
Q 112	serial printer
Q 113	dot matrix printer
Q 114	daisywheel printer
Q 115	laser printer
Q 116	font
Q 117	print head
Q 118	paper loader
Q 119	soundproof printer hood
Q 120	plotter
Q 121	a scanner
Q 122	letter-quality
Q 123	the ribbon can be easily changed
Q 124	a low level of noise
Q 125	maintenance contract
Q 126	preventative maintenance
Q 127	any worn-out or defective part will be replaced free of charge
Q 128	adjustment
Q 129	provided the machine is regularly inspected
Q 130	hardware cannot be repaired on site
Q 131	the hard disk is damaged
Q 132	the fault was due to a voltage reduction
Q 133	the breakdown was due to a software fault
Q 134	power supply
Q 135	user manual
Q 136	component
Q 137	casing
Q 138	the cassette recorder was not connected to the computer
Q 139	the function key was not working
Q 140	you should have listed the contents of the disk
Q 141	this fax machine normally sends A4 pages in less than 12 seconds

Q 142	the workstation is out of order
Q 143	the fault is in the 16-bit processor
Q 144	the processor ought to drive up to 8 workstations
Q 145	the user was unaware that the service was not free
Q 146	packet switching

R — Names of countries and cities

R	1	Aachen
R	2	Africa
R	3	Alexandria
R	4	Algeria
R	5	Algiers
R	6	Amsterdam
R	7	Antwerp
R	8	Argentina
R	9	Arnhem
R	10	Asia
R	11	Athens
R	12	Australia
R	13	Austria
R	14	Avignon
R	15	Baden-Baden
R	16	Baghdad
R	17	Bahrain
R	18	Barcelona
R	19	Basel
R	20	Bayreuth
R	21	Beirut
R	22	Belfast
R	23	Belgium
R	24	Belgrade
R	25	Berlin
R	26	Berne
R	27	Bilbao
R	28	Bochum
R	29	Bolivia
R	30	Bombay
R	31	Bonn

R	32	Bordeaux
R	33	Brasilia
R	34	Brazil
R	35	Bregenz
R	36	Bremen
R	37	Bremerhaven
R	38	Brunswick
R	39	Brussels
R	40	Bucharest
R	41	Budapest
R	42	Bulgaria
R	43	Buenos Aires
R	44	Cadiz
R	45	Cairo
R	46	Canada
R	47	Canary Islands
R	48	Cape Town
R	49	Chad
R	50	Chile
R	51	China
R	52	Cologne
R	53	Colombia
R	54	Constance
R	55	Copenhagen
R	56	Cordoba
R	57	Corinth
R	58	Costa Rica
R	59	Cuba
R	60	Czechoslovakia
R	61	Damascus
R	62	Delhi
R	63	Denmark
R	64	Dijon
R	65	Djakarta
R	66	Dortmund
R	67	Dresden
R	68	Dubai
R	69	Dublin
R	70	Dunkirk
R	71	Düsseldorf
R	72	Ecuador
R	73	Edinburgh
R	74	E.E.C. (European Economic Community)

R 75 Egypt
R 76 Eindhoven
R 77 England
R 78 Erfurt
R 79 Ethiopia
R 80 Europe
R 81 Falkland Islands
R 82 Finland
R 83 Florence
R 84 France
R 85 Frankfurt
R 86 Freiburg
R 87 Gdansk
R 88 Geneva
R 89 Genoa
R 90 Ghana
R 91 Giessen
R 92 Gotha
R 93 Göttingen
R 94 Graz
R 95 Great Britain
R 96 Greece
R 97 Groningen
R 98 Guyana
R 99 The Hague
R 100 Halle
R 101 Hamburg
R 102 Hanover
R 103 Havana
R 104 Heidelberg
R 105 Helsinki
R 106 Holland
R 107 Honduras
R 108 Hungary
R 109 Iceland
R 110 India
R 111 Indonesia
R 112 Innsbruck
R 113 Interlaken
R 114 Iran
R 115 Iraq
R 116 Ireland
R 117 Israel

R 118	Istanbul
R 119	Italy
R 120	Ivory Coast
R 121	Jamaica
R 122	Japan
R 123	Jena
R 124	Jerusalem
R 125	Jordan
R 126	Kaiserslautern
R 127	Karl Marx Stadt (Chemnitz)
R 128	Karlsruhe
R 129	Kassel
R 130	Kiel
R 131	Kitzbühel
R 132	Klagenfurt
R 133	Koblenz
R 134	Krakow
R 135	Lausanne
R 136	Lebanon
R 137	Leipzig
R 138	Libya
R 139	Lille
R 140	Lima
R 141	Linz
R 142	Lisbon
R 143	Ljubljana
R 144	London
R 145	Lübeck
R 146	Lucerne
R 147	Lugano
R 148	Luxembourg
R 149	Lyons
R 150	Maastricht
R 151	Magdeburg
R 152	Mainz
R 153	Malaysia
R 154	Malta
R 155	Mannheim
R 156	Marseilles
R 157	Mecca
R 158	Mexico
R 159	Mexico City
R 160	Milan

R 161	Monaco
R 162	Montevideo
R 163	Montreux
R 164	Morocco
R 165	Moscow
R 166	Munich
R 167	Münster
R 168	Naples
R 169	Netherlands
R 170	New Delhi
R 171	New York
R 172	New Zealand
R 173	Nicaragua
R 174	Nice
R 175	Northern Ireland
R 176	Norway
R 177	Nuremberg
R 178	Oslo
R 179	Ostend
R 180	Padua
R 181	Panama
R 182	Paraguay
R 183	Paris
R 184	Passau
R 185	Peking
R 186	Peru
R 187	Philippines
R 188	Piraeus
R 189	Poland
R 190	Portugal
R 191	Prague
R 192	Qatar
R 193	Recife
R 194	Reykjavik
R 195	Riyadh
R 196	Rio de Janeiro
R 197	Rome
R 198	Rostock
R 199	Rotterdam
R 200	Rumania
R 201	Russia
R 202	Saarbrücken
R 203	Saint Petersburg (Leningrad)

R 204	Salzburg
R 205	Sardinia
R 206	Saudi Arabia
R 207	Scotland
R 208	Seville
R 209	Sicily
R 210	Singapore
R 211	South Africa
R 212	South America
R 213	South Korea
R 214	Spain
R 215	Split
R 216	Steyr
R 217	Stockholm
R 218	Strasbourg
R 219	Stuttgart
R 220	Sweden
R 221	Switzerland
R 222	Syria
R 223	Tangiers
R 224	Teheran
R 225	Tel Aviv
R 226	Thailand
R 227	The Hague
R 228	Thessalonika
R 229	Tokyo
R 230	Toronto
R 231	Toulon
R 232	Toulouse
R 233	Trier
R 234	Tripoli
R 235	Tunis
R 236	Tunisia
R 237	Turin
R 238	Turkey
R 239	Ulm
R 240	United Arab Emirates
R 241	United Kingdom
R 242	United States
R 243	Utrecht
R 244	Vancouver
R 245	Venezuela
R 246	Venice

R 247 Vienna
R 248 Wales
R 249 Warsaw
R 250 Weimar
R 251 West Indies
R 252 Wismar
R 253 Wolfsburg
R 254 Yugoslavia
R 255 Zagreb
R 256 Zaragoza
R 257 Zürich
R 258 Zwickau

S — Abbreviations

S   1   a/c
S   2   Bros
S   3   Co.
S   4   c/o
S   5   doz.
S   6   ed. (edition)
S   7   E.C.
S   8   e.g.
S   9   enc.
S 10   etc.
S 12   inst.
S 13   Ltd.
S 14   p.p.
S 15   V.A.T.

Index

cut **N31**

damage **D59, F18, F19, F20, F21, F24, F25, F26, F27, F33, F34, F43, F45, F46, F57, F60, F64, F76, F81, F82, P21, Q131**
damage-proof **D98**
data **Q15, Q57**
database **Q53, Q54**
date **A100, A105, D1, D10, D18, D21, E51, I94, K107, Q21**
dead **D112**
dealers **G27**
dealt **F62**
Dear **A1, A2, A3, A4, A5**
debit **E31, E96, O28**
debtor **E61**
declaration **D124, O43**
decline **M66, M68**
decrease **M43, M69, M70**
deducted **E16, E18, E25, I28**
deduction **E17**
defective **B40, Q127**
degree **H7, I68**
delay **D4, D7, D27, E100, E103, E114, O16**
delegate **I16**
delete **C53, Q92**
deliver **C7, C15, D5, D11, D16, D18, D20, D23, D24, D25, D34, D118, E7, E8, F1**
delivery **B42, B86, B94, C38, C40, C44, C58, D1, D2, D3, D4, D6, D7, D8, D9, D10, D17, D19, D21, D22, F13, O42**
demand **B56, G17, H7, M65, M66**
demolished **J23**
departing **K2**
department **E27, I18, I86, J11, J26, J37, P6**
departure **K53, K59, K107**
deposit **K105, O3**
deputy **J36**
designs **B70**
despatch **D33, D38, D39, D40, D41, D43, D57, J11**
despite **E104**
destination **D58**
detached **L7**
detailed **H54**
details **A71, A85, B54, B64, B94, G62, G84, I46, K38, L24**

detrimental **M 73**
develop **G19, M36**
development **M40, M49**
dial **N13, N27, N28, N29**
dialling **N32, N34**
dictaphone **Q3**
died **J43**
different **F16, I15**
difficult **H87**
difficulties **F36, F49, M67**
dimensions **D115**
dining-car **K17**
diploma **I67, I99**
director **J36, J38, J43**
directory **N20, N21, N22, Q84, Q85**
disappointed **F8**
disc **Q13, Q14**
discount **B78, B80, B81, B82, B83, E15, E16, E24, F72, K43, L17**
discretion **H72**
discussion **A75**
disk **Q59, Q69, Q78, Q79, Q82, Q83, Q86, Q87, Q89, Q101, Q102, Q104, Q131, Q140**
dismissed **H18**
display **G21**
disposal **G58**
disposition **H24**
distinction **I82**
dividend **M57**
documentary **E41, E42, E43, E48**
documents **D40, D63, E37, E39, G64**
domestic **H63, M38, M41**
domicile **B112**
draft **E48, E65, E84, E89**
draw **B27, O15**
drawing **B71, F6**
drinks **K58**
drive **Q14**
drums **D84**
dry **D99**
DTP **Q51**
due **B41, C36, D4, E26, E34, E105, E110, E119**
dues **D141**
dutiable **D123**
duties **H46, I5, J45**

ESPAÑOL

Materias

Introducción

Este libro va dirigido a los que tienen que escribir o simplemente entender correspondencia comercial en inglés, francés, alemán, italiano o español. Contiene expresiones clave en cada uno de estos cinco idiomas, en secciones que se han diseñado para facilitar el uso al máximo. Además de estas expresiones, el libro también contiene el vocabulario necesario para hacer llamadas telefónicas y realizar operaciones bancarias o de correos. Se dan también listas de los nombres de países y ciudades en los distintos idiomas.

Nuestra intención ha sido que sea de utilidad no sólo a los que manejan la correspondencia comercial en su trabajo sino también a estudiantes y profesores de dicha materia. Los autores han cuidado de no favorecer ningún idioma en particular y el libro está compuesto de tal manera que sirve tanto a la secretaria francesa que tenga que escribir cartas en inglés como al estudiante que hable español que desee entender cartas en alemán o italiano. En total, son posibles diez combinaciones de los distintos idiomas, lo cual hace que el libro sea de gran utilidad para las empresas de importación-exportación.

Cómo emplear el libro

El libro se divide en cinco secciones distintas, que corresponden a los cinco idiomas utilizados. Cada una de estas secciones está subdividida en capítulos tales como *Solicitudes y ofertas*, *Pedidos*, etc. Dentro de cada capítulo, cada expresión lleva una letra y un número clave (**A36, B45**, etc.), los cuales corresponden a la expresión apropiada en cada uno de los demás idiomas.

Si tomamos, por ejemplo, la expresión inglesa **B45** 'the samples must be returned within 2 weeks', encontraremos bajo la misma letra y número en la sección española, la expresión 'las muestras deberán devolverse en un plazo máximo de dos semanas', en la sección alemana, la expresión 'die Muster müssen binnen 2 Wochen zurückgeschickt werden', etc.

Hay que tener en cuenta que cuando uno busque y no encuentre una expresión, bien podría existir una expresión sinónima.

Para que el usuario pueda localizar una palabra o una expresión particular con la máxima rapidez, se ha incluido un índice para cada idioma; dicho índice hace referencia a la letra y al número correspondiente.

Las palabras y expresiones entre corchetes en la sección inglesa indican la versión norteamericana del término.

A — Expresiones generales

A	1	Muy señor nuestro:
A	2	Muy señores nuestros:
A	3	Estimado Sr. X:
A	4	Estimada Sra. X:
A	5	Estimada Srta. X:
A	6	a la atención de
A	7	confidencial
A	8	asunto:
A	9	acusamos recibo de su atenta carta
A	10	hemos recibido su atenta carta
A	11	de 3 del corriente
A	12	con referencia a su carta
A	13	su referencia
A	14	nuestra referencia
A	15	una empresa con la que tenemos contacto nos ha facilitado su dirección
A	16	nos apresuramos a contestar su carta de
A	17	todavía no hemos recibido respuesta a nuestra carta de
A	18	con referencia a nuestra conversación telefónica de
A	19	me complace saber que
A	20	nuestro representante nos ha informado que
A	21	por recomendación de nuestro representante
A	22	lamentamos saber que
A	23	hemos recibido su carta a través de
A	24	nos interesa saber que
A	25	su carta antes mencionada
A	26	su carta mencionada a continuación
A	27	les haremos saber por teléfono
A	28	les haremos saber por telegrama
A	29	con referencia a nuestra reunión de
A	30	. . . nos ha informado
A	31	lamentamos comunicarles
A	32	tenemos el gusto de informarles
A	33	nos ha interesado saber que
A	34	adjuntamos nuestro catálogo
A	35	por la presente confirmamos
A	36	hagan el favor de comunicarnos
A	37	sírvanse averiguar la razón de

A	38	se requiere la información para
A	39	tan pronto como les sea posible
A	40	en cuanto hayamos recibido
A	41	con referencia a nuestra carta
A	42	con referencia a nuestra llamada telefónica
A	43	lamentamos profundamente que
A	44	nos ha extrañado que
A	45	les agradeceríamos nos mandasen
A	46	confiamos en que estas medidas serán de su agrado
A	47	esperamos les sea posible
A	48	sentimos no haber contestado antes
A	49	tenemos la oportunidad de
A	50	adjuntamos
A	51	en sobre aparte
A	52	en la misma recogida postal
A	53	a vuelta de correo
A	54	les devolvemos
A	55	que nos mandaron
A	56	nos permitimos sugerirles que
A	57	pueden estar seguros de que . . .
A	58	al referirnos a nuestra correspondencia anterior
A	59	no les extrañará que
A	60	tendremos mucho gusto en
A	61	caso de que no sea posible
A	62	nos acaban de comunicar que
A	63	estamos seguros de que comprenderán que
A	64	sírvanse
A	65	como ya saben Vds.
A	66	en contestación a su atenta carta
A	67	según nuestros archivos
A	68	nos permitimos recordarles que
A	69	sentimos tener que recordarles que
A	70	según nos solicitaron en su carta de
A	71	precisaremos información detallada sobre sus productos
A	72	nos agradaría conocer su opinión sobre este asunto
A	73	consideramos importante que Vds.
A	74	estamos tramitando enviarles
A	75	como consecuencia de nuestra conversación con su representante
A	76	puesto que estamos iniciando nuestras relaciones comerciales
A	77	según se desprende de su carta
A	78	nos permitimos señalarles que

A 79	me gustaría entrevistarme con X
A 80	nos vemos obligados a cancelar nuestra reunión del . . .
A 81	a su entera satisfacción
A 82	nuestra sede central está en
A 83	nuestra sede central se ha trasladado a
A 84	haremos todo lo que esté en nuestras manos para resolver el asunto
A 85	cuyos detalles exponemos a continuación
A 86	nuestro gerente se encuentra realizando un viaje de negocios
A 87	les agradeceremos nos contesten cuanto antes
A 88	confiamos en que Vds. comprenderán nuestra posición
A 89	les rogamos nos disculpen por las molestias que les hemos causado
A 90	esto no ha sido considerado debidamente
A 91	les sugerimos que vuelvan a considerar el asunto
A 92	quedamos gratamente impresionados por
A 93	nos es imposible aceptar
A 94	encontrarán detalles de
A 95	en el caso de que podamos servirles en algo
A 96	haremos todo cuanto podamos
A 97	nos damos cuenta de que
A 98	ya hemos cursado instrucciones para que
A 99	tan pronto como estén listas las mercancías
A 100	cuando conozcan la fecha
A 101	en caso de que se decidan por ello
A 102	en caso de que
A 103	de haberlo sabido
A 104	en un futuro próximo
A 105	en una fecha posterior
A 106	nos agradaría recibir esta información
A 107	adjuntamos sobre de respuesta franqueado
A 108	adjuntamos cupón internacional de respuesta
A 109	en caso de necesidad
A 110	puntualmente
A 111	el Sr. X nos ha aconsejado que nos dirijamos a Vds.
A 112	hasta la fecha no hemos tenido mucho éxito
A 113	por vía terrestre
A 114	por vía aérea
A 115	certificado
A 116	les rogamos tengan precaución
A 117	dentro de dos semanas
A 118	cuyos nombres les remitiríamos con mucho gusto

A 119	a juzgar por sus informes
A 120	estaríamos dispuestos a
A 121	estamos seguros de que
A 122	nos interesaría
A 123	quedamos a la espera de una pronta respuesta
A 124	confiamos en haberles sido de utilidad
A 125	quedamos muy agradecidos por
A 126	esperamos que sigan
A 127	les saluda cordialmente
A 128	les saluda atentamente
A 129	anexo(s)
A 130	firmado
A 131	P.P.

B — Solicitudes y ofertas

B	**1**	tenemos entendido que Vds. fabrican
B	**2**	nos especializamos en la fabricación de
B	**3**	somos propietarios de
B	**4**	estamos buscando un proveedor de confianza
B	**5**	sírvanse enviarnos información detallada sobre
B	**6**	nos interesan particularmente los siguientes artículos
B	**7**	sírvanse mandarme cualquier información que consideren oportuna
B	**8**	para poder elegir el producto que más me convenga
B	**9**	varios clientes nuestros han expresado interés por
B	**10**	sírvanse enviarnos prospectos de sus mercancías
B	**11**	hagan el favor de mandarnos su último catálogo
B	**12**	su prospecto más reciente
B	**13**	su última lista de precios
B	**14**	nos hemos enterado de su empresa a través de publicaciones especializadas
B	**15**	somos clientes de Vds. desde hace muchos años
B	**16**	según se desprende de su anuncio
B	**17**	se van agotando nuestras existencias
B	**18**	se han agotado nuestras existencias
B	**19**	¿pueden suministrar en almacén?
B	**20**	tenemos en existencia

B	**21**	su solicitud con referencia a nuestros productos
B	**22**	necesitamos el suministro lo más tarde el 2 de abril
B	**23**	para facilitar la introducción de su producto en el mercado
B	**24**	estamos dispuestos a hacerles una oferta especial
B	**25**	en el curso de una reciente visita a la feria de muestras
B	**26**	vi una muestra de sus productos
B	**27**	permítannos que señalemos a su atención
B	**28**	a condición de que . . .
B	**29**	sírvanse mandarnos una selección de sus productos
B	**30**	contamos con poder pedir estos productos con regularidad
B	**31**	en grandes cantidades
B	**32**	les rogamos nos informen si admiten compras a prueba
B	**33**	¿de cuánto tiempo disponemos para la prueba del producto?
B	**34**	esperamos con anticipación su oferta
B	**35**	nos interesan sus productos
B	**36**	la calidad de los productos es de suma importancia
B	**37**	con tal que no varíen los precios de las materias primas
B	**38**	nuestros productos se someten a pruebas rigurosas a fin de asegurar su calidad
B	**39**	todos nuestros productos llevan una garantía de dos años
B	**40**	garantizamos la sustitución gratuita de piezas defectuosas
B	**41**	debido a materiales o montaje defectuosos
B	**42**	hasta tres meses después de la fecha de entrega
B	**43**	aceptamos pedidos de cantidades mínimas de
B	**44**	las muestras son gratuitas
B	**45**	las muestras deberán devolverse en un plazo máximo de dos semanas
B	**46**	las muestras serán cargadas a su cuenta
B	**47**	junto con las muestras
B	**48**	hagan el favor de remitirnos muestras de sus productos
B	**49**	lamentablemente no es posible hacerles un envío a prueba
B	**50**	con derecho a devolución de las mercancías no vendidas
B	**51**	a prueba
B	**52**	deseamos ampliar nuestra gama actual
B	**53**	a las cuatro semanas de haber efectuado el pedido
B	**54**	sírvanse precisarnos detalles de sus productos
B	**55**	se desprende de su prospecto
B	**56**	debido a la fuerte demanda de nuestra clientela
B	**57**	los artículos ya están obsoletos
B	**58**	ya no fabricamos estos artículos en serie
B	**59**	nos permitimos sugerirles que se pongan en contacto con
B	**60**	10 motores, tipo . . .

B 61 en las siguientes medidas y cantidades

B 62 sírvanse participarnos cotizaciones de

B 63 nos interesaría ver sus últimos modelos

B 64 detalles de sus últimos modelos

B 65 con tal que nos resulten satisfactorios tanto el precio como la calidad

B 66 los pesos y tamaños están indicados en el catálogo ilustrado

B 67 para pedidos de más de

B 68 para un pedido de un mínimo de

B 69 en los siguientes colores

B 70 de los siguientes diseños

B 71 de acuerdo con el dibujo adjunto

B 72 ¿está disponible su catálogo en francés?

B 73 hemos visto material publicitario suyo

B 74 hagan el favor de mandarnos sus precios al por mayor

B 75 precios al por menor

B 76 nuestros precios están indicados en la lista adjunta

B 77 nuestros precios se indican en la muestra

B 78 los precios cotizados no incluyen descuentos

B 79 les cotizamos los precios mínimos

B 80 concedemos un descuento del . . . % en los precios que se indican en el catálogo

B 81 estamos dispuestos a concederles una rebaja de introducción del . . . %

B 82 ¿están dispuestos a concedernos un descuento especial?

B 83 descuento comercial

B 84 les rogamos nos informen de las condiciones de pago

B 85 nuestros precios siguen vigentes hasta el 8 de mayo

B 86 los precios cotizados incluyen entrega a la dirección indicada antes

B 87 los precios se deben cotizar en libras esterlinas

B 88 los precios vigentes en el momento del envío

B 89 los precios indicados en su carta

B 90 los precios se indican a continuación

B 91 si sus precios son competitivos

B 92 a un precio de . . . por unidad

B 93 a un precio especial de . . .

B 94 sírvanse informarnos sobre precios y plazos de entrega

B 95 estos son los precios más bajos que podemos ofrecerles

B 96 les podemos conceder un descuento de exportación del . . . %

B 97 nuestros precios incluyen el seguro

B 98   nuestros precios se encuentran por debajo de los de nuestros competidores

B 99   el precio por unidad

B 100   en fábrica

B 101   en almacén

B 102   nuestros precios se entienden f.o.b. Londres

B 103   embalaje incluido

B 104   embalaje excluido

B 105   porte pagado a Madrid

B 106   franco frontera

B 107   flete pagado hasta frontera

B 108   c. & f. (costo y flete)

B 109   franco en vagón

B 110   c.i.f. (costos, seguro y flete)

B 111   f.a.s. (franco al costado del barco)

B 112   franco a domicilio

B 113   franco en el puerto

B 114   franco en almacén

B 115   nos complace hacerles la siguiente oferta

B 116   ¿estarían dispuestos a aceptar un plazo de pago de tres semanas?

B 117   trabajamos con un margen de ganancia muy reducido

B 118   para grandes pedidos

B 119   la presente oferta es válida durante 5 días

B 120   sólo nos consideramos obligados por esta oferta en el caso de aceptarse el pedido antes del 5 de marzo

B 121   en el caso de quedar sin venderse las mercancías

B 122   se reserva el derecho de variar los precios

B 123   les agradecemos su solicitud con referencia a nuestros productos

B 124   si la calidad de los productos nos satisface plenamente

B 125   les haremos un pedido de prueba

B 126   si resultan satisfactorios los productos

B 127   pediremos mayores cantidades

B 128   para los primeros pedidos

B 129   para pedidos posteriores

B 130   mientras no se agoten las existencias

B 131   su pedido será servido a su entera satisfacción

B 132   nuestras condiciones de venta son

B 133   la pronta y esmerada ejecución de su pedido

B 134   les ofrecemos los productos indicados por Vds., como sigue

B 135 si los precios les resultan aceptables
B 136 con las siguientes condiciones

C — Pedidos

C 1 hemos estudiado su oferta
C 2 hemos estudiado detalladamente sus muestras
C 3 las mercancías ofrecidas en su catálogo se ajustan a nuestras necesidades
C 4 si nos satisface su primer envío
C 5 en relación con las muestras que nos enviaron Vds., les hacemos un pedido de . . .
C 6 queremos hacerles el siguiente pedido
C 7 el pedido ha de servirse sin demora
C 8 estamos dispuestos a hacerles un pedido con regularidad
C 9 el pedido se hace según sus precios de catálogo
C 10 queremos pedir 5 de cada uno de los siguientes artículos
C 11 adjunto les enviamos nuestro pedido núm. 8765 de . . .
C 12 sírvanse mandarnos inmediatamente los siguientes artículos
C 13 debemos insistir en que los artículos se suministren de las existencias
C 14 nos hacen falta las mercancías dentro de diez días
C 15 si no les es posible entregar dentro de dicho plazo
C 16 nos referimos a nuestro pedido del 5 de mayo
C 17 con referencia a nuestro pedido núm. 9675
C 18 sus precios nos parecen algo elevados
C 19 si Vds. rebajaran su oferta en un . . . %
C 20 estaríamos dispuestos a hacerles el siguiente pedido
C 21 sus precios son más altos que los de nuestro proveedor anterior
C 22 podemos adquirir las mercancías de otro proveedor a precios más ventajosos
C 23 tenemos compromiso con otro proveedor
C 24 ya hemos cubierto nuestras necesidades
C 25 nos llegó tarde su oferta
C 26 la muestra que se nos suministró no era de una calidad adecuada
C 27 si pueden suministrar los artículos de una calidad superior
C 28 si es posible suministrar en cantidades más reducidas

C	29	sírvanse comunicarnos la cantidad máxima que podrían suministrar inmediatamente
C	30	tenemos que modificar algo su pedido
C	31	esperamos que tal modificación les resulte aceptable
C	32	el artículo núm . . . no está disponible en este momento
C	33	debido a ciertos problemas que hemos experimentado con nuestro proveedor
C	34	debido a una huelga
C	35	debido a una escasez de materias primas
C	36	debido a una insuficiencia de personal
C	37	estamos atrasados en la producción
C	38	por lo cual nos resulta imposible garantizar la entrega antes del 4 de marzo
C	39	estamos dispuestos a reponer los artículos
C	40	se reserva el derecho de no efectuar el envío
C	41	queremos aumentar la cantidad pedida a . . .
C	42	no podemos aprovechar su oferta
C	43	no podemos aceptar sus condiciones de pago
C	44	no podemos aceptar sus condiciones de entrega
C	45	no podemos considerar su oferta
C	46	no nos hacen falta dichos artículos en este momento
C	47	no disponemos de almacenaje suficiente
C	48	no podemos aceptar su oferta en este momento
C	49	nuestra cartera de pedidos está completa
C	50	nos resulta imposible empezar a fabricar antes de agosto
C	51	nos vemos obligados a cancelar nuestro pedido
C	52	hemos cancelado nuestro pedido por telegrama
C	53	sírvanse cancelar los siguientes artículos de nuestro pedido
C	54	se reserva el derecho de cancelar el pedido
C	55	hemos recibido hoy mismo su pedido
C	56	confirmamos su pedido del 12 de mayo
C	57	les despacharemos su pedido lo antes posible
C	58	las mercancías de su pedido están listas para el envío
C	59	las mercancías de su pedido están listas para ser recogidas
C	60	estamos a la espera de sus instrucciones
C	61	sírvanse tomar las medidas necesarias para recoger las mercancías
C	62	se ha iniciado la manufactura de las mercancías
C	63	tengan la amabilidad de confirmar lo antes posible el pedido antes mencionado
C	64	esperamos estar en condiciones de servir su pedido dentro de unos diez días

D — Entregas, transportes, aduanas

D	1	confirmamos la fecha de entrega precisada en su carta
D	2	esperamos sus instrucciones en cuanto a la entrega
D	3	se precisa entrega inmediata
D	4	el retraso en el envío se debe a
D	5	los artículos se pueden suministrar inmediatamente
D	6	nos urge la entrega
D	7	el retraso en el envío nos ha ocasionado graves problemas
D	8	sírvanse comunicarnos cuándo se efectuará el envío
D	9	nuestro plazo de entrega más corto sería de un mes
D	10	haremos todo lo posible para efectuar el envío en la fecha prevista
D	11	podemos efectuar el suministro antes de la fecha prevista
D	12	nuestros agentes expedidores son
D	13	las mercancías estarán dispuestas para el envío a principios de mayo
D	14	las mercancías están listas para ser recogidas
D	15	en cuanto recibamos su pedido se expedirán las mercancías
D	16	se pueden expedir las mercancías en contenedores
D	17	se efectuará el envío dentro de 4 meses
D	18	sírvanse comunicarnos si les sería posible efectuar el envío para esta fecha
D	19	el plazo de entrega es de 4 meses
D	20	las mercancías se han de expedir para finales del mes que viene
D	21	ha de respetarse la fecha de entrega precisada en nuestra carta
D	22	la entrega ha de efectuarse puntualmente
D	23	no podemos aceptar las mercancías si no se entregan en la fecha convenida
D	24	no nos será posible entregar las mercancías dentro del plazo convenido de 2 meses
D	25	se pueden entregar las mercancías para el 5 de agosto
D	26	todavía no se han recibido los géneros
D	27	sírvanse comunicarnos el motivo de este retraso
D	28	porte pagado
D	29	el envío consta de

D 30 el envío se efectuó en el barco Berlín
D 31 el barco ha de llegar a Dóver el 21 de julio
D 32 confiamos en que el envío les llegará en buenas condiciones
D 33 todavía no nos ha llegado el envío que efectuaron Vds. el 15 de marzo
D 34 el envío que prometieron efectuar el 13 de febrero
D 35 enviaremos todas las mercancías en un solo lote
D 36 el envío consta de dos cajas, pesando cada una 50 kilos
D 37 el envío de las mercancías
D 38 se les han despachado hoy mismo las mercancías
D 39 las mercancías están listas para el envío
D 40 hemos remitido los documentos de expedición a nuestro banco
D 41 las mercancías se despacharon el 9 de junio
D 42 las cajas han sido recogidas por la agencia de transportes
D 43 en cuanto recibamos sus instrucciones, les enviaremos el aviso de expedición
D 44 hemos entregado las mercancías solicitadas a la agencia de transportes
D 45 su pedido no especifica el modo de expedición
D 46 como carga aérea
D 47 por carga aérea
D 48 por ferrocarril
D 49 por avión
D 50 por barco
D 51 por carretera
D 52 mercancías en tránsito
D 53 porte pagado
D 54 porte no incluido
D 55 porte incluido
D 56 portes
D 57 el puerto de embarque
D 58 el puerto de destino
D 59 para reducir al mínimo los daños en el tránsito
D 60 el conocimiento de embarque
D 61 la factura de flete
D 62 la factura consular
D 63 los documentos de embarque
D 64 la nota de consignación aérea
D 65 el expediente de valoración
D 66 el certificado de origen no estaba en regla
D 67 nos resulta imposible embalar las mercancías de la manera

		deseada por Vds.
D	**68**	es imprescindible que las mercancías se embalen con el máximo cuidado
D	**69**	es preciso que el embalaje sea consistente
D	**70**	el embalaje no es de la calidad requerida
D	**71**	sírvanse notificarnos si disponen de otro tipo de embalaje
D	**72**	el embalaje de las mercancías es deficiente
D	**73**	sírvanse prestar especial atención al embalaje
D	**74**	no podemos aceptar sus quejas sobre deficiencias en el embalaje
D	**75**	no se admite la devolución de las cajas
D	**76**	las cajas estarán numeradas consecutivamente
D	**77**	sentimos no poder aceptar solicitudes de embalajes especiales
D	**78**	tenemos que insistir en que las mercancías vayan embaladas en
D	**79**	el papel de embalaje
D	**80**	el cartón ondulado
D	**81**	virutas de madera
D	**82**	forrado de
D	**83**	contenedores
D	**84**	bidones
D	**85**	fardos
D	**86**	cajones
D	**87**	cajas
D	**88**	latas/botes
D	**89**	tarros
D	**90**	paletas
D	**91**	toneles
D	**92**	cajones de madera
D	**93**	sacos
D	**94**	no se admite la devolución de las cajas de cartón
D	**95**	los cajones serán marcados de la siguiente manera
D	**96**	resistente a los golpes
D	**97**	impermeable
D	**98**	irrompible
D	**99**	manténgase en lugar seco
D	**100**	manténgase en lugar fresco
D	**101**	manténgase boca arriba
D	**102**	arriba
D	**103**	abajo
D	**104**	frágil
D	**105**	abrir aquí

D 106	levantar aquí
D 107	frágil
D 108	atención
D 109	inflamable
D 110	peso neto
D 111	peso bruto
D 112	peso muerto
D 113	la carga
D 114	la descarga
D 115	pesos y medidas
D 116	el peso bruto se especifica en cada cajón
D 117	los derechos aduaneros corren a cargo del comprador
D 118	suministrado a Londres, derechos aduaneros pagados
D 119	sujeto a derechos aduaneros
D 120	se nos ha cobrado . . . en concepto de derechos aduaneros por estos artículos
D 121	los derechos de aduana de estas mercancías correrán a cargo de Vds.
D 122	derechos de aduana a pagar por el consignatario
D 123	valor arancelario
D 124	la declaración de aduana
D 125	los gastos de aduana
D 126	el despacho de aduana
D 127	hemos recibido la factura aduanera
D 128	la aduana de Aquisgrán impuso una multa al envío
D 129	nos hace falta el recibo de la aduana
D 130	la aduana de Dóver ha incautado el envío
D 131	han entrado en vigor nuevos reglamentos aduaneros
D 132	nosotros nos hacemos cargo de los trámites de aduana
D 133	una multa de la aduana
D 134	un almacén de depósito aduanero
D 135	un almacén de depósito
D 136	en depósito aduanero
D 137	el almacenamiento
D 138	el deterioro
D 139	el hurto
D 140	los derechos de aeropuerto
D 141	los derechos portuarios
D 142	los gastos de transbordo
D 143	los aranceles
D 144	nosotros nos hacemos cargo de los gastos de aduana

E — Facturas, pagos y recordatorios

E	1	acusamos recibo del envío
E	2	el envío llegó ayer a nuestra fábrica
E	3	las mercancías llegaron en buen estado
E	4	el suministro llegó bien
E	5	las mercancías que pedimos el 4 de abril llegaron puntualmente
E	6	adjuntamos la factura núm . . .
E	7	incluimos la factura correspondiente a las mercancías suministradas el 3 de mayo
E	8	la factura adjunta corresponde a las mercancías entregadas contra su pedido número . . .
E	9	les rogamos liquiden su factura lo antes posible
E	10	les rogamos liquiden su factura no más tarde del 12 de mayo
E	11	sírvanse abonar el importe de la factura en la cuenta núm. . . .
E	12	les rogamos liquiden la factura a vuelta de correo
E	13	enviamos adjunto un extracto de cuenta
E	14	el importe de la cuenta es . . .
E	15	el descuento está incluido en la cifra
E	16	en nuestros precios ya se han incluido los descuentos
E	17	habiéndose descontado un . . . %
E	18	hemos descontado el . . . % habitual de su factura
E	19	nos permitimos señalarles que hay un error en la factura
E	20	se ha cometido un error al sumar las cifras de la factura número
E	21	sírvanse enviarnos una factura corregida
E	22	les agradeceríamos hicieran el debido ajuste en la factura
E	23	les agradeceríamos corrigiesen el extracto de cuenta
E	24	en la factura se ha descontado sólo un . . . %
E	25	se ha descontado . . . de la factura
E	26	la equivocación fue debida a un error mecanográfico
E	27	un error por parte de nuestro departamento de contabilidad
E	28	un descuido involuntario
E	29	confirmamos el nuevo saldo de . . .
E	30	adjuntamos una nota de abono

E	31	una nota de cargo
E	32	les agradeceríamos una pronta liquidación
E	33	esperamos les sea posible liquidar la cuenta en el curso de la semana que viene
E	34	sírvanse mandarnos el importe de la cuenta en los próximos días
E	35	nos permitimos recordarles que nuestras condiciones de pago son
E	36	véanse nuestras condiciones de pago
E	37	documentos contra aceptación
E	38	contra reembolso
E	39	documentos contra pago
E	40	pago por adelantado
E	41	la carta de crédito
E	42	una carta de crédito a su favor
E	43	la letra de cambio
E	44	revocable
E	45	irrevocable
E	46	confirmado
E	47	sin confirmar
E	48	la letra
E	49	la letra a la vista
E	50	la letra a un plazo a la vista
E	51	le letra a un plazo con/del fecha
E	52	pagar contra recibo de bienes
E	53	al tipo de cambio vigente
E	54	al contado
E	55	billetes
E	56	monedas
E	57	moneda de curso legal
E	58	el giro bancario
E	59	el portador
E	60	el acreedor
E	61	el deudor
E	62	el pagaré
E	63	el crédito comercial
E	64	pagadero en el banco
E	65	una letra a 60 días a la vista
E	66	un crédito de . . . a abrir en el banco . . .
E	67	hemos cursado instrucciones a nuestro banco para que giren a su favor la cantidad de . . .
E	68	hemos girado a su favor la cantidad de . . .
E	69	hemos abonado esta cantidad en su cuenta

E 70	hemos cursado instrucciones a nuestro banco para que abonen en su cuenta la cantidad de . . .
E 71	hemos transferido la cantidad de . . . a su cuenta
E 72	para liquidar la cuenta
E 73	nuestra cuenta en el banco . . .
E 74	adjunto enviamos un cheque por el valor de . . .
E 75	un cheque cruzado
E 76	un cheque abierto
E 77	un giro postal
E 78	se ha cobrado el cheque
E 79	un cheque a su favor
E 80	adjuntamos un cheque por el valor de . . . en liquidación de su factura
E 81	£600 menos £45 en concepto de embalaje
E 82	adjuntamos un cheque por la mitad del importe
E 83	la transferencia bancaria
E 84	el giro
E 85	se ha abonado dicha cantidad en su cuenta
E 86	sírvanse enviarnos un recibo lo antes posible
E 87	acusamos recibo du su pago
E 88	les agradecemos el pago
E 89	aceptamos su letra
E 90	se ha abonado en nuestra cuenta la cantidad de . . .
E 91	les agradecemos haber liquidado la factura tan rápidamente
E 92	hemos recibido su aviso de pago
E 93	hace más de un mes que venció el plazo de pago de su cuenta
E 94	la factura queda sin saldar
E 95	esperamos su pago
E 96	su cuenta sigue arrojando un saldo negativo de . . .
E 97	las facturas pendientes han de saldarse para finales de este mes
E 98	no hemos recibido el saldo de nuestro extracto de cuenta de septiembre
E 99	por si se hubiera extraviado nuestro extracto de cuenta, incluimos una copia
E 100	sírvanse comunicarnos el motivo de la demora en el pago
E 101	puesto que hace ya tiempo que venció el plazo para saldar la cuenta
E 102	todavía no hemos recibido ninguna contestación a nuestra petición de pago
E 103	les rogamos tomen las medidas pertinentes lo antes posible

E 104   pese a nuestras repetidas peticiones de pago
E 105   a fin de saldar la cuenta pendiente
E 106   nuestros avisos han pasado desapercibidos
E 107   en el futuro, la factura ha de saldarse sin demora
E 108   todavía nos deben Vds.
E 109   hemos de recordarles que sólo en el caso de primeros pedidos concedemos un plazo de pago de dos semanas
E 110   nos permitimos señalarles que el plazo de pago venció el 4 de julio
E 111   ésta es nuestra última petición de pago
E 112   hemos de insistir en la liquidación inmediata de la cuenta
E 113   en el caso de que no recibamos su pago para principios del mes que viene
E 114   su demora en el pago es inaceptable
E 115   se extravió la factura
E 116   tomaremos medidas legales
E 117   nuestro departamento legal se encargará de recuperar la cantidad adeudada
E 118   recurriremos a la vía judicial para la recuperación
E 119   nos vemos obligados a tomar medidas para recuperar la cantidad pendiente
E 120   por vía judicial
E 121   hemos confiado el asunto a nuestro departamento legal
E 122   estamos dispuestos a concederles un plazo adicional de 12 días para efectuar el pago
E 123   pueden hacernos un pago parcial
E 124   Vds. han solicitado una prórroga del plazo de pago
E 125   confiamos en que Vds. comprenderán nuestra situación
E 126   estamos dispuestos a prorrogar el plazo de pago

F — Reclamaciones

F 1   las mercancías que se enviaron el 3 del mes corriente no fueron las que habíamos pedido
F 2   lamentamos tener que quejarnos de su envío núm. . . . .
F 3   nos permitimos señalarles un error en el envío que recibimos ayer
F 4   los artículos eran de colores distintos a los pedidos

F	5	eran de tallas distintas a las pedidas
F	6	no correspondían a los diseños que les enviamos
F	7	la calidad de las mercancías no llegó a satisfacernos
F	8	nos decepcionó la calidad de las mercancías
F	9	por las razones expuestas no podemos aceptar esta mercancía
F	10	los artículos resultaron ser defectuosos
F	11	nos enviaron Vds. 500 . . . en vez de los 250 que pedimos
F	12	ha habido un error en la ejecución del pedido
F	13	el contenido de los cajones no corresponde a la nota de entrega
F	14	faltaba del envío el artículo núm. . . .
F	15	los géneros no corresponden a las muestras
F	16	los artículos parecen haber sido confeccionados de manera distinta
F	17	los cajones llegaron rotos
F	18	las mercancías fueron deterioradas por un incendio
F	19	los géneros fueron dañados por malos tratos en el tránsito
F	20	los géneros llegaron dañados
F	21	muy estropeado
F	22	varios artículos llegaron rayados
F	23	roto
F	24	(ligeramente) deteriorado
F	25	dañado por el calor
F	26	dañado por el agua
F	27	los géneros deben de haberse dañado en el transporte
F	28	deben de haberse embalado sin el debido cuidado
F	29	el material de embalaje era de calidad inferior
F	30	los cajones deberían haberse reforzado con tiras metálicas
F	31	los cajones estaban mal construidos
F	32	los artículos están oxidados
F	33	los daños se produjeron entre la aduana británica y nuestra fábrica
F	34	los daños se produjeron antes de la llegada de las mercancías a Dóver
F	35	les rogamos nos envíen un repuesto cuanto antes
F	36	esto nos ha ocasionado grandes dificultades, dado que nos urgían las mercancías
F	37	nos urgen los restantes artículos
F	38	sentimos informarles que todos los artículos tendrán que reponerse
F	39	estamos dispuestos a quedarnos con las mercancías
F	40	a un precio reducido de . . . por unidad

F 41	nos vemos obligados a devolver el suministro entero
F 42	nos vemos obligados a devolver parte del suministro
F 43	hemos dispuesto la devolución de todos los artículos dañados en el tránsito
F 44	no tenemos más remedio que anular el pedido
F 45	consentimos en aceptar las mercancías dañadas si Vds. por su parte están dispuestos a rebajar el precio en un . . . %
F 46	sólo podemos vender las mercancías dañadas a un precio sensiblemente inferior al normal
F 47	todos los artículos tendrán que reponerse
F 48	esperamos que se evitarán tales errores en el futuro
F 49	esto nos ha ocasionado grandes dificultades con algunos clientes
F 50	nos permitimos sugerirles que se pongan en contacto con el agente expedidor
F 51	la compañía naviera
F 52	la compañía ferroviaria
F 53	la línea aérea
F 54	a nuestro parecer, les incumbe a Vds. hacer las indagaciones que sean necesarias
F 55	nos vemos obligados a pedirles que nos indemnicen por las pérdidas que hemos sufrido
F 56	insistimos en que Vds. nos indemnicen
F 57	nos vemos obligados a pedirles que nos abonen el valor de los artículos dañados
F 58	en lo que a los próximos pedidos se refiere, nos vemos en la obligación de reconsiderar nuestra posición
F 59	se ha investigado su reclamación
F 60	dado que el daño ocurrió en el transporte
F 61	les rogamos remitan el asunto a . . .
F 62	ésta es la primera vez que hemos tratado con dicho agente de transportes
F 63	nuestro seguro cubre los desperfectos mencionados por Vds.
F 64	nuestra garantía cubre este daño
F 65	según los términos de nuestra garantía
F 66	Vds. tienen derecho a que se les reembolse la cantidad abonada
F 67	les ofrecemos nuestras más sinceras disculpas por este error
F 68	estamos dispuestos a reponer las mercancías por otras de calidad parecida
F 69	adjuntamos un cheque por el valor de . . . como

reembolso
F 70 se repondrán las mercancías a nuestro cargo
F 71 sentimos que nuestro envío no les haya satisfecho
F 72 estamos dispuestos a ofrecerles un descuento del . . . %
F 73 les hemos concedido una rebaja del . . . % en el importe de la cuenta
F 74 hemos examinado las mercancías meticulosamente
F 75 no se ha descubierto ningún defecto en las mercancías
F 76 no podemos aceptar responsabilidad por los daños causados
F 77 según pueden constatar Vds. al leer las condiciones del contrato
F 78 sentimos comunicarles que no admitimos la devolución de las mercancías
F 79 les rogamos remitan el asunto a la compañía de seguros
F 80 nos permitimos señalarles que ha vencido el plazo de vigencia de la garantía
F 81 les rogamos se dirijan a la compañía naviera para que ésta certifique los daños
F 82 nos hace falta un informe de los agentes de transportes en el que se especifiquen los daños
F 83 dadas las circunstancias, no podemos aceptar su queja

G — Representaciones

G 1 buscamos un representante para vender nuestros productos en el extranjero
G 2 buscamos un representante que se encargue de la venta de nuestros productos
G 3 buscamos un representante para nuestra sucursal de . . .
G 4 el representante debe trabajar exclusivamente para nuestra firma
G 5 se ha de comprometer a no trabajar para nuestros competidores
G 6 y debe limitar sus actividades a este territorio
G 7 su principal tarea sería la de presentar nuestros catálogos y muestras a los clientes
G 8 el puesto requiere conocimientos especializados
G 9 se busca un representante especializado

G 10   no se requieren conocimientos especializados

G 11   nosotros mismos formamos a nuestros representantes

G 12   somos una pequeña empresa, dedicada a la fabricación de
. . .

G 13   dichos artículos disfrutan de un potencial de venta
excelente

G 14   nos han informado que Vd. tiene una larga experiencia en
la venta de artículos de esta clase

G 15   ¿sería Vd. capaz de introducir dichos artículos en el
mercado italiano?

G 16   tenemos intención de lanzar este producto al mercado
alemán

G 17   tenemos la impresión de que existe una fuerte demanda de
tales productos en el extranjero

G 18   Vd. representa ya a varias compañías británicas

G 19   su trabajo consistiría en ampliarnos este mercado

G 20   estaríamos dispuestos a gastar un promedio de . . . al año
en la publicidad

G 21   se requiere la exhibición de una amplia gama de nuestros
productos en sus salas de exposiciones

G 22   el representante recibirá material publicitario gratis

G 23   gozamos de la representación en exclusiva

G 24   la representación en exclusiva

G 25   somos comisionistas

G 26   buscamos oficinas de venta en España

G 27   somos concesionarios

G 28   representantes de venta

G 29   representantes con dedicación plena

G 30   representantes con dedicación parcial

G 31   el intermediario

G 32   el consignatario

G 33   la remesa de surtidos

G 34   los géneros consignados

G 35   el agente de exportación

G 36   el agente de compras

G 37   el principal

G 38   estamos seguros de que sus productos tendrán una fácil
salida en este país

G 39   tenemos entendido que Vds. buscan un representante en
Francia

G 40   tenemos una larga experiencia en este campo

G 41   deseamos ofrecerles nuestros servicios como
representantes

G 42 hemos representado a muchas empresas similares en gran beneficio suyo

G 43 estamos muy bien conectados con los grandes almacenes londinenses

G 44 tenemos intención de intensificar nuestros esfuerzos en el mercado alemán

G 45 estamos dispuestos a hacernos cargo del servicio posventa

G 46 no tenemos compromisos en este país con ninguna otra empresa

G 47 nos comprometemos a no representar a ningún competidor suyo

G 48 también estaríamos dispuestos a aconsejar en cuestiones de marketing y publicidad

G 49 disponemos de una extensa red de contactos en Francia

G 50 estamos dispuestos a concederles la representación

G 51 el contrato tendrá una duración inicial de . . . años

G 52 el contrato puede prorrogarse por otro año

G 53 el contrato lo puede rescindir cualquiera de las partes

G 54 avisándose con . . . meses de antelación

G 55 hay un período de prueba de . . . meses

G 56 la representación es inicialmente a prueba

G 57 estamos dispuestos a concederles la representación en exclusiva

G 58 nos complacemos en poner un coche a su disposición

G 59 sírvanse notificarnos dentro de . . . semanas si son aceptables estas condiciones

G 60 ya hemos llegado a un acuerdo de representación con otra entidad

G 61 estamos dispuestos a concederles la representación francesa de nuestros productos

G 62 les remitiremos todos los detalles de nuestra gama de productos

G 63 sus folletos habrán de traducirse al francés y al inglés

G 64 confiamos en que Vds. harán traducir estos documentos

G 65 nosotros estamos dispuestos a hacer traducir el material, si Vds. prefieren

G 66 nosotros facilitaremos el material publicitario

G 67 corriendo los gastos por nuestra cuenta

G 68 los gastos corren por cuenta de nuestra compañía

G 69 los gastos corren por cuenta del representante

G 70 la zona del representante

G 71 facilitaremos prospectos en francés

G 72 realizaremos una campaña de publicidad intensiva

G 73   estamos dispuestos a asumir una parte del coste

G 74   toda actividad llevada a término por el representante

G 75   los géneros se venden a comisión

G 76   nuestros representantes trabajan a comisión

G 77   le aseguramos un sueldo base de . . . más una comisión del . . . %

G 78   no acostumbramos asegurar un sueldo base

G 79   nuestra comisión habitual para representantes en el extranjero es del . . . %

G 80   dicha comisión se paga por todo pedido que se haga a través de Vd. o de sus intermediarios

G 81   la comisión se paga por todo pedido procedente de su territorio

G 82   la comisión es pagadera al recibo del importe de la cuenta

G 83   la comisión ha de incluir todos sus gastos

G 84   con tal que nos remita Vd. todos los pormenores de sus gastos

G 85   se le reembolsarán todos los gastos contra presentación de los recibos correspondientes

G 86   se reembolsarán los gastos incurridos con motivo de atenciones a los clientes

G 87   la comisión será de un . . . % de las ventas que Vd. realice

G 88   aseguramos una comisión del . . . % de las ventas que Vd. realice

G 89   la comisión por ventas

G 90   Vd. percibirá trimestralmente el importe de las comisiones

G 91   la comisión se paga por todo pedido que se efectúe

G 92   preferimos saldar la cuenta al final de cada trimestre

G 93   preferimos extractos de cuenta mensuales

H — Referencias

H 1   el señor X ha solicitado el puesto de . . . en nuestra empresa

H 2   nos dio su nombre como referencia

H 3   les agradeceríamos tuvieran a bien proporcionarnos informes sobre el señor X

H 4   información sobre su carácter así como sus capacidades

H 5   su formalidad
H 6   ¿han quedado satisfechos con su prestación?
H 7   el puesto requiere un alto grado de integridad
H 8   el trabajo exige esfuerzo
H 9   necesitamos una persona capaz de adaptarse a las circunstancias
H 10   cualquier información que proporcionen Vds. se tratará con la máxima confidencia
H 11   lleva 5 años trabajando en nuestra compañía
H 12   lleva sólo un corto plazo de tiempo trabajando aquí
H 13   trabaja con nosotros desde que se graduó del colegio
H 14   recibió una formación profesional en esta compañía como . . .
H 15   trabajó en esta empresa de junio de 19 . . . a agosto de 19 . . .
H 16   después de 3 años salió de nuestra empresa para trabajar en el extranjero
H 17   fue empleado como . . .
H 18   le despedimos hace 4 años
H 19   se le dio el despido en abril de 19 . . .
H 20   era un trabajador muy competente
H 21   era un trabajador de toda confianza
H 22   honrado y muy trabajador
H 23   puntual
H 24   tiene un carácter agradable
H 25   es especialista en . . .
H 26   es ambicioso
H 27   sin duda por este motivo ha solicitado este puesto
H 28   en el momento actual quedan limitadas las posibilidades de ser ascendido en nuestra compañía
H 29   ha demostrado que es capaz de trabajar por su propia iniciativa
H 30   siempre ha gozado de buena salud
H 31   no era muy trabajador
H 32   no era de confianza
H 33   se ausentaba del trabajo con frecuencia
H 34   con frecuencia llegaba tarde al trabajo
H 35   no era muy puntual
H 36   pecaba por falta de cuidado en su trabajo
H 37   por razones de salud
H 38   estaba mal de salud
H 39   y esto ha incidido en su trabajo
H 40   por consiguiente dudo en recomendarle

H 41	ha demostrado poca iniciativa y trabaja con lentitud
H 42	es de poca confianza
H 43	su rendimiento era satisfactorio, por lo general
H 44	su prestación ha sido siempre de primera calidad
H 45	su prestación ha sido siempre de primerísima calidad
H 46	desempeñó sus deberes a nuestra entera satisfacción
H 47	no dudamos en recomendarle
H 48	su rendimiento era con frecuencia poco satisfactorio
H 49	lamentamos no estar en condiciones de proporcionarles información alguna sobre el aspirante
H 50	le conocemos desde hace poco tiempo
H 51	le conocemos desde hace diez años
H 52	nos alegra que él nos haya dado como referencia
H 53	así que nos permitimos sugerirles que se dirijan a . . .
H 54	ellos estarán en condiciones de facilitarles información más detallada sobre él
H 55	la compañía . . . acaba de hacernos un pedido importante
H 56	nos han rogado les concedamos un crédito
H 57	han citado el nombre de Vds. como referencia
H 58	dado que ésta es la primera vez que hemos tenido relaciones comerciales con esta empresa
H 59	les agradeceríamos nos proporcionasen información sobre su solvencia
H 60	y sobre sus perspectivas a largo plazo
H 61	a medio plazo
H 62	a corto plazo
H 63	sobre su competitividad en el mercado nacional
H 64	el mercado exterior
H 65	¿cuál es su reputación, tanto en el mercado nacional como en el exterior?
H 66	información sobre su solvencia y su fiabilidad
H 67	les agradeceríamos cualquier información que pudieran facilitarnos sobre dicha compañía
H 68	parece que Vds. conocen la empresa desde hace tiempo
H 69	¿les parece prudente que les concedamos un crédito de . . .?
H 70	sin garantías
H 71	les garantizamos la máxima confidencia en este asunto
H 72	trataremos la información facilitada por Vds. con la máxima discreción
H 73	tendremos mucho gusto en devolverles el favor
H 74	hace 6 años que tenemos contactos con esta empresa
H 75	mantenemos relaciones comerciales con la compañía desde hace 5 años

H 76 son clientes nuestros regulares

H 77 mantenemos relaciones comerciales desde hace muchos años

H 78 la empresa goza de una reputación inmejorable

H 79 se encuentra en una buena situación financiera

H 80 la compañía disfruta de recursos financieros muy amplios

H 81 dicha compañía es de toda confianza

H 82 la compañía siempre ha cumplido puntualmente con sus obligaciones

H 83 estamos seguros de que Vds. pueden concederles el mencionado crédito con toda confianza

H 84 nos hemos visto obligados a enviar varios avisos a esta empresa en los últimos meses

H 85 todavía nos deben la cantidad de . . .

H 86 todavía no han saldado la cuenta del año pasado

H 87 se encuentran en dificultades financieras

H 88 no disponen de capital suficiente

H 89 no estimamos prudente conceder crédito a esta compañía

H 90 estimamos que es necesario proceder con sumo cuidado

H 91 no podemos responder de la autenticidad de esta información

H 92 puesto que desconocemos la citada empresa

H 93 no disponemos de información suficiente sobre dicha empresa

H 94 tenemos la impresión de que la compañía se fundó hace poco

H 95 sentimos no estar en condiciones de aconsejarles en este asunto

H 96 lamentamos no poder facilitarles la información que solicitan Vds.

H 97 nuestras relaciones con la compañía son demasiado recientes

H 98 por consiguiente, les aconsejamos se dirijan a . . .

I — Solicitudes de trabajo y anuncios

I	1	somos una empresa de buena reputación situada en el sur de Inglaterra
I	2	se busca . . .
I	3	se necesita . . .
I	4	se tienen vacantes para . . .
I	5	para incorporarse al trabajo el 8 de octubre
I	6	para sustituir a uno de nuestros representantes
I	7	para sustituir a nuestro director de exportación que se jubila
I	8	se necesita alguien que tenga experiencia en el campo de las ventas al exterior
I	9	se necesita vendedor con experiencia
I	10	la persona que necesitamos ha de tener entre 25 y 35 años
I	11	y ha de tener una experiencia de no menos de 5 años en el campo de . . .
I	12	es recomendable que sepa inglés
I	13	es imprescindible que sepa idiomas extranjeros
I	14	la persona nombrada ha de ser capaz de trabajar en equipo
I	15	ha de ser capaz de adaptarse a las necesidades de diversos clientes
I	16	así como delegar la responsabilidad
I	17	se busca una persona capaz de adaptarse a diversas circunstancias
I	18	para dirigir nuestro departamento de exportación
I	19	el puesto incluye un coche de la empresa
I	20	estamos dispuestos a pagar un salario de no menos de . . .
I	21	el salario se ajustará a la edad y a la experiencia
I	22	remuneración a convenir
I	23	un salario de no menos de . . . anuales
I	24	al mes
I	25	el salario neto es de . . .
I	26	el salario bruto es de . . .
I	27	se pagan primas
I	28	se descuenta un . . . % en concepto de impuestos
I	29	en concepto de cotización para la seguridad social
I	30	el salario está exento de impuestos

I 31   la empresa corre con los gastos de alojamiento

I 32   seis semanas de vacaciones al año

I 33   vacaciones pagadas

I 34   semana laboral de 35 horas

I 35   semana laboral de 6 días

I 36   se practica un horario flexible

I 37   los aspirantes deben estar dispuestos a trabajar horas extraordinarias

I 38   existe un régimen de pensiones propio de la empresa

I 39   sírvanse facilitar los nombres de dos personas a quienes se pudiera acudir para pedir una referencia

I 40   una de las referencias ha de ser la empresa en la que actualmente trabaja Vd.

I 41   también nos hace falta una referencia de parte de su banco

I 42   según se desprende de su anuncio en . . .

I 43   según informaciones recibidas de ciertos colegas profesionales

I 44   he leído su anuncio en el número de . . . de la semana pasada

I 45   me dirijo a Vds. a fin de solicitar este puesto

I 46   tengan la amabilidad de enviarme más informaciones sobre el puesto

I 47   junto con un formulario de solicitud

I 48   según se desprende del curriculum vitae adjunto

I 49   tengo mucha experiencia en este tipo de trabajo

I 50   además he asistido a varias conferencias sobre este tema

I 51   tengo la seguridad de reunir las condiciones necesarias para desempeñar este papel

I 52   trabajo en la actualidad en una empresa exportadora

I 53   busco un puesto parecido

I 54   ahora quiero cambiar de puesto

I 55   quisiera conseguir un puesto en una empresa más grande

I 56   con relaciones internacionales

I 57   para mejorar mis posibilidades profesionales

I 58   por razones personales

I 59   busco un puesto de más responsabilidad

I 60   quiero trabajar en el extranjero

I 61   quisiera ampliar mis posibilidades de ascenso

I 62   busco un puesto que tenga mejores perspectivas

I 63   quiero aprovechar mis conocimientos de idiomas

I 64   hablo correctamente francés y alemán

I 65   tengo conocimientos básicos del inglés

I 66   tengo títulos en . . .

I 67   soy diplomado en . . .
I 68   soy licenciado en . . .
I 69   mi velocidad en mecanografía es de . . . pulsaciones por minuto
I 70   mi velocidad en taquigrafía es de . . . palabras por minuto
I 71   tengo experiencia en el manejo de microcomputadores
I 72   he utilizado un procesador de textos
I 73   nací en . . .
I 74   fui al colegio en . . .
I 75   donde aprobé las siguientes asignaturas
I 76   en las siguientes asignaturas
I 77   cursé estudios en la Universidad de . . .
I 78   donde me especialicé en . . .
I 79   y donde estudié como asignatura secundaria
I 80   me licencié en las siguientes asignaturas
I 81   aprobé el examen del Estado
I 82   con sobresaliente
I 83   me suspendieron en las siguientes materias
I 84   luego pasé 4 años trabajando en una empresa exportadora
I 85   pasé 3 años en el extranjero
I 86   me ascendieron a jefe de departamento en 19 . . .
I 87   me quedé en paro en 19 . . .
I 88   sigo desempleado desde entonces
I 89   en la escuela nocturna cursé estudios en . . .
I 90   he recibido formación profesional como secretaria bilingüe
I 91   en caso de que tengan a bien concederme una entrevista
I 92   puedo presentarme a una entrevista en cualquier momento
I 93   sólo dispongo de los viernes para acudir a una entrevista
I 94   me permito preguntar si sería posible aplazar la fecha de la entrevista
I 95   estaré disponible a partir del 16 de junio
I 96   confío en que mi solicitud sea considerada
I 97   incluyo referencias de mi patrono anterior
I 98   incluyo copias de las referencias facilitadas por mis dos patronos anteriores
I 99   así como copias de mis certificados de diploma
I 100   abajo se dan los nombres de dos personas que están dispuestas a dar referencias sobre mí
I 101   las siguientes personas han tenido la amabilidad de acceder a dar referencias sobre mí
I 102   les agradecería tuvieran a bien no dirigirse a mi patrono actual
I 103   antes de la entrevista

I **104** sin mi consentimiento previo
I **105** incluyo un sobre franqueado y con dirección
I **106** incluyo cupón internacional de respuesta
I **107** no duden Vds. en pedir cualquier información suplementaria que necesiten
I **108** he solicitado el puesto de . . .
I **109** con lo cual le agradeceré se digne dar referencias sobre mí

J — Cambio de domicilio social

J **1** nuestra oficina central ya no se encuentra en Londres
J **2** nuestra oficina central se ha trasladado a Frankfurt
J **3** acabamos de abrir una nueva sucursal en Madrid
J **4** debido al progresivo incremento de nuestros negocios
J **5** nos hemos trasladado a un local nuevo más amplio en Burdeos
J **6** esto nos permite mejorar el servicio a todos nuestros clientes
J **7** les aseguramos que no dejaremos de mantener el alto nivel de servicio que siempre hemos ofrecido a nuestra clientela
J **8** hemos cambiado de dirección
J **9** y de aquí en adelante será como sigue
J **10** hagan el favor de dirigir toda correspondencia a esta nueva dirección
J **11** hagan el favor de comunicar este cambio de dirección a su departamento de envíos
J **12** tenemos un nuevo número de teléfono
J **13** en adelante nuestro número de teléfono será el...
J **14** hemos cambiado nuestra razón social
J **15** el actual nombre de la firma es...
J **16** nos hemos fusionado con la firma...
J **17** a partir del 14 de mayo nuestra nueva razón social será...
J **18** ya no nos dedicamos a esta actividad
J **19** ya no fabricamos estos artículos
J **20** hace tres años que dejamos de fabricar estos artículos
J **21** hoy día nos especializamos sólo en la fabricación de...
J **22** los señores...y Cía. se han encargado de la producción de dichos artículos

J	23	nuestra fábrica de Turín ha de ser demolida en marzo
J	24	y vamos a trasladar la producción a Zurich
J	25	nos hemos visto obligados a cerrar nuestra fábrica de Birmingham
J	26	hemos cerrado nuestro departamento de exportación
J	27	nos permitimos sugerirles que se pongan en contacto con la casa matriz
J	28	nuestra empresa afiliada de París
J	29	nuestra compañía ha sido adquirida por...
J	30	...han adquirido el...% de las acciones de nuestra empresa
J	31	la compañía queda disuelta
J	32	suspendimos nuestras operaciones comerciales hace 6 meses
J	33	la compañía está en quiebra
J	34	hemos entrado en liquidación
J	35	el señor...ha sido ascendido al puesto de...
J	36	él es ahora subdirector
J	37	es director de nuestro nuevo departamento de exportación en Viena
J	38	ha sido nombrado para el consejo de dirección
J	39	ha sido trasladado a otra sucursal
J	40	el señor...ya no trabaja en esta compañía
J	41	se ha trasladado a otra empresa
J	42	se jubiló en agosto
J	43	nuestro director gerente, el señor..., falleció hace seis meses
J	44	ha sido sustituido por el señor...
J	45	sus responsabilidades han sido asumidas por el señor...

K — Viajes y reservas de hoteles

K	1	quisiera reservar un asiento en el tren París – Heidelberg
K	2	que sale de París a las 13,45 y que llega a Heidelberg a las 19,55
K	3	el rápido
K	4	el expreso transeuropeo (TEE)
K	5	¿es necesario reservar billete en este tren?
K	6	la reserva de billetes es necesaria en todos los expresos

K	7	este servicio no funciona los días de fiesta
K	8	sólo hay servicio los días laborables
K	9	el tren de cercanías
K	10	el tren especial
K	11	el tren suplementario
K	12	el tren sale del andén número 6
K	13	un asiento de ventanilla
K	14	en un compartimiento para no fumadores
K	15	litera
K	16	el coche-cama
K	17	el vagón-restaurante
K	18	el bar
K	19	el control de pasaportes en el tren
K	20	¿quiere viajar en primera?
K	21	un asiento en un compartimiento de primera clase
K	22	¿a qué hora llega el tren a...?
K	23	adjunto una copia de mi itinerario previsto
K	24	un billete sencillo
K	25	un billete reducido de ida y vuelta en el día
K	26	un billete de ida y vuelta
K	27	un billete de andén
K	28	¿hay que pagar un suplemento en este tren?
K	29	¿hay consigna en la estación?
K	30	¿dónde está la consigna automática?
K	31	¿dónde está la oficina de objetos perdidos?
K	32	¿este billete es válido para todos los itinerarios de autobús?
K	33	este billete no es transferible
K	34	¿se puede comprar un abono mensual para el autobús?
K	35	una tarjeta para varios viajes
K	36	¿a qué hora sale el barco de Calais?
K	37	el ferry
K	38	sírvanse enviarme detalles de su servicio de ferry para coches
K	39	el hovercraft
K	40	un camarote para dos
K	41	un camarote de primera
K	42	quiero reservar una plaza para un coche y dos pasajeros
K	43	¿se ofrecería un descuento para un grupo de 20?
K	44	en el ferry Dóver-Calais
K	45	¿a qué hora es el vuelo número...a...?
K	46	un vuelo chárter
K	47	un vuelo regular

K 48 quiero reservar 3 asientos en el primer vuelo disponible a...

K 49 ¿de qué terminal sale el vuelo?

K 50 ¿se sirven comidas durante el vuelo?

K 51 la clase turista

K 52 la clase Club

K 53 sírvase confirmar el billete 24 horas antes de la salida

K 54 ¿se incluyen los derechos de aeropuerto en el precio?

K 55 el equipaje de mano

K 56 la azafata

K 57 el auxiliar de vuelo

K 58 se sirven bebidas durante el vuelo

K 59 los señores pasajeros deben presentarse a la facturación al menos 45 minutos antes de la salida

K 60 busco una habitación de un precio medio

K 61 quiero reservar una habitación invidivual con baño

K 62 una habitación doble

K 63 una habitación con dos camas

K 64 con ducha

K 65 con servicios y ducha

K 66 sírvanse comunicarme el precio de una habitación individual

K 67 en plena temporada

K 68 al principio de la temporada

K 69 al final de la temporada

K 70 del 19 al 30 de abril

K 71 ¿se aceptan reservas para grupos?

K 72 quiero organizar un congreso en octubre para nuestros representantes

K 73 y busco un hotel adecuado cerca del aeropuerto

K 74 agradeceríamos se mandase un autocar al aeropuerto a buscarnos

K 75 deseamos que el autocar nos lleve al hotel

K 76 el precio de una habitación doble por tres noches es...

K 77 estos son los precios, todo incluido

K 78 desayuno incluido

K 79 la media pensión

K 80 la pensión completa

K 81 incluidos el servicio y el impuesto sobre el valor añadido (IVA)

K 82 la propina

K 83 por favor denos los precios con todo incluido

K 84 todas las habitaciones disponen de calefacción central

K 85	todas las habitaciones disponen de agua corriente fría y caliente
K 86	se sirve el desayuno hasta las 10
K 87	el hotel dispone de su propio aparcamiento
K 88	el aparcamiento subterráneo
K 89	el aparcamiento de varios niveles
K 90	hay aparcamiento muy cerca
K 91	el hotel se encuentra en una zona tranquila
K 92	dispone de salas de reuniones
K 93	dispone de una sala de conferencias para 100 personas
K 94	está cerca del centro de la ciudad
K 95	¿a cuánto está el hotel del aeropuerto?
K 96	¿hay servicio de autobuses al aeropuerto?
K 97	está a sólo unos minutos del centro de la ciudad
K 98	se encuentra en la periferia en una zona tranquila
K 99	cerca del río
K 100	tiene ascensor
K 101	el conserje nocturno
K 102	tiene una agencia de cambios
K 103	les escribo para confirmar mi reserva
K 104	sírvanse enviarme la carta y una lista de vinos
K 105	hagan el favor de notificarme si requieren Vds. un depósito
K 106	hagan el favor de enviar la factura a mi empresa, a los señores...
K 107	lamento tener que cambiar mi fecha de salida
K 108	y no llegaré a...hasta el 21 de julio
K 109	me veo obligado a cancelar mi reserva en su hotel

L — Inmuebles: ventas y alquileres

L 1	se vende casa
L 2	se alquila casa
L 3	el piso
L 4	el apartamento
L 5	un ático

L	6	la villa
L	7	el chalet
L	8	el bungalow
L	9	el chalet adosado
L	10	la casa de ciudad
L	11	dos dormitorios, salón-comedor, cocina, cuarto de baño, garaje, jardín
L	12	queremos alquilar una casa por un año y medio aproximadamente
L	13	sírvanse comunicarnos el alquiler correspondiente a tal piso
L	14	el alquiler es de…al mes
L	15	al año
L	16	si están dispuestos a alquilar el piso por dos años
L	17	les podemos ofrecer un descuento del…%
L	18	se busca un local comercial en el centro de la ciudad
L	19	se desea comprar una propiedad en el centro de la ciudad
L	20	estamos dispuestos a pagar un máximo de…
L	21	bien situada
L	22	en una zona residencial
L	23	en zonas verdes/en medio de zonas ajardinadas
L	24	para más información, dirigirse a…
L	25	se ofrecen hipotecas
L	26	se ofrecen préstamos
L	27	a un…% de interés
L	28	libre de intereses
L	29	a un alquiler de…mensuales
L	30	al precio de…por metro cuadrado
L	31	podemos negociar una hipoteca
L	32	podemos negociar préstamos a través de nuestra compañía de seguros
L	33	tenemos varias casas de veraneo en el sur de Francia a la venta
L	34	vuelos de inspección gratis
L	35	la propiedad colectiva (en régimen de uso alterno)

M — Asuntos financieros

M	1	la reunión se celebrará en la sede central de la compañía
M	2	la junta general anual
M	3	la junta general anual se celebrará este año el día 3 de julio
M	4	la junta general ordinaria
M	5	se ha convocado la junta extraordinaria
M	6	el orden del día de la junta general anual
M	7	puntos a tratar
M	8	otros asuntos
M	9	participaron en la junta las siguientes personas
M	10	el director general
M	11	el presidente
M	12	el jefe de ventas
M	13	el director de exportación
M	14	el representante en el extranjero
M	15	el jefe de personal
M	16	los enlaces sindicales
M	17	los miembros del sindicato
M	18	los accionistas
M	19	el consejo de administración
M	20	las actas fueron levantadas por . . .
M	21	el presidente dio la bienvenida a los señores accionistas
M	22	y presentó la memoria correspondiente al ejercicio del año pasado
M	23	y presentó las actas de la última junta
M	24	hemos incrementado nuestra producción
M	25	ha aumentado la producción
M	26	nuestra producción ha aumentado en un . . . % en comparación con el año pasado
M	27	y hemos creado nuevos puestos de trabajo
M	28	nuestra cifra de ventas aumentó en un . . . %
M	29	el incremento en la cifra de ventas
M	30	incrementamos nuestras exportaciones en un . . . %
M	31	debido a un aumento en las inversiones
M	32	hemos invertido grandes cantidades en nuestras fábricas
M	33	hemos aumentado nuestra participación en el mercado
M	34	nuestras mercancías tuvieron una buena salida en los mercados de otros países europeos

M	35	a fin de consolidar nuestra posición en el mercado
M	36	debemos reforzar nuestra posición en el mercado
M	37	el mercado exterior
M	38	el mercado nacional
M	39	nuestros mercados más importantes son Francia e Italia
M	40	ha habido una evolución favorable en nuestras ventas a Alemania
M	41	con ventas nacionales de . . .
M	42	nuestras ventas totales aumentaron de . . . a . . .
M	43	nuestras ventas totales disminuyeron de . . . a . . .
M	44	esperamos buenas posibilidades de venta a largo plazo
M	45	hemos explotado al máximo nuestra capacidad disponible
M	46	debemos mantener nuestro liderazgo del sector
M	47	nuestro programa de inversión a largo plazo
M	48	nos permitirá mejorar la calidad de nuestros productos
M	49	nuestro programa de desarrollo
M	50	a corto plazo
M	51	a medio plazo
M	52	esperamos un aumento en nuestra cifra de ventas
M	53	nuestro activo aumentó en un . . . %
M	54	el préstamo
M	55	el disponible aumentó en un . . . %
M	56	la compañía incrementó su capital social a . . .
M	57	los dividendos pagados por acción fueron de . . .
M	58	el rédito
M	59	los beneficios
M	60	los beneficios netos
M	61	los beneficios después de impuestos
M	62	la compañía incrementó sus beneficios en un . . . % en el primer trimestre
M	63	la tasa de crecimiento
M	64	la recesión económica general
M	65	ha reducido la demanda
M	66	y en la segunda mitad del año disminuyó la demanda
M	67	y nos hemos encontrado con dificultades de venta
M	68	y ha disminuido la producción
M	69	debemos contar con una ligera disminución en la producción
M	70	y han disminuido las exportaciones
M	71	esto ha reducido nuestras posibilidades de crecimiento
M	72	el incremento en el precio de la energía y otras materias primas
M	73	ha tenido un efecto nefasto

M 74 también ha aumentado la competencia
M 75 debido a la competencia de otras empresas del ramo
M 76 hemos perdido competitividad
M 77 también eran muy elevados los gastos de personal
M 78 durante el ejercicio pasado la compañía sufrió pérdidas totales de . . .
M 79 las pérdidas fueron considerables en ciertos sectores

N – Uso del teléfono

N 1 quisiera hablar con el señor . . .
N 2 no cuelgue Vd.
N 3 está comunicando
N 4 le pongo
N 5 diga/oiga
N 6 adiós
N 7 el señor . . . no está
N 8 ¿quiere Vd. dejar un recado?
N 9 ¿le puede dar el siguiente recado?
N 10 esto es un mensaje grabado
N 11 ¿sería tan amable de ponerme con la extensión . . . , por favor?
N 12 llamo desde una cabina
N 13 cuelgue Vd. y vuelva a marcar
N 14 una llamada local
N 15 una conferencia/una llamada a larga distancia
N 16 una llamada internacional
N 17 una llamada de cobro revertido
N 18 quisiera poner una conferencia a cobro revertido a . . .
N 19 quisiera poner una conferencia de persona a persona
N 20 la guía telefónica
N 21 tendrá Vd. que consultar el número en la guía
N 22 información
N 23 ¿me puede dar el número de los señores . . . ?
N 24 ¿me puede dar el prefijo de Manchester?
N 25 se oye mal
N 26 voy a tener que colgar
N 27 Vd. mismo puede marcar el número
N 28 tendré que volver a marcar

N 29   me he equivocado/he marcado mal
N 30   hay un cruce
N 31   me han cortado
N 32   el tono
N 33   la señal de estar comunicando
N 34   tiene que suprimir el cero cuando marque el número
N 35   llamo desde Inglaterra
N 36   volveré a llamar más tarde

O – Banco y correos

O 1   quisiera abrir una cuenta de ahorros
O 2   una cuenta corriente
O 3   una cuenta de depósito
O 4   una cuenta conjunta
O 5   se ha abierto una cuenta a su nombre
O 6   ¿cuál es el índice actual de interés?
O 7   ¿a cuánto ascienden los gastos bancarios?
O 8   el talonario
O 9   una orden de pago permanente
O 10   tengo la cuenta en el banco . . .
O 11   mi número de cuenta es . . .
O 12   tengo una cuenta en la caja postal de ahorros
O 13   quisiera hacer una transferencia de . . . a mi cuenta
O 14   quiero cancelar mi cuenta
O 15   quiero sacar/retirar
O 16   para sacar cantidades de esa magnitud hay una corta demora
O 17   quiero ingresar en mi cuenta la cantidad de . . .
O 18   su cuenta está en números rojos
O 19   y su máximo límite de crédito es de . . .
O 20   ha rebasado Vd. ya esta cantidad
O 21   quiero cobrar este cheque
O 22   ¿es posible cambiar aquí estos cheques de viajero?
O 23   quiero ingresar este cheque en mi cuenta
O 24   quisiera un extracto de cuenta
O 25   los extractos de cuenta le serán enviados mensualmente
O 26   ¿cuál es mi saldo actual?

O 27 el haber/el saldo positivo
O 28 el debe/el saldo negativo
O 29 un crédito a largo plazo
O 30 a corto plazo
O 31 el portador
O 32 la caja de ahorros
O 33 la sociedad inmobiliaria
O 34 la tarjeta de crédito
O 35 la tarjeta Eurocheque
O 36 cinco sellos de . . . ptas., por favor
O 37 quiero mandar este paquete a Francia
O 38 por correo aéreo
O 39 por correo normal
O 40 como paquete postal
O 41 por correo certificado
O 42 urgente
O 43 hay que rellenar una declaración de aduana
O 44 quisiera poner un telegrama a . . .
O 45 por télex
O 46 lista de correos
O 47 quisiera un giro postal por el valor de . . .
O 48 apartado de correos
O 49 código postal

P – Seguros

P 1 quiero hacerme un seguro
P 2 el seguro personal
P 3 el seguro inmobiliario
P 4 la compañía de seguros
P 5 el asegurado, el señor . . . nos ha pedido que
P 6 hemos entregado su carta a nuestro departamento de
       reclamaciones
P 7 se incluye el documento de cobertura
P 8 necesito un formulario para la concertación de un seguro
P 9 recibirá Vd. la póliza en breve
P 10 la póliza ha de ser expedida por nuestra oficina central
P 11 incluimos los términos de la póliza
P 12 el número de la póliza es . . .

P 13 haga el favor de comunicarnos el nombre del asegurado
P 14 el plazo de vigencia de la póliza es . . .
P 15 quiero renovar mi póliza
P 16 he cancelado la póliza
P 17 la suma asegurada asciende a . . .
P 18 la prima mensual es de . . .
P 19 la póliza cubre
P 20 la reclamación del seguro
P 21 los daños
P 22 fuerza mayor
P 23 el seguro contra incendios
P 24 el seguro del coche
P 25 el seguro a terceros
P 26 una póliza de seguros a todo riesgo
P 27 el seguro de viaje
P 28 necesita una carta verde
P 29 debe notificar el accidente a nuestra oficina central
P 30 debe obtener los nombres de testigos
P 31 el seguro de accidentes
P 32 el seguro de equipaje
P 33 el seguro de enfermedad
P 34 el agente de seguros

Q – Terminología de oficina e informática

Q 1 el archivo
Q 2 el fichero
Q 3 el dictáfono
Q 4 la mesa
Q 5 el télex
Q 6 la máquina de escribir con memoria
Q 7 el microordenador
Q 8 la pantalla
Q 9 el procesador de textos
Q 10 el teclado
Q 11 la tecla
Q 12 la terminal del ordenador

Q 13 el disquete/el disco flexible
Q 14 la unidad de disco/el drive
Q 15 el banco de datos
Q 16 la memoria
Q 17 el chip de silicona/la pastilla
Q 18 el microprocesador
Q 19 la calculadora de bolsillo
Q 20 el corrector líquido
Q 21 el fechador
Q 22 el clip/el sujetapapeles
Q 23 la grapa
Q 24 la grapadora
Q 25 el sacapuntas
Q 26 la máquina de franquear
Q 27 el bloc de notas
Q 28 la carpeta
Q 29 la impresora
Q 30 la fotocopiadora
Q 31 informática
Q 32 videotex
Q 33 el sistema se ajusta a las normas internacionales de telecomunicaciones
Q 34 el usuario puede acceder al sistema desde su oficina, por vía telefónica
Q 35 el usuario puede acceder a la guía de teléfonos electrónica desde la terminal
Q 36 el módem proporciona el interface con la red de telecomunicaciones
Q 37 diálogo entre ordenadores
Q 38 el sistema incluye las funciones de transmisión de mensajes y correo electrónicos
Q 39 este modelo cuenta con la posibilidad de efectuar la fusión de dos ficheros de correo
Q 40 servicio Teletex
Q 41 fax
Q 42 este sistema permite conectar un ordenador a la red de télex
Q 43 tiene la función que permite volver a efectuar una llamada automáticamente
Q 44 envía mensajes fuera de las horas punta
Q 45 una teleconferencia
Q 46 en línea/interactivo
Q 47 (en) tiempo real

Q	48	diseño asistido por ordenador
Q	49	fabricación asistida por ordenador
Q	50	enseñanza asistida por ordenador
Q	51	publicación de libros en la oficina
Q	52	sistema experto
Q	53	base de datos
Q	54	base de datos relacional
Q	55	cada día se actualiza la información
Q	56	hoja electrónica de cálculo
Q	57	los datos se almacenan por ficheros y éstos son controlados por el sistema
Q	58	la información almacenada se clasifica por páginas numeradas
Q	59	cualquier ordenador compatible puede leer el disco
Q	60	este modelo es compatible con IBM
Q	61	este modelo funciona con MS–DOS y no es compatible con PC–DOS
Q	62	clon
Q	63	sistema operativo o de explotación
Q	64	mensajes de error
Q	65	byte/bitio
Q	66	kilobyte
Q	67	megabyte
Q	68	este modelo tiene 512 K de RAM/de memoria de acceso directo
Q	69	la capacidad de memoria del disco es de 1000 K
Q	70	software
Q	71	paquete de software
Q	72	este paquete viene en disco
Q	73	la configuración puede adaptarse a sus necesidades
Q	74	y existe una versión en italiano
Q	75	el programa posee un menú dirigido por el cursor
Q	76	el cursor se mueve utilizando el ratón
Q	77	lápiz luminoso
Q	78	disco de sistema
Q	79	disco de trabajo
Q	80	de doble cara
Q	81	doble densidad
Q	82	es necesario estructurar el disco
Q	83	un disco de 3 pulgadas y media
Q	84	directorio de disco
Q	85	subdirectorio
Q	86	disco emisor

Q	87	disco receptor
Q	88	copia de seguridad
Q	89	se puede reproducir el fichero del disco A en el disco B
Q	90	el programa está protegido
Q	91	transferir el texto
Q	92	eliminar el texto
Q	93	añadir el texto
Q	94	existe un diccionario para verificar y corregir la ortografía
Q	95	fusionar ficheros
Q	96	el texto se puede enviar directamente a la impresora
Q	97	hardware
Q	98	ordenador personal
Q	99	miniordenador
Q	100	unidad central
Q	101	disco flexible/disquette
Q	102	disco duro/disco rígido
Q	103	CD ROM (ROM = memoria de sólo lectura)
Q	104	vídeo disco
Q	105	periféricos
Q	106	pantalla monocromática
Q	107	pantalla a color
Q	108	pantalla de cristal líquido
Q	109	pantalla de plasma
Q	110	la pantalla visualiza 25 líneas de 80 caracteres
Q	111	impresora en paralelo
Q	112	impresora en serie
Q	113	impresora de matriz de puntos
Q	114	impresora de margarita
Q	115	impresora láser
Q	116	juego de caracteres
Q	117	cabeza de impresión
Q	118	cargador de papel
Q	119	peana insonora de la impresora
Q	120	programa de análisis
Q	121	lector
Q	122	de calidad
Q	123	la cinta se cambia con facilidad
Q	124	bajo nivel de ruido
Q	125	contrato de mantenimiento
Q	126	mantenimiento preventivo
Q	127	las piezas estropeadas o defectuosas se reemplazarán gratuitamente
Q	128	ajuste

Q 129	siempre que la máquina se revise regularmente
Q 130	no se puede reparar el hardware allí donde está instalado
Q 131	el disco duro está dañado
Q 132	el fallo fue debido a una bajada de corriente
Q 133	la avería fue debida a un fallo de software
Q 134	alimentación eléctrica
Q 135	manual del usuario
Q 136	componente
Q 137	caja
Q 138	la grabadora no estaba conectada al ordenador
Q 139	la tecla de función no funcionaba
Q 140	debería haber listado el contenido del disco
Q 141	este fax envía normalmente las páginas de A4 en menos de 12 segundos
Q 142	la estación de trabajo no funciona
Q 143	el fallo está en el procesador de 16 bits
Q 144	el procesador puede gobernar hasta 8 estaciones de trabajo
Q 145	el usuario no sabía que el servicio no era gratuito
Q 146	conmutación de paquetes

R — Nombres de países y ciudades

R	1	Aquisgrán
R	2	Africa
R	3	Alejandría
R	4	Argelia
R	5	Argel
R	6	Amsterdam
R	7	Amberes
R	8	Argentina
R	9	Arnhem
R	10	Asia
R	11	Atenas
R	12	Australia
R	13	Austria
R	14	Aviñón

R	15	Baden-Baden
R	16	Bagdad
R	17	Islas Bahrein
R	18	Barcelona
R	19	Basilea
R	20	Bayreuth
R	21	Beirut
R	22	Belfast
R	23	Bélgica
R	24	Belgrado
R	25	Berlín
R	26	Berna
R	27	Bilbao
R	28	Bochum
R	29	Bolivia
R	30	Bombay
R	31	Bonn
R	32	Burdeos
R	33	Brasilia
R	34	Brasil
R	35	Bregenz
R	36	Bremen
R	37	Bremerhaven
R	38	Brunswick
R	39	Bruselas
R	40	Bucarest
R	41	Budapest
R	42	Bulgaria
R	43	Buenos-Aires
R	44	Cádiz
R	45	Cairo
R	46	Canadá
R	47	Islas Canarias
R	48	Ciudad del Cabo
R	49	Chad
R	50	Chile
R	51	China
R	52	Colonia
R	53	Colombia
R	54	Constanza
R	55	Copenhague
R	56	Córdoba
R	57	Corinto

R 58	Costa Rica
R 59	Cuba
R 60	Checoslovaquia
R 61	Damasco
R 62	Delhi
R 63	Dinamarca
R 64	Dijon
R 65	Djakarta
R 66	Dortmund
R 67	Dresde
R 68	Dubai
R 69	Dublín
R 70	Dunquerque
R 71	Düsseldorf
R 72	Ecuador
R 73	Edimburgo
R 74	CEE
R 75	Egipto
R 76	Eindhoven
R 77	Inglaterra
R 78	Erfurt
R 79	Etiopía
R 80	Europa
R 81	Islas Malvinas
R 82	Finlandia
R 83	Florencia
R 84	Francia
R 85	Frankfurt
R 86	Freiburgo
R 87	Gdansk
R 88	Ginebra
R 89	Génova
R 90	Ghana
R 91	Gießen
R 92	Gotha
R 93	Göttingen
R 94	Graz
R 95	Gran Bretaña
R 96	Grecia
R 97	Groningen
R 98	Guyana
R 99	La Haya
R 100	Halle

R 101	Hamburgo
R 102	Hannover
R 103	La Habana
R 104	Heidelberg
R 105	Helsinki
R 106	Holanda
R 107	Honduras
R 108	Hungría
R 109	Islandia
R 110	India
R 111	Innsbruck
R 112	Interlaken
R 113	Irán
R 114	Irak
R 115	Irlanda
R 116	Israel
R 117	Estambul
R 118	Italia
R 119	Costa de Marfil
R 120	Jamaica
R 121	Indonesia
R 122	el Japón
R 123	Jena
R 124	Jerusalén
R 125	Jordania
R 126	Kaiserslautern
R 127	Karl Marx Stadt (Chemnitz)
R 128	Karlsruhe
R 129	Kassel
R 130	Kiel
R 131	Kitzbühel
R 132	Klagenfurt
R 133	Koblenz
R 134	Cracovia
R 135	Lausana
R 136	Líbano
R 137	Leipzig
R 138	Libia
R 139	Lila
R 140	Lima
R 141	Linz
R 142	Lisboa
R 143	Ljubljana

R 144	Londres
R 145	Lübeck
R 146	Lucerna
R 147	Lugano
R 148	Luxemburgo
R 149	Lyon
R 150	Maastricht
R 151	Magdeburgo
R 152	Mainz
R 153	Malasia
R 154	Malta
R 155	Mannheim
R 156	Marsella
R 157	Meca
R 158	México
R 159	Ciudad de México
R 160	Milán
R 161	Mónaco
R 162	Montevideo
R 163	Montreux
R 164	Marruecos
R 165	Moscú
R 166	Munich
R 167	Münster
R 168	Nápoles
R 169	Países Bajos
R 170	Nueva Delhi
R 171	Nueva York
R 172	Nueva Zelandia
R 173	Nicaragua
R 174	Niza
R 175	Irlanda del Norte
R 176	Noruega
R 177	Nuremberg
R 178	Oslo
R 179	Ostende
R 180	Padua
R 181	Panamá
R 182	Paraguay
R 183	París
R 184	Passau
R 185	Pekín
R 186	Perú

R 187	las Filipinas
R 188	Pireo
R 189	Polonia
R 190	Portugal
R 191	Praga
R 192	Qatar
R 193	Recife
R 194	Reykjavik
R 195	Riad
R 196	Río de Janeiro
R 197	Roma
R 198	Rostock
R 199	Rotterdam
R 200	Rumania
R 201	Rusia
R 202	Saarbrücken
R 203	San Petersburgo (Leningrado)
R 204	Salzburgo
R 205	Cerdeña
R 206	Arabia Saudita
R 207	Escocia
R 208	Sevilla
R 209	Sicilia
R 210	Singapur
R 211	Africa del Sur
R 212	América del Sur
R 213	la Corea del Sur
R 214	España
R 215	Split
R 216	Steyr
R 217	Estocolmo
R 218	Estrasburgo
R 219	Stuttgart
R 220	Suecia
R 221	Suiza
R 222	Siria
R 223	Tánger
R 224	Teherán
R 225	Tel Aviv
R 226	Tailandia
R 227	La Haya
R 228	Tesalónica
R 229	Tokio

R 230	Toronto
R 231	Tolón
R 232	Toulouse
R 233	Trier
R 234	Trípoli
R 235	Túnez
R 236	Túnez
R 237	Turín
R 238	Turquía
R 239	Ulm
R 240	Emiratos Arabes Unidos
R 241	Reino Unido
R 242	Estados Unidos
R 243	Utrecht
R 244	Vancouver
R 245	Venezuela
R 246	Venecia
R 247	Viena
R 248	País de Gales
R 249	Varsovia
R 250	Weimar
R 251	las Antillas
R 252	Wismar
R 253	Wolfsburgo
R 254	Yugoslavia
R 255	Zagreb
R 256	Zaragoza
R 257	Zürich
R 258	Zwickau

S—Abreviaturas

S 1 cta.
S 2 Hnos.
S 3 Cía.
S 4 a/c
S 5 dna.
S 6 ed.
S 7 CE
S 8 p.ej.
S 9 adj.
S 10 etc.
S 11 a saber
S 12 cte.
S 13 S.A.
S 14 p.p.
S 15 I.V.A.

Indice

FRANÇAIS

Table des matières

Introduction

Le présent ouvrage s'adresse à quiconque ayant à rédiger ou comprendre des lettres d'affaires en anglais, français, allemand, italien ou espagnol. Il contient des tournures importantes dans chacune des cinq langues, réparties en sections pour en faciliter l'usage. En plus de ces tournures, l'ouvrage contient le vocabulaire nécessaire pour faire des appels téléphoniques et des transactions en banque ou à la poste; vous y trouverez également des listes de pays et de villes dans chaque langue.

Le but de l'ouvrage est d'être utile non seulement à ceux qui s'occupent de la correspondance commerciale dans leur vie professionelle mais aussi à ceux qui étudient ou enseignent ce sujet. Les auteurs ont cherché aussi à éviter de favoriser une langue plus qu'une autre, et l'ouvrage est donc structuré de façon à être aussi utile à la secrétaire française désirant écrire des lettres en anglais qu'à l'étudiant italien désirant comprendre des lettres en allemand. En tout, il est possible de faire dix combinaisons semblables utilisant les cinq langues figurant dans cet ouvrage, ce qui en fait un instrument de travail indispensable à toute entreprise s'occupant de l'import-export.

Mode d'utilisation

Il y a une section pour chacune des cinq langues et chaque section est divisée à nouveau en sous-sections telles que *Demandes et offres, Commandes* etc. Dans chaque sous-section une lettre et nombre clefs se rapportent à chaque tournure (**A36**, **B45** etc.) correspondant exactement à la tournure équivalente dans chacune des autres langues. A titre d'exemple, si l'on prend la tournure anglaise **B45** 'the samples must be returned within 2 weeks', on trouvera sous la même combinaison de lettre et nombre dans la section française la tournure 'les échantillons doivent être renvoyés dans un délai de 2 semaines', et dans la section allemande 'die Muster müssen binnen 2 Wochen zurückgeschickt werden' etc.

Pour repérer vite et sans difficulté un mot ou une tournure particuliers un index est fourni pour chaque langue, qui se réfère directement à la lettre et au nombre clefs.

Il est important de se rappeler que si l'on ne trouve pas une tournure particulière il faut envisager son remplacement par un synonyme.

Les mots et tournures entre crochets dans la section anglaise indiquent qu'ils appartiennent à l'anglais américain.

A — Expressions générales

A	1	Monsieur
A	2	Messieurs
A	3	(Cher) Monsieur
A	4	Madame
A	5	Mademoiselle
A	6	à l'attention de
A	7	Confidentiel
A	8	Objet
A	9	nous accusons réception de votre lettre
A	10	nous vous remercions de votre lettre
A	11	du 3 courant
A	12	nous nous référons à votre lettre
A	13	V/Réf
A	14	N/Réf
A	15	votre nom nous a été donné par des relations d'affaires
A	16	nous nous empressons de répondre à votre lettre du
A	17	nous n'avons pas reçu de réponse à notre lettre du
A	18	à la suite de notre conversation téléphonique du
A	19	je suis heureux d'apprendre que
A	20	notre représentant nous a appris que
A	21	suivant les recommandations de notre représentant
A	22	nous sommes désolés d'apprendre que
A	23	votre lettre nous a été transmise par
A	24	nous sommes intéressés d'apprendre que
A	25	votre lettre mentionnée ci-dessus
A	26	votre lettre mentionnée ci-dessous
A	27	nous vous ferons savoir par téléphone
A	28	nous vous ferons savoir par télégramme
A	29	à la suite de notre réunion du
A	30	nous avons appris par l'intermédiaire de
A	31	nous sommes au regret de vous informer que
A	32	nous avons le plaisir de vous informer que
A	33	nous avons été intéressés d'apprendre que
A	34	veuillez trouver ci-joint notre catalogue
A	35	nous confirmons par la présente
A	36	veuillez nous faire part de
A	37	veuillez trouver la raison pour laquelle
A	38	nous avons besoin de ces renseignements pour
A	39	dans les plus brefs délais

A	40	dès que nous aurons reçu
A	41	suite à notre lettre
A	42	suite à notre appel téléphonique
A	43	nous regrettons vivement que
A	44	nous notons avec surprise que
A	45	nous vous saurions gré de nous faire parvenir
A	46	nous espérons que vous approuverez ces mesures
A	47	nous espérons qu'il vous sera possible de
A	48	nous nous excusons de ne pas avoir répondu plus tôt à
A	49	nous avons eu l'opportunité de
A	50	nous joignons à cette lettre
A	51	sous pli séparé
A	52	par le même courrier
A	53	par retour de courrier
A	54	nous vous renvoyons
A	55	que vous nous avez envoyé
A	56	nous nous permettons de suggérer que
A	57	vous pouvez être assuré que
A	58	en nous référant à notre correspondance antérieure
A	59	cela ne vous étonnera pas
A	60	nous serons très heureux de
A	61	au cas où ceci ne serait pas possible
A	62	nous venons d'apprendre que
A	63	nous sommes persuadés que vous comprendrez que
A	64	voulez-vous avoir l'amabilité de
A	65	comme vous le savez
A	66	en réponse à votre lettre
A	67	d'après notre documentation
A	68	nous nous permettons de vous rappeler que
A	69	nous sommes au regret de devoir vous rappeler que
A	70	comme vous l'avez demandé dans votre lettre du
A	71	nous aurons besoin de renseignements sur vos produits
A	72	nous serions heureux de connaître vos idées sur cette question
A	73	à notre avis il est important pour vous de
A	74	nous nous chargeons de vous faire parvenir
A	75	à la suite de notre discussion avec votre représentant
A	76	comme nous entrons en relations d'affaires avec vous
A	77	nous notons d'après votre lettre que
A	78	nous tenons à vous signaler que
A	79	je voudrais prendre rendez-vous avec Monsieur X.
A	80	nous serons dans l'obligation d'annuler notre rendez-vous du

A 81	à votre entière satisfaction
A 82	notre siège social est situé à
A 83	notre siège social a été transféré à
A 84	nous ferons de notre mieux pour régler la question
A 85	détails comme suit
A 86	notre directeur est actuellement en voyage d'affaires
A 87	veuillez nous informer de votre décision le plus vite possible
A 88	nous espérons que vous comprendrez la situation dans laquelle nous nous trouvons
A 89	nous regrettons le dérangement que nous avons pu vous causer
A 90	ceci n'a pas été suffisament pris en considération
A 91	nous vous conseillons de reconsidérer
A 92	nous avons été impressionnés par
A 93	nous ne pouvons accepter
A 94	vous trouverez les détails de
A 95	si nous pouvons vous être utiles de quelque façon
A 96	nous ferons l'impossible pour
A 97	nous comprenons bien que
A 98	nous avons donné des instructions pour que
A 99	dès que les marchandises seront prêtes
A 100	quand vous saurez la date
A 101	si vous vous décidiez à suivre cette ligne de conduite
A 102	au cas où
A 103	si nous avions su ceci
A 104	dans un proche avenir
A 105	à une date ultérieure
A 106	nous vous serions obligés de bien vouloir nous faire parvenir ces renseignements
A 107	nous joignons une enveloppe timbrée pour la réponse à cette lettre
A 108	nous joignons un coupon-réponse international à cette lettre
A 109	en cas de besoin
A 110	à l'heure
A 111	Monsieur X nous a mis en rapport avec vous
A 112	Jusq'ici nous n'avons pas connu beaucoup de succès
A 113	par voie maritime
A 114	par avion
A 115	(en) recommandé
A 116	nous vous demandons d'apporter un soin special à
A 117	dans un délai de 15 jours

A 118   dont nous serions heureux de vous envoyer les noms
A 119   à en juger par leurs rapports
A 120   nous serions prêts à
A 121   nous sommes convaincus que
A 122   nous nous intéressons à . . .
A 123   dans l'espoir d'une prompte réponse
A 124   nous espérons avoir pu vous être utiles
A 125   nous sommes fort reconnaissants
A 126   nous espérons que vous continuerez à
A 127   nous vous prions d'agréer, Monsieur, nos salutations
distinguées (l'expression de nos sentiments distingués/
respectueux/amicaux)
A 128   nous vous prions d'agréer, Monsieur, nos salutations
distinguées (l'expression de nos sentiments distingués/
respectueux/amicaux)
A 129   P.J.
A 130   signé
A 131   P.pon.

B — Demandes de renseignements et offres

B   1   nous avons appris que vous fabriquez des
B   2   nous nous spécialisons dans la fabrication de
B   3   nous sommes propriétaires de
B   4   nous recherchons un fournisseur digne de confiance
B   5   veuillez nous envoyer des renseignements complets sur
B   6   nous nous intéressons principalement aux articles suivants
B   7   veuillez m'envoyer les renseignements susceptibles de
m'aider
B   8   pour faire le choix le plus approprié à mes besoins
B   9   plusieurs de nos clients ont montré de l'intérêt pour
B 10   veuillez nous envoyer des brochures illustrant vos
marchandises
B 11   veuillez nous envoyer votre dernier catalogue
B 12   votre nouvelle brochure
B 13   votre dernier tarif

B 14 nous avons eu connaissance de votre firme par la presse commerciale

B 15 nous sommes clients de votre firme depuis de nombreuses années

B 16 nous voyons d'après votre annonce

B 17 notre stock de marchandises sera bientôt épuisé

B 18 nous sommes en rupture de stock

B 19 pouvez-vous livrer immédiatement sur stock?

B 20 nous avons en stock

B 21 votre demande de renseignements concernant nos produits

B 22 nous avons besoin des marchandises pour le 2 avril au plus tard

B 23 pour nous aider à lancer votre produit sur le marché

B 24 nous sommes prêts à vous faire une offre spéciale

B 25 lors d'une récente visite à la foire commerciale

B 26 j'ai vu des échantillons de vos produits

B 27 nous nous permettons d'attirer spécialement votre attention sur

B 28 à condition que

B 29 veuillez nous envoyer un choix d'articles de votre gamme

B 30 nous avons l'intention de passer commande régulièrement pour ces marchandises

B 31 en quantités importantes

B 32 veuillez nous faire savoir si vous permettez un achat à titre d'essai

B 33 pour combien de temps pourrons-nous garder ce produit à titre d'essai?

B 34 votre offre nous intéresse et nous serons heureux de la recevoir

B 35 nous sommes intéressés par vos produits

B 36 la qualité des marchandises est à nos yeux de première importance

B 37 à condition que les prix des matières premières restent inchangés

B 38 nos produits sont soigneusement contrôlés pour en assurer la qualité

B 39 tous nos produits sont garantis pour deux ans

B 40 nous remplaçons gratuitement toute pièce défectueuse

B 41 attribuable à des imperfections de fabrication ou de matériaux

B 42 jusqu'à 3 mois après la livraison

B 43 nous acceptons des commandes pour des quantités minimales de

B 44 nos échantillons sont offerts gratuitement
B 45 les échantillons doivent etre renvoyés dans un délai de quinze jours
B 46 nous vous facturerons les échantillons
B 47 avec les échantillons
B 48 veuillez nous envoyer des échantillons de vos produits
B 49 nous ne pouvons pas offrir cet article à titre d'essai
B 50 avec la possibilité de reprise des invendus
B 51 à l'essai
B 52 nous désirons développer notre gamme actuelle
B 53 dans un délai de 4 semaines après commande
B 54 veuillez nous envoyer des détails précis sur vos produits
B 55 nous avons vu d'après votre brochure que
B 56 à la suite d'une forte demande de la part de nos clients
B 57 ces articles sont maintenant désuets
B 58 nous ne fabriquons plus ces articles en grande série
B 59 nous vous proposons de contacter
B 60 10 moteurs, type . . .
B 61 dans les tailles et quantités suivantes
B 62 veuillez nous faire une proposition de prix pour . . .
B 63 nous serions heureux de voir vos tout derniers modèles
B 64 détails de vos modèles récents
B 65 à condition que la qualité et les prix soient satisfaisants
B 66 les poids et mesures sont indiqués dans le catalogue illustré
B 67 pour des quantités de plus de
B 68 pour une commande minimale de
B 69 dans les coloris suivants
B 70 dans les motifs suivants
B 71 conformément au dessin que nous joignons à cette lettre
B 72 disposez-vous d'un catalogue rédigé en français?
B 73 nous avons vu votre matériel publicitaire
B 74 veuillez nous donner vos prix de gros
B 75 prix de détail
B 76 nos prix figurent sur la liste ci-incluse
B 77 nos prix sont marqués sur l'échantillon
B 78 les prix indiqués sont sans remise
B 79 ce sont nos meilleurs prix
B 80 nous accordons une remise de . . . % sur les prix catalogue
B 81 nous pouvons accorder une remise de . . . % sur les nouvelles commandes
B 82 pouvez-vous nous consentir une remise spéciale?
B 83 remise au détaillant
B 84 veuillez indiquer vos conditions de paiement

B 85   nos prix sont fermes jusqu'au 8 mai
B 86   les prix offerts doivent comprendre la livraison à cette adresse
B 87   veuillez indiquer vos prix en livres sterling
B 88   prix courant au moment de l'expédition
B 89   les prix indiqués dans votre lettre
B 90   prix comme suit
B 91   si vos prix sont compétitifs
B 92   au prix de . . . la pièce
B 93   au prix spécial de . . .
B 94   veuillez indiquer les prix et les délais de livraison
B 95   ce sont les meilleurs prix que nous puissions offrir
B 96   nous accordons une remise de . . . % sur les exportations
B 97   nos prix comprennent l'assurance
B 98   nos prix sont plus bas que ceux de nos concurrents
B 99   prix par article
B 100   départ usine
B 101   départ entrepôt
B 102   nos prix sont F.O.B. Londres
B 103   emballage compris
B 104   emballage non compris
B 105   port payé jusqu'à Madrid
B 106   franco frontière
B 107   port payé jusqu'à la frontière
B 108   Coût et Fret
B 109   franco rail
B 110   C.A.F. (Coût, Assurance, Fret)
B 111   franco quai
B 112   franco domicile
B 113   franco port
B 114   franco entrepôt
B 115   nous avons le plaisir de vous faire l'offre suivante
B 116   pouvez-vous nous accorder un crédit de 3 semaines
B 117   nous travaillons à marge bénéficiaire réduite
B 118   pour des commandes en gros
B 119   l'offre est valable pour 5 jours
B 120   l'offre est valable sous réserve d'acceptation avant le 5 mars
B 121   sous réserve de non-vente des marchandises
B 122   nous nous réservons le droit de modifier les prix
B 123   nous vous remercions de votre demande de renseignements concernant nos marchandises

B 124	si nous sommes satisfaits de la qualité de vos marchandises
B 125	nous vous passerons une commande d'essai
B 126	si les marchandises nous donnent satisfaction
B 127	nous passerons des commandes plus importantes
B 128	pour les premières commandes
B 129	pour les commandes suivantes
B 130	tant que durent nos stocks
B 131	votre commande sera exécutée à votre entière satisfaction
B 132	nos conditions de vente sont les suivantes
B 133	l'exécution prompte et soigneuse de votre commande
B 134	nous vous offrons les marchandises que vous avez spécifiées aux conditions suivantes
B 135	si les prix vous paraissent acceptables
B 136	aux conditions suivantes

C — Commandes

C	**1**	nous avons examiné votre offre
C	**2**	nous avons soigneusement examiné vos échantillons
C	**3**	les articles dans votre catalogue correspondent à nos besoins
C	**4**	nous sommes satisfaits de votre premier envoi
C	**5**	nous désirons passer commande sur la base des échantillons
C	**6**	nous désirons vous confier la commande suivante
C	**7**	la commande doit être livrée immédiatement
C	**8**	nous sommes prêts à vous passer une commande permanente
C	**9**	la commande est basée sur vos prix catalogue
C	**10**	nous désirons commander 5 exemplaires de chacun des articles suivants
C	**11**	veuillez trouver ci-joint notre commande No. 8765 pour
C	**12**	veuillez nous envoyer immédiatement les articles suivants
C	**13**	nous tenons à ce que que les marchandises soient livrées sur stock
C	**14**	nous avons besoin des articles d'ici 10 jours

C 15 si vous ne pouvez pas livrer dans ce délai
C 16 nous nous référons à notre commande du 5 mai
C 17 en nous référant à notre commande No. 9675
C 18 vos prix nous semblent assez élevés
C 19 si vous pouviez nous consentir un rabais de . . . % sur votre offre
C 20 nous serions prêts à vous confier la commande suivante
C 21 vos prix sont plus élevés que ceux de notre ex-fournisseur
C 22 nous pouvons obtenir ces articles chez un autre fournisseur à un prix plus favorable
C 23 nous sommes engagés vis-à-vis d'un autre fournisseur
C 24 nous avons déjà paré à nos besoins
C 25 votre offre nous est parvenue trop tard
C 26 votre échantillon n'était pas d'une qualité suffisante
C 27 si vous pouvez nous offrir ces articles de meilleure qualité
C 28 si vous pouvez fournir ces articles en quantités plus petites
C 29 veuillez nous indiquer la quantité maximale que vous pourriez livrer immédiatement
C 30 nous devons apporter une légère modification à votre commande
C 31 nous osons espérer que cette modification vous paraît acceptable
C 32 l'article No. 487 n'est pas disponible en ce moment
C 33 à cause de certains ennuis avec notre fournisseur
C 34 à cause d'une grève
C 35 à cause d'une pénurie de matières premières
C 36 par suite d'un manque de personnel
C 37 nous sommes en retard sur la production
C 38 nous ne pouvons donc garantir la livraison d'ici le 4 mars
C 39 nous sommes prêts à échanger les articles
C 40 nous nous réservons le droit de refuser la livraison
C 41 nous désirons porter la quantité à
C 42 nous ne pouvons accepter votre offre
C 43 nous ne pouvons accepter vos conditions de paiement
C 44 nous ne pouvons accepter vos conditions de livraison
C 45 nous ne pouvons prendre votre offre en considération
C 46 en ce moment nous n'avons pas besoin de ces articles
C 47 nous n'avons pas d'espace libre pour emmagasiner
C 48 nous ne pouvons accepter votre commande en ce moment
C 49 notre carnet de commandes est complet
C 50 nous ne pouvons commencer la fabrication avant août
C 51 nous désirons annuler notre commande
C 52 nous avons annulé notre commande par télégramme

C	53	veuillez retirer les articles suivants de notre commande
C	54	nous nous réservons le droit d'annuler la commande
C	55	nous avons bien reçu aujourd'hui votre commande pour nos marchandises
C	56	nous confirmons votre commande du 12 mai
C	57	nous exécuterons votre commande dans les plus brefs délais
C	58	votre commande est maintenant prête pour livraison
C	59	votre commande attend maintenant son enlèvement
C	60	nous attendons vos instructions complémentaires
C	61	veuillez faire retirer ces marchandises
C	62	nous avons commencé la fabrication des marchandises
C	63	veuillez confirmer la commande mentionnée ci-dessus aussitôt que possible
C	64	nous avons besoin approximativement de dix jours pour exécuter votre commande

D — Livraison, transport, douane

D	1	nous confirmons la date de livraison stipulée dans votre lettre
D	2	nous attendons vos instructions à l'égard de la livraison
D	3	nous devons insister pour avoir une livraison immédiate
D	4	le retard dans la livraison a été causé par
D	5	nous pouvons livrer ces marchandises immédiatement
D	6	nous avons besoin de cette livraison d'urgence
D	7	le retard dans la livraison nous a occasionné des ennuis considérables
D	8	veuillez nous faire savoir quand la livraison sera effectuée
D	9	notre délai de livraison le plus court serait d'un mois
D	10	nous ferons tout notre possible pour respecter la date de livraison
D	11	nons pouvons livrer les marchandises avant la date convenue
D	12	nos transitaires sont
D	13	nous ferons en sorte que les marchandises soient prêtes à être expédiées pour début mai
D	14	les marchandises attendent l'enlèvement

D 15 dès que nous aurons reçu votre commande nous expédierons les marchandises

D 16 nous pouvons livrer les marchandises en conteneurs

D 17 la livraison sera effectuée dans un délai de 4 mois

D 18 veuillez nous faire savoir si vous pouvez livrer les marchandises avant cette date

D 19 le délai de livraison est de 4 mois

D 20 les marchandises doivent être livrées avant la fin du mois prochain

D 21 les dates de livraison doivent être conformes à celles qui ont été données dans notre lettre

D 22 la livraison doit être faite dans le délai convenu

D 23 nous ne pouvons accepter les marchandises si elles ne nous parviennent pas dans le délai convenu

D 24 il ne sera pas possible de livrer les marchandises dans le délai convenu de 2 mois

D 25 nous pouvons livrer pour le 5 août

D 26 nous n'avons pas encore reçu les marchandises

D 27 veuillez nous faire connaître les raisons de ce retard

D 28 port payé

D 29 l'expédition se compose de

D 30 l'expédition a été faite par vapeur Berlin

D 31 le bateau devrait arriver à Douvres le 21 juillet

D 32 nous espérons que l'expédition vous parviendra en bon état

D 33 nous n'avons pas encore reçu l'expédition du 15 mars

D 34 l'expédition que vous vous êtes engagés à faire pour le 13 février

D 35 nous enverrons toutes les marchandises en une seule expédition

D 36 l'expédition comprend 2 caisses de 50 kilos chacune

D 37 l'expédition des marchandises

D 38 les marchandises vous ont été expédiées aujourd'hui

D 39 les marchandises sont prêtes pour l'expédition

D 40 nous avons remis les documents d'expédition à notre banque

D 41 les marchandises seront expédiées le 9 juin

D 42 les caisses ont été réceptionnées par le transporteur

D 43 dès que nous aurons reçu vos instructions, nous vous enverrons notre avis d'expédition

D 44 nous avons remis les marchandises que vous avez commandées à notre transporteur

D 45 votre commande ne précise pas le moyen de transport

D 46 comme fret aérien
D 47 par transport aérien
D 48 par chemin de fer
D 49 par avion
D 50 par bateau/par mer
D 51 par camion
D 52 marchandises en transit
D 53 fret payé
D 54 fret non compris
D 55 fret compris
D 56 coût du fret
D 57 port d'expédition
D 58 port de destination
D 59 afin de réduire au minimum les dommages en cours de route
D 60 le connaissement
D 61 l'avis de fret
D 62 la facture consulaire
D 63 les documents d'expédition
D 64 la lettre de transport aérien (L.T.A.)
D 65 le certificat de valeur
D 66 le certificat d'origine n'était pas en règle
D 67 nous ne pouvons emballer les marchandises de la façon que vous avez demandée
D 68 il est essentiel d'emballer soigneusement les marchandises
D 69 l'emballage doit être solide
D 70 l'emballage est inférieur à ce que nous attendions
D 71 veuillez nous informer si vous avez un autre type d'emballage
D 72 l'emballage de vos marchandises est d'une qualité médiocre
D 73 nous vous prions de prêter toute votre attention à l'emballage
D 74 nous ne pouvons accepter vos observations sur l'emballage défectueux
D 75 les caisses d'emballage ne sont pas reprises
D 76 les caisses d'emballage seront numérotées consécutivement
D 77 nous ne pouvons accepter des demandes d'emballage spécial
D 78 nous devons insister pour que les marchandises soient emballées dans
D 79 le papier d'emballage

D 80	le carton ondulé
D 81	copeaux de bois
D 82	garni de
D 83	contenants
D 84	tonnelets
D 85	balles
D 86	caisses à claire-voie
D 87	caisses
D 88	bidons
D 89	pots
D 90	palettes
D 91	barils
D 92	caisses en bois
D 93	sacs
D 94	les cartons ne sont pas repris
D 95	les caisses à claire-voie doivent être marquées comme suit
D 96	antichoc
D 97	imperméable/étanche à l'eau
D 98	à l'épreuve des dégâts/résistant
D 99	craint l'humidité/garder au sec
D 100	tenir au frais
D 101	dessus
D 102	dessus/haut
D 103	dessous/fond
D 104	manipuler avec soin
D 105	ouvrir ici
D 106	lever ici
D 107	fragile
D 108	attention
D 109	inflammable
D 110	poids net
D 111	poids brut
D 112	poids mort
D 113	le chargement
D 114	le déchargement
D 115	poids et dimensions
D 116	le poids brut est marqué sur chaque caisse
D 117	droits devant être payés par l'acheteur
D 118	livrés à Londres, franco de douane
D 119	passible de droits
D 120	nous avons dû payer un droit de . . . sur les articles
D 121	vous devrez payer les droits d'entrée sur les marchandises
D 122	droits devant être payés par le destinataire

D 123 la valeur imposable des marchandises
D 124 la déclaration en douane
D 125 frais de douane
D 126 le dédouanement
D 127 nous avons reçu la facture douanière
D 128 le bureau de douane d'Aix-la-Chapelle a infligé une amende sur l'expédition
D 129 nous avons besoin du reçu des douanes
D 130 la douane de Douvres a saisi l'expédition
D 131 de nouveaux règlements douaniers sont entrés en vigueur
D 132 nous nous occuperons des formalités douanières
D 133 une amende douanière
D 134 un entrepôt de douane
D 135 un entrepôt de douane
D 136 en entrepôt
D 137 entreposage
D 138 les déchets
D 139 le charpadage
D 140 taxes d'aéroport
D 141 droits de port
D 142 frais de manutention
D 143 tarifs douaniers
D 144 nous payerons les frais de dédouanement

E — Factures, paiements et rappels

E 1 nous accusons réception des marchandises
E 2 l'expédition est arrivée hier à notre usine
E 3 les marchandises sont arrivées en bon état
E 4 l'expédition nous est parvenue sans dommage
E 5 les articles commandés le 4 avril sont arrivés dans le délai prévu
E 6 veuillez trouver ci-joint notre facture No . . .
E 7 nous remettons sous ce pli notre facture pour les marchandises qui vous ont été livrées le 3 mai

E	8	la facture ci-jointe couvre les marchandises livrées contre votre commande No . . .
E	9	nous vous prions de bien vouloir régler au plus tôt notre facture
E	10	nous vous prions de bien vouloir régler la facture avant le 12 mai
E	11	nous vous prions de créditer le compte No . . . du montant de la facture
E	12	nous vous prions de bien vouloir régler la facture par retour du courrier
E	13	nous vous remettons sous ce pli notre relevé
E	14	la somme globale à payer est de . . .
E	15	la remise est déjà comprise dans le montant
E	16	la remise a déjà été déduite
E	17	après déduction de 6%
E	18	nous avons déduit de votre facture la remise habituelle de 7%
E	19	nous sommes obligés de vous signaler qu'il y a une erreur dans votre facture
E	20	vous avez fait une erreur en totalisant votre facture No . . .
E	21	veuillez nous envoyer une facture rectifiée
E	22	nous vous prions de bien vouloir rectifier la facture en conséquence
E	23	nous serions heureux que vous rectifiez le relevé
E	24	votre facture accorde un escompte commercial de 3% seulement
E	25	nous avons déduit . . . du montant de la facture
E	26	l'erreur était attribuable à une faute de frappe
E	27	une erreur dans notre service-comptabilité
E	28	une omission
E	29	nous confirmons le solde recifié de . . .
E	30	nous remettons sous ce pli une note de crédit
E	31	une note de débit
E	32	nous vous serions obligés de bien vouloir nous régler immédiatement
E	33	nous espérons recevoir votre règlement d'ici 8 jours
E	34	voudriez-vous bien nous régler la somme due dans les prochains jours
E	35	nous aimerions vous rappeler que nos conditions de paiement sont . . .
E	36	nous vous référons à nos conditions de paiement
E	37	documents contre acceptation

E	38	contre remboursement
E	39	documents contre paiement
E	40	paiement à l'avance
E	41	la lettre de crédit documentaire
E	42	une lettre de crédit documentaire en notre faveur
E	43	la lettre de change documentaire
E	44	révocable
E	45	irrévocable
E	46	confirmé
E	47	non confirmé
E	48	la traite documentaire
E	49	la traite à vue
E	50	la traite à vue limitée dans le temps
E	51	la traite à date fixe
E	52	paiement contre livraison des marchandises
E	53	au cours du change actuel
E	54	comptant
E	55	billets
E	56	monnaie
E	57	cours légal
E	58	le virement postal
E	59	le bénéficiaire
E	60	le créancier
E	61	le débiteur
E	62	le billet à ordre
E	63	le crédit commercial
E	64	payable à la banque
E	65	une traite de 60 jours
E	66	un crédit de . . . à ouvrir à la banque . . .
E	67	nous avons demandé à notre banque de vous régler la somme due
E	68	nous avons versé la somme de . . . à votre compte
E	69	nous avons crédité votre compte de cette somme
E	70	nous avons demandé à notre banque de verser sur votre compte la somme de . . .
E	71	nous avons viré sur votre compte la somme de . . .
E	72	en règlement de votre compte
E	73	notre compte en banque
E	74	nous joignons un chèque de . . .
E	75	un chèque barré
E	76	un chèque non barré
E	77	un mandat postal
E	78	le chèque a été encaissé

E 79 un chèque tiré sur votre compte

E 80 nous vous remettons sous ce pli un chèque de . . . en règlement de votre facture

E 81 £600, moins £45 pour l'emballage

E 82 nous vous remettons sous ce pli un chèque pour la moitié du montant

E 83 le virement bancaire

E 84 l'effet bancaire

E 85 votre compte a été crédité du montant . . .

E 86 veuillez nous envoyer un acquit aussitôt que possible

E 87 nous avons bien reçu votre paiement

E 88 nous vous remercions de votre paiement

E 89 nous avons accepté votre traite

E 90 votre paiement du montant de . . . a bien été reçu par notre banque

E 91 nous vous remercions de votre paiement rapide

E 92 nous avons reçu votre avis de versement

E 93 votre compte est en souffrance depuis plus de 4 semaines

E 94 notre facture reste toujours impayée

E 95 nous attendons votre versement

E 96 votre compte montre un solde débiteur de . . .

E 97 les factures impayées doivent être réglées avant la fin de ce mois

E 98 nous n'avons pas reçu le solde de notre relevé de septembre

E 99 puisqu'il est possible que notre relevé ait pu s'égarer, nous en joignons une copie

E 100 veuillez nous faire connaître les raisons du retard dans le paiement

E 101 comme le montant dû est considérablement en retard

E 102 nous n'avons pas jusqu'ici eu de réponse à notre demande de paiement

E 103 voudriez-vous bien donner votre attention immédiate à cette affaire

E 104 malgré nos demandes répétées de paiement

E 105 pour récupérer la somme due

E 106 vous n'avez pas répondu à nos rappels

E 107 à l'avenir nos factures devront être réglées immédiatement

E 108 vous nous devez toujours . . .

E 109 nous sommes obligés de vous rappeler que nous n'accordons un crédit de 15 jours que sur les premières commandes

E 110   nous nous permettons d'attirer votre attention sur le fait que le paiement était échu le 4 juillet

E 111   ceci est notre dernière demande de paiement

E 112   nous devons insister maintenant pour un paiement immédiat

E 113   si nous ne recevons pas votre paiement avant le début du mois prochain

E 114   le retard de votre paiement est tout à fait inacceptable

E 115   la facture s'est égarée

E 116   nous prendrons des mesures légales

E 117   notre avocat recouvrera la somme

E 118   nous ferons recouvrer la somme due par notre avoué

E 119   nous sommes obligés d'entamer des poursuites pour récupérer la somme due

E 120   par des moyens légaux

E 121   nous avons remis l'affaire entre les mains de nos avoués

E 122   nous vous accorderons encore un délai de 12 jours pour régler votre compte

E 123   vous pouvez nous envoyer un acompte

E 124   vous avez demandé une prorogation du délai de paiement

E 125   nous espérons que vous apprécierez notre situation

E 126   nous sommes prêts à accorder un délai supplémentaire

F — Réclamations

F 1   les marchandises livrées le 3 courant n'étaient pas celles que nous avions commandées

F 2   nous sommes au regret de devoir nous plaindre de votre expédition No . . .

F 3   nous voudrions signaler une erreur dans l'expédition que nous avons reçue hier

F 4   les articles n'étaient pas du bon coloris

F 5   les tailles n'étaient pas bonnes

F 6   ils n'étaient pas conformes aux dessins que nous vous avions envoyés

F 7   la qualité des marchandises était inférieure à celle que nous attendions

F 8   nous avons été déçus par la qualité des marchandises

F	**9**	c'est pour ces raisons que nous ne pouvons pas accepter les articles
F	**10**	les articles étaient défectueux
F	**11**	vous nous en avez envoyé 500 . . . . au lieu des 250 que nous avions commandés
F	**12**	il s'est produit une erreur dans l'exécution de votre commande
F	**13**	le contenu des caisses à claire-voie n'est pas conforme au bon de livraison
F	**14**	l'article No . . . était manquant dans l'expédition
F	**15**	les marchandises ne sont pas conformes aux échantillons
F	**16**	les articles semblent être d'une construction différente
F	**17**	les caisses à claire-voie étaient cassées
F	**18**	les marchandises ont été endommagées par le feu
F	**19**	les marchandises ont été abîmées par une manipulation peu soigneuse
F	**20**	les marchandises sont arrivées en mauvais état
F	**21**	très endommagé
F	**22**	plusieurs articles étaient éraflés
F	**23**	cassé
F	**24**	légèrement abîmé
F	**25**	détérioré par la chaleur
F	**26**	endommagé par l'eau
F	**27**	les marchandises ont dû être abîmées au cours du transit
F	**28**	elles ont dû être mal emballées
F	**29**	les matériaux d'emballage étaient d'une qualité inférieure
F	**30**	les caisses à claire-voie auraient dû être renforcées par des bandes métalliques
F	**31**	les caisses à claire-voie étaient mal construites
F	**32**	les articles sont rouillés
F	**33**	les avaries se sont produites entre la douane britannique et notre usine
F	**34**	les avaries se sont produites avant l'arrivée des marchandises à Douvres
F	**35**	nous nous trouvons dans l'obligation de vous demander de nous envoyer un remplacement aussitôt que possible
F	**36**	ceci nous a occasionné des difficultés considérables parce que nous avions un besoin urgent des marchandises
F	**37**	nous avons un besoin urgent des articles restants
F	**38**	nous regrettons que tous les articles devront être remplacés
F	**39**	nous sommes prêts à garder les marchandises
F	**40**	à un prix réduit de . . . par article

F 41 nous renvoyons l'expédition entière

F 42 nous renvoyons une partie de l'expédition

F 43 nous renvoyons tous les articles abîmés en cours de route

F 44 nous devons maintenant annuler la commande

F 45 nous sommes prêts à accepter les marchandises endommagées si vous nous accordez une réduction de prix de 25%

F 46 nous ne pouvons vendre les marchandises endommagées qu'à un prix considérablement réduit

F 47 tous les articles devront être remplacés

F 48 nous espérons que vous ferez en sorte qu'une pareille erreur ne se reproduise pas à l'avenir

F 49 ceci nous a causé de graves difficultés avec certains de nos clients

F 50 nous vous conseillons de vous adresser aux transitaires

F 51 la compagnie maritime

F 52 la société des chemins de fer

F 53 la ligne aérienne

F 54 nous pensons qu'il est de votre responsabilité de chercher de plus amples renseignements

F 55 nous sommes dans l'obligation de vous demander de compenser nos pertes

F 56 nous sommes obligés d'insister pour obtenir un dédommagement

F 57 nous devons vous demander de nous créditer de la valeur des marchandises endommagées

F 58 nous aurons à reconsidérer notre position en ce qui concerne de futures commandes

F 59 nous avons vérifié votre réclamation

F 60 puisque les avaries se sont produites en cours de route

F 61 nous vous prions, en cette matière, de vous référer à . . .

F 62 c'est la première fois que nous traitons avec cette compagnie de transports

F 63 notre assurance couvre les défauts que vous mentionnez

F 64 notre garantie couvre ces avaries

F 65 selon les conditions de notre garantie

F 66 vous pouvez vous faire rembourser la somme déjà payée

F 67 nous vous prions d'accepter toutes nos excuses pour cette erreur

F 68 nous sommes prêts à échanger les marchandises contre celles d'une qualité semblable

F 69 nous remettons sous ce pli un chèque de . . . à titre de remboursement

F 70   nous remplacerons à nos frais

F 71   nous sommes désolés que vous ne soyez pas satisfaits de notre expédition

F 72   nous sommes prêts à vous offrir une remise de 10%

F 73   nous avons réduit votre facture de 15%

F 74   nous avons vérifié très soigneusement les marchandises

F 75   nous ne pouvons constater aucun défaut dans les marchandises

F 76   nous ne pouvons accepter aucune responsabilité pour les dommages

F 77   comme vous le verrez d'après les conditions du contrat

F 78   nous regrettons de ne pas pouvour reprendre les marchandises

F 79   nous vous conseillons de signaler l'affaire à la compagnie d'assurances

F 80   nous devons vous signaler que la période de garantie a expiré

F 81   vous devez demander à la compagnie maritime de certifier les dommages

F 82   nous exigeons un rapport des transitaires dressant une liste des dommages

F 83   dans ces circonstances nous ne pouvons pas accepter votre réclamation

G — Agences

G 1   nous recherchons un agent pour vendre nos marchandises à l'étranger

G 2   il nous faut un représentant pour assurer la vente de nos produits

G 3   nous recherchons un représentant pour notre succursale à . . .

G 4   l'agent doit travailler exclusivement pour nous

G 5   il doit accepter de ne pas travailler pour nos concurrents

G 6   et doit limiter ses activités à cette région

G 7   sa tâche principale serait de présenter nos catalogues et échantillons à notre clientèle

G 8   le poste exige des connaissances spécialisées

G	9	il nous faut un représentant spécialisé
G	10	nous n'exigeons pas de connaissances spécialisées
G	11	nous assurons nous-mêmes la formation de nos représentants
G	12	nous sommes une petite entreprise fabriquant . . .
G	13	le potentiel de vente de ces articles est excellent
G	14	nous avons appris que vous possédez une expérience considérable dans la vente de ce genre d'article
G	15	vous serait-il possible d'introduire ces marchandises sur le marché italien?
G	16	nous désirons lancer ce produit sur le marché allemand
G	17	il nous semble qu'il y a une demande considérable pour ces marchandises à l'étranger
G	18	vous représentez déjà plusieurs sociétés britanniques
G	19	votre tâche serait de développer ce marché pour notre maison
G	20	nous serions prêts à dépenser en moyenne . . . par an pour la publicité
G	21	nous nous attendons à ce que vous exposiez une gamme complète de nos produits dans vos salles d'exposition
G	22	nous fournirons gratuitement au représentant tout le matériel de publicité
G	23	nous sommes les agents exclusifs
G	24	l'agence exclusive
G	25	nous sommes des commissionnaires
G	26	nous cherchons des bureaux de vente en Espagne
G	27	nous avons un contrat de franchise pour la vente
G	28	agents de vente
G	29	agents à plein temps
G	30	agents à temps partiel
G	31	l'intermédiaire
G	32	le destinataire
G	33	le stock de consignation
G	34	marchandises en dépôt
G	35	l'agent d'exportation
G	36	l'agent pour les achats
G	37	le commettant
G	38	nous sommes convaincus que vous produits s'écouleront bien dans ce pays
G	39	nous avons appris que vous cherchez un représentant en France
G	40	nous avons une grande expérience dans ce genre de travail

G 41 nous aimerions offrir nos services pour cette représentation

G 42 nous avons représenté avec succès un bon nombre de maisons semblables

G 43 nous entretenons de bonnes relations avec les grands magasins de Londres

G 44 nous avons l'intention de concentrer de façon intensive nos efforts sur le marché allemand

G 45 nous sommes prêts à continuer à assurer le service après-vente

G 46 nous ne sommes liés à aucune autre firme dans ce pays

G 47 nous acceptons de ne représenter aucun de vos concurrents

G 48 nous serions aussi prêts à vous donner conseil en matière de marketing et de publicité des marchandises

G 49 nous avons de nombreux contacts en France

G 50 nous sommes prêts à vous offrir la représentation

G 51 le contrat initial se limite à . . . ans

G 52 le contrat peut être renouvelé pour une autre année

G 53 le contrat est résiliable par l'une ou l'autre des parties

G 54 avec un préavis de . . . mois

G 55 il y a une période d'essai de . . . mois

G 56 la représentation vous est confiée à titre d'essai

G 57 nous vous accorderons les droits exclusifs de vente

G 58 nous pouvons mettre une voiture à votre disposition

G 59 veuillez nous faire savoir dans un délai de . . . semaines si ces conditions vous paraissent acceptables

G 60 nous avons déjà signé un contrat de représentation avec une autre maison

G 61 nous pouvons vous confier la représentation de nos produits en France

G 62 nous vous enverrons une documentation détaillée de tous nos produits

G 63 il faudra traduire nos brochures en anglais et en français

G 64 nous espérons que vous pourrez vous occuper de la traduction de ces documents

G 65 si vous préférez, nous pouvons nous occuper nous-mêmes de la traduction

G 66 nous fournirons le matériel de publicité

G 67 à nos frais

G 68 les frais seront payés par notre maison

G 69 les frais sont à la charge du représentant

G 70 le territoire du représentant

G	71	nous fournirons des brochures en français
G	72	nous effectuerons une campagne publicitaire intensive
G	73	nous sommes d'accord pour prendre à notre charge une partie des frais
G	74	toute affaire conclue par le représentant
G	75	les marchandises sont vendues à la commission
G	76	nos représentants travaillent à la commission
G	77	nous offrons un salaire fixe de . . . avec en plus une commission de . . . %
G	78	ce n'est pas dans nos habitudes d'offrir un salaire fixe
G	79	la commission habituelle pour nos représentants à l'étranger est de . . .
G	80	cette commission est payable sur toutes les commandes conclues par vous ou vos intermédiaires
G	81	cette commission est payable sur toutes les commandes venant de votre territoire
G	82	la commission est payée à la réception de la facture
G	83	la commission comprendra les frais que vous pourrez avoir
G	84	à condition que vous nous envoyiez un résumé détaillé de vos frais
G	85	nous vous rembourserons vos frais contre remise de vos reçus
G	86	les frais de réception des clients seront remboursés
G	87	la commission représentera . . . % de la valeur des marchandises vendues
G	88	nous offrons une commission de . . . % pour toute affaire que vous négocierez
G	89	la commission sur les ventes
G	90	la commission sera payée trimestriellement
G	91	une commission est payable sur toutes les commandes
G	92	nous préférons solder notre compte avec vous à la fin de chaque trimestre
G	93	nous préférons des relevés mensuels

H — Références

H	1	M. X a posé sa candidature au poste de . . . dans notre société
H	2	il a donné votre nom comme référence

H	3	nous vous serions reconnaissants de bien vouloir nous fournir des renseignements sur M. X
H	4	des renseignements sur son caractère et ses capacités
H	5	s'il est digne de confiance
H	6	avez-vous été satisfaits de ses services?
H	7	le poste exige un haut degré d'intégrité
H	8	ce poste est exigeant
H	9	nous cherchons quelqu'un capable de s'adapter
H	10	nous considérerons tout renseignement fourni par vous comme strictement confidentiel
H	11	il travaille pour notre société depuis 5 ans
H	12	il ne travaille pour nous que depuis peu de temps
H	13	il est avec nous depuis qu'il a quitté l'école
H	14	nous lui avons donné la formation de . . .
H	15	il a travaillé pour nous du 19 juin . . . au 19 août . . .
H	16	il a quitté notre société au bout de 3 ans pour partir travailler à l'étranger
H	17	il était employé en qualité de . . .
H	18	il a été congédié il y a 4 ans
H	19	il a été licencié le 19 avril . . .
H	20	il s'est avéré un ouvrier compétent
H	21	il était tout à fait digne de confiance
H	22	honnête et assidu
H	23	ponctuel
H	24	il est d'une nature agréable
H	25	il est spécialisé dans . . .
H	26	il est ambitieux
H	27	il n'y a aucun doute que c'est pour cette raison qu'il a posé sa candidature à ce poste
H	28	les possibilités d'avancement sont limitées dans notre société en ce moment
H	29	il a fait preuve d'une initiative considérable dans son travail
H	30	il avait toujours une bonne santé
H	31	il n'était pas un très bon travailleur
H	32	il n'était pas très sérieux
H	33	il était souvent absent de son travail
H	34	il était souvent en retard pour son travail
H	35	il n'était pas très ponctuel
H	36	il était souvent assez négligent dans son travail
H	37	pour des raisons de santé
H	38	il n'avait pas une bonne santé
H	39	et ceci a affecté son travail

H 40   par conséquent j'ai quelque hésitation à vous le recommander

H 41   il a fait preuve de peu d'initiative et il travaille lentement

H 42   on ne peut pas du tout compter sur lui

H 43   en général son travail était satisfaisant

H 44   son travail était toujours de très bonne qualité

H 45   son travail était toujours de première qualité

H 46   il s'est toujours acquitté de ses fonctions à notre entière satisfaction

H 47   nous n'avons aucune hésitation à le recommander

H 48   son travail laissait souvent à désirer

H 49   il nous semble que nous ne pouvons vous donner aucun renseignement sur ce candidat

H 50   nous ne le connaissons que depuis peu de temps

H 51   nous le connaissons depuis 10 ans

H 52   et nous avons plaisir à lui servir de références

H 53   nous vous proposons donc de vous adresser à . . .

H 54   ils devraient être en mesure de vous donner de plus amples renseignements à son sujet

H 55   la société . . . vient de nous confier une commande importante

H 56   ils ont demandé qu'on leur fasse crédit

H 57   votre nom a été donné comme référence

H 58   comme c'est la première fois que nous traitons avec cette maison

H 59   nous vous serions reconnaissants de bien vouloir nous renseigner sur sa situation financière

H 60   et sur leurs perspectives à long terme

H 61   à moyen terme

H 62   à court terme

H 63   sur leur compétitivité sur le marché domestique

H 64   le marché extérieur

H 65   quelle est leur réputation dans notre pays et à l'étranger?

H 66   des renseignements sur leur crédit et leur véracité

H 67   nous vous serions reconnaissants de nous envoyer tout renseignement éventuel sur la société

H 68   nous croyons savoir que vous connaissez la maison depuis un certain temps

H 69   pourrions-nous, à votre avis, leur accorder un crédit de . . .

H 70   sans garantie

H 71   nous vous assurons de notre discrétion complète à cet égard

H 72 nous utiliserons vos renseignements avec la plus grande discrétion

H 73 nous serons toujours heureux de vous rendre un service réciproque

H 74 nous connaissons cette maison depuis 6 ans

H 75 nous traitons avec cette maison depuis 5 ans

H 76 ils comptent parmi nos clients réguliers

H 77 nous entretenons des relations commerciales avec eux depuis de nombreuses années

H 78 la société jouit d'une réputation excellente

H 79 elle bénéficie d'une bonne situation financière

H 80 la société possède des ressources financières considérables

H 81 cette maison est complètement digne de confiance

H 82 la compagnie s'est toujours acquittée promptement de ses obligations

H 83 nous sommes sûrs que vous pouvez accorder ce crédit sans hésitation

H 84 nous avons été obligés d'envoyer plusieurs rappels à cette maison durant ces derniers mois

H 85 ils nous doivent toujours la somme de . . .

H 86 ils n'ont toujours pas réglé nos factures de l'année dernière

H 87 ils se trouvent dans une situation financière difficile

H 88 ils manquent de capitaux

H 89 il ne serait pas prudent d'accorder un crédit à cette maison

H 90 nous vous conseillons d'être prudents

H 91 nous déclinons toute responsabilité en vous communiquant ces renseignements

H 92 comme nous ne connaissons pas cette maison

H 93 nous ne possédons pas beaucoup d'information au sujet de cette maison

H 94 nous croyons que la société n'a été fondée que récemment

H 95 il nous semble que nous ne sommes pas assez bien placés pour vous conseiller sur cette affaire

H 96 nous regrettons de ne pas pouvoir fournir les renseignements que vous demandez

H 97 nous n'avons pas connu la maison suffisament longtemps

H 98 nous devons donc vous renvoyer à . . .

I — Demandes et annonces d'emploi

I	1	nous sommes une compagnie bien implantée, basée dans le sud de l'Angleterre
I	2	nous cherchons . . .
I	3	nous recherchons . . .
I	4	nous embauchons des . . .
I	5	pour commencer le 8 octobre
I	6	pour remplacer l'un de nos représentants
I	7	pour remplacer le chef de notre service-export qui prend sa retraite
I	8	nous recherchons une personne ayant de l'expérience dans le domaine de la vente à l'exportation
I	9	nous recherchons un vendeur expérimenté
I	10	la personne que nous recherchons sera âgée de 25 à 35 ans
I	11	et aura un minimum de 5 ans d'expérience dans le domaine de . . .
I	12	connaissance de l'anglais souhaitée
I	13	une connaissance de langues étrangères est essentielle
I	14	la personne choisie doit être capable de travailler en équipe
I	15	il/elle doit pouvoir s'adapter aux besoins de différents clients
I	16	et de déléguer les responsabilités
I	17	nous recherchons une personne capable de très bien s'adapter
I	18	pour assurer la direction de notre service-export
I	19	une voiture de fonction est offerte avec le poste
I	20	nous sommes prêts à offrir un salaire d'au moins . . .
I	21	rémunération en fonction de l'âge et de l'expérience
I	22	rémunération négociable
I	23	une rémunération d'au moins . . . par an
I	24	par mois
I	25	le salaire net est de . . .
I	26	le salaire brut est de . . .
I	27	une prime est payable
I	28	le prélèvement fiscal est d'environ . . . %
I	29	pour la sécurité sociale
I	30	le salaire n'est pas imposable

I 31   un logement sera fourni à titre gratuit par la compagnie
I 32   6 semaines de congé par an
I 33   congés payés
I 34   une semaine de 35 heures
I 35   6 jours par semaine
I 36   un horaire mobile est en vigueur
I 37   les candidats doivent être prêts à faire des heures supplémentaires
I 38   la compagnie dispose de son propre régime de retraite
I 39   veuillez nous donner les noms de deux personnes qui seraient prêts à vous servir de références
I 40   l'une des vos références doit être celle de votre employeur actuel
I 41   nous exigeons également une référence de votre banque
I 42   je vois d'après votre annonce dans . . .
I 43   j'ai appris par certains de mes associés
I 44   j'ai lu votre annonce dans l'édition de la semaine dernière du . . .
I 45   j'aimerais poser ma candidature à ce poste
I 46   veuillez m'envoyer des renseignements plus complets sur ce poste
I 47   accompagnés d'un dossier de candidature
I 48   comme vous le verrez d'après le curriculum vitae ci-joint
I 49   j'ai une expérience considérable dans ce genre de travail
I 50   j'ai aussi assisté à plusieurs conférences sur ce sujet
I 51   je me sens capable de satisfaire aux exigences de ce poste
I 52   je travaille actuellement pour une maison exportatrice
I 53   je cherche un poste similaire
I 54   je désire maintenant changer de poste
I 55   je désire travailler pour une organisation plus importante
I 56   ayant des relations internationales
I 57   pour améliorer mes perspectives de carrière
I 58   pour des raisons personnelles
I 59   je cherche un poste offrant plus de responsabilité
I 60   je désire travailler à l'étranger
I 61   je désire améliorer mes chances de promotion
I 62   je cherche un poste qui offre de meilleures possibilités de carrière
I 63   je désire utiliser ma connaissance de langues étrangères
I 64   je parle couramment le français et l'allemand
I 65   j'ai une connaissance de base de l'anglais
I 66   j'ai des qualifications en . . .
I 67   je suis titulaire d'un diplôme de . . .

I **68** je suis titulaire d'une licence en . . .
I **69** je tape . . . mots par minute
I **70** je prends en sténo . . . mots par minute
I **71** j'ai l'habitude de travailler avec les micro-ordinateurs
I **72** j'ai utilisé un système de traitement de textes
I **73** je suis né à . . .
I **74** j'ai été à l'école à . . .
I **75** où j'ai été reçu aux examens suivants
I **76** dans les matières suivantes
I **77** je suis allé à l'université de . . .
I **78** où j'ai étudié . . . comme matière principale
I **79** et . . . comme matière secondaire
I **80** j'ai obtenu ma licence dans les matières suivantes . . .
I **81** j'ai été reçu à l'examen d'état
I **82** avec mention très bien
I **83** j'ai été recalé dans les matières suivantes . . .
I **84** j'ai travaillé ensuite pendant 4 années dans une société
        exportatrice
I **85** j'ai passé trois années à l'étranger
I **86** j'ai été promu responsable du service en 19 . . .
I **87** j'ai été licencié en 19 . . .
I **88** depuis lors je suis au chômage
I **89** j'ai suivi des cours du soir de . . .
I **90** j'ai reçu une formation de secrétaire bilingue
I **91** au cas où vous désireriez me convoquer pour un entretien
I **92** je suis disponible à tout moment pour un entretien éventuel
I **93** je ne suis disponible que le vendredi pour venir à un
        entretien
I **94** serait-il possible de renvoyer l'entretien à une date
        ultérieure?
I **95** je serai disponible à partir du 16 juin
I **96** j'espère que ma candidature sera favorablement reçue
I **97** je vous remets ci-inclus une lettre de recommandation de
        mon ancien employeur
I **98** je vous remets ci-inclus copies des certificats qui m'ont été
        délivrés par mes deux derniers employeurs
I **99** et copies de mes diplômes
I **100** les noms de deux références sont donnés ci-dessous
I **101** les personnes suivantes m'ont permis de donner leurs noms
         comme références
I **102** je vous serais reconnaissant de ne pas vous adresser à mon
         employeur actuel
I **103** avant l'entretien

I 104	sans mon accord préalable
I 105	je remets ci-joint une enveloppe timbrée à mon nom
I 106	je remets ci-joint un coupon-réponse international
I 107	je serais heureux de vous donner tout autre renseignement dont vous auriez besoin
I 108	j'ai posé ma candidature au poste de . . .
I 109	et je vous serais fort reconnaissant de bien vouloir me servir de référence

J — Changement d'adresse etc.

J	1	notre siège social n'est plus situé à Londres
J	2	notre siège social a été transféré à Francfort
J	3	nous venons d'ouvrir une nouvelle succursale à Madrid
J	4	à cause de la croissance régulière de nos affaires
J	5	nous avons transféré nos bureaux dans de nouveaux locaux plus spacieux à Bordeaux
J	6	ceci signifie que nous serons en mesure d'offrir un meilleur service à tous nos clients
J	7	nous vous assurons que nous maintiendrons la même haute qualité de nos services
J	8	notre adresse a changé
J	9	et est maintenant la suivante
J	10	veuillez faire suivre toute correspondance à cette adresse
J	11	veuillez informer votre service d'expédition de ce changement d'adresse
J	12	notre numéro de téléphone a changé
J	13	notre numéro de téléphone est maintenant...
J	14	nous avons changé le nom de notre maison
J	15	le nom de la maison est maintenant...
J	16	nous avons fusionné avec...
J	17	à partir du 14 mai nous serons connus sous le nouveau nom de...
J	18	nous ne sommes plus dans ce genre d'affaires
J	19	nous ne fabriquons plus ces articles
J	20	nous avons cessé la production de ces articles il y a 3 ans
J	21	nous ne nous spécialisons maintenant que dans la fabrication de...

J	22	la fabrication de ces articles a été reprise par la société...
J	23	notre usine à Turin sera démolie en mars
J	24	et nous transférons la production à Zurich
J	25	nous avons été obligés de fermer notre usine à Birmingham
J	26	nous avons fermé notre service export
J	27	nous vous proposons de vous mettre en relation avec notre société mère
J	28	notre société associée à Paris
J	29	nous avons été repris par...
J	30	...ont acquis...% de nos actions
J	31	la compagnie s'est retirée des affaires
J	32	nous avons cessé notre commerce il y a 6 mois
J	33	la compagnie a fait faillite
J	34	le syndic a été prié d'intervenir
J	35	M...a été promu au poste de...
J	36	il est maintenant sous-directeur
J	37	il est chef de notre nouveau service-export à Vienne
J	38	il a été nommé au Conseil d'Administration
J	39	il a été transféré dans une autre succursale
J	40	M...ne travaille plus pour cette maison
J	41	il est parti dans une autre compagnie
J	42	il a pris sa retraite en août
J	43	notre P.D.G., M...est décédé il y a 6 mois
J	44	il a été remplacé par M...
J	45	ses fonctions ont été reprises par M...

K — Voyages et réservation d'hôtel

K	1	je voudrais réserver une place dans le train Paris/ Heidelberg
K	2	départ de Paris à 13h45, arrivée à Heidelberg à 19h55
K	3	le rapide
K	4	le T.E.E.
K	5	est-il nécessaire de réserver une place dans ce train?
K	6	les réservations sont nécessaires sur tous les rapides
K	7	ce train ne circule pas les jours fériés

K	8	ce train ne circule que les jours ouvrables
K	9	le train local
K	10	le train spécial
K	11	le train supplémentaire
K	12	le train part du quai No.6
K	13	une place côté fenêtre
K	14	dans un compartiment non-fumeurs
K	15	la couchette
K	16	le wagon-lit
K	17	le wagon-restaurant
K	18	la voiture-buffet
K	19	le contrôle des passeports aura lieu dans le train
K	20	désirez-vous voyager en première classe?
K	21	une place dans un compartiment première classe
K	22	à quelle heure le train arrive-t-il à . . .?
K	23	je joins sous ce pli une copie de mon itinéraire projeté
K	24	un aller simple
K	25	un aller-retour valable 24 heures
K	26	un aller-retour
K	27	le ticket de quai
K	28	doit-on payer un supplément pour ce train?
K	29	y a-t-il une consigne dans la gare?
K	30	où sont les consignes automatiques?
K	31	où est le bureau des objets trouvés?
K	32	ce ticket est-il valable sur toutes les lignes d'autobus?
K	33	ce billet est strictement personnel
K	34	est-ce que je peux obtenir une carte d'abonnement mensuel pour l'autobus?
K	35	un abonnement
K	36	à quelle heure le bateau quitte-t-il Calais?
K	37	le ferry
K	38	veuillez m'envoyer des renseignements sur vos services de ferry pour voitures
K	39	l'aéroglisseur
K	40	une cabine pour deux personnes
K	41	une cabine première classe
K	42	je voudrais réserver une place pour une automobile et deux passagers
K	43	pouvez-vous offrir une réduction de prix pour un groupe de 20 personnes?
K	44	sur le ferry Douvres/Calais
K	45	à quelle heure est le vol No...pour...?
K	46	le vol charter

K	47	le vol régulier
K	48	je voudrais retenir 3 places sur le premier vol disponible
K	49	de quel terminal l'avion part-il?
K	50	sert-on des repas au cours du vol?
K	51	la classe économique
K	52	la classe club
K	53	veuillez confirmer vos réservations 24 heures avant le départ
K	54	est-ce que les taxes d'aéroport sont comprises dans le prix?
K	55	les bagages à main
K	56	l'hôtesse de l'air
K	57	le steward
K	58	des boissons sont servies pendant le vol
K	59	les passagers doivent se présenter au bureau 45 minutes avant le départ
K	60	je cherche une chambre à un prix modéré
K	61	je voudrais réserver une chambre pour une personne avec bain
K	62	une chambre pour 2 personnes
K	63	une chambre à deux lits
K	64	avec douche
K	65	avec douche et W.C.
K	66	veuillez me faire savoir le prix d'une chambre pour une personne
K	67	pendant la haute saison
K	68	au début de la saison
K	69	à l'arrière-saison
K	70	du 19 au 30 avril
K	71	acceptez-vous des réservations de groupe?
K	72	je désire organiser une conférence pour nos représentants chargés de la vente en octobre
K	73	et je cherche un hôtel convenable près de l'aéroport
K	74	nous voulons qu'un car vienne nous chercher à l'aéroport
K	75	nous désirons être emmenés en car jusqu'à l'hôtel
K	76	le prix d'une chambre pour deux personnes pour trois nuits est de . . .
K	77	ces prix sont tout compris
K	78	petit-déjeuner compris
K	79	la demi-pension
K	80	la pension complète
K	81	service et T.V.A. compris
K	82	le pourboire

K	83	veuillez nous donner le prix tout compris
K	84	chauffage central dans toutes les chambres
K	85	eau froide et chaude dans toutes les chambres
K	86	le petit-déjeuner est servi jusqu'à 10 heures
K	87	l'hôtel possède son propre parking
K	88	le parking souterrain
K	89	un parking à plusieurs niveaux
K	90	il y a un parking à proximité
K	91	l'hôtel est situé dans un quartier calme
K	92	l'hôtel a des salles de conférences disponibles
K	93	l'hôtel a une salle de conférences pouvant accueillir jusqu'à 100 personnes
K	94	l'hôtel est proche du centre-ville
K	95	à quelle distance se trouve l'hôtel de l'aéroport?
K	96	y a-t-il un service d'autobus pour l'aéroport?
K	97	il n'est qu'à quelques minutes du centre-ville
K	98	il est situé dans une banlieue calme
K	99	près de la rivière
K	100	il y a un ascenseur
K	101	le concierge de nuit
K	102	il y a un bureau de change
K	103	je voudrais confirmer ma réservation (par écrit)
K	104	veuillez m'envoyer votre carte ainsi que celle des vins
K	105	veuillez me faire savoir si vous exigez une caution
K	106	veuillez envoyer la note à ma société MM . . .
K	107	malheureusement j'ai dû changer la date de mon départ
K	108	et n'arriverai pas avant le 21 juillet
K	109	je suis obligé d'annuler ma réservation dans votre hôtel

L — Immobilier: vente et location

L	1	maison à vendre
L	2	maison à louer
L	3	l'appartement
L	4	l'appartement
L	5	appartement à grand standing
L	6	la villa
L	7	la maison individuelle

L   8   le bungalow
L   9   la maison jumelée/la villa mitoyenne
L 10   la maison en ville
L 11   2 chambres, salle de séjour, cuisine, salle de bain, garage, jardin
L 12   nous souhaitons louer une maison pendant 18 mois approximativement
L 13   veuillez nous indiquer le loyer d'un tel appartement
L 14   le loyer est de . . . par mois
L 15   par an
L 16   si vous êtes prêt à louer l'appartement pendant 2 ans
L 17   nous pouvons vous offrir une réduction de . . . %
L 18   nous cherchons des locaux à l'usage de bureaux en centre-ville
L 19   nous désirons acheter une maison en centre-ville
L 20   nous sommes prêts à payer un maximum de . . .
L 21   dans un emplacement attrayant
L 22   dans un quartier résidentiel
L 23   dans la zone verte
L 24   pour de plus amples renseignements s'adresser à . . .
L 25   emprunt-logement disponible
L 26   prêts disponibles
L 27   à un taux d'intérêt de . . . %
L 28   sans intérêt
L 29   à un loyer de . . . par mois
L 30   au prix de . . . le mètre carré
L 31   nous pouvons arranger un emprunt-logement
L 32   un prêt peut être arrangé par notre compagnie d'assurances
L 33   nous avons un certain nombre de résidences secondaires
L 34   vols d'inspection gratuits
L 35   la multipropriété

M — Rapports financiers

M   1   la réunion aura lieu au siège social de la société
M   2   l'Assemblée Générale Annuelle
M   3   notre Assemblée Générale Annuelle aura lieu cette année le 3 juillet

M	4	l'Assemblée Générale Ordinaire
M	5	une Assemblée Extraordinaire a été convoquée
M	6	l'ordre du jour de l'Assemblée Générale Annuelle
M	7	questions à débattre dans l'ordre du jour
M	8	autres questions à l'ordre du jour
M	9	ont participé à la réunion les personnes suivantes
M	10	le directeur général
M	11	le président
M	12	le directeur commercial
M	13	le directeur des exportations
M	14	le représentant à l'étranger
M	15	le directeur du personnel
M	16	les représentants des ouvriers
M	17	les membres du syndicat
M	18	les actionnaires
M	19	le conseil d'administration/le conseil exécutif
M	20	le procès-verbal a été pris par . . .
M	21	le président a accueilli les actionnaires à l'assemblée
M	22	et a présenté le rapport de l'exercice précédent
M	23	et a présenté le procès-verbal de la dernière assemblée
M	24	nous avons augmenté la production
M	25	la production a augmenté
M	26	nous avons augmenté notre production de . . . % par rapport à l'année précédente
M	27	et avons créé de nouveaux emplois
M	28	notre chiffre d'affaires a augmenté de . . . %
M	29	l'augmentation du chiffre d'affaires
M	30	nous avons augmenté nos exportations de . . . %
M	31	dû à un accroissement des investissements
M	32	nous avons investi des sommes considérables dans nos usines
M	33	nous avons augmenté notre part du marché
M	34	nos marchandises ont trouvé des débouchés faciles dans d'autres pays européens
M	35	en vue de consolider notre situation sur le marché
M	36	nous devons affermir notre place sur le marché
M	37	le marché extérieur
M	38	le marché intérieur
M	39	nos plus grands débouchés sont la France et l'Italie
M	40	il y a eu un développement favorable dans nos ventes en Allemagne
M	41	avec des ventes intérieures de . . .
M	42	nos ventes totales ont augmenté de . . . à . . .

M	43	nos ventes totales ont baissé de . . . à . . .
M	44	à long terme, nous envisageons de bonnes possibilités commerciales
M	45	nous avons utilisé nos ressources disponibles au maximum
M	46	nous devons conserver notre place de leader dans ce secteur
M	47	notre programme d'investissements à long terme
M	48	nous permettra d'améliorer la qualité de nos produits
M	49	notre programme de développement
M	50	à court terme
M	51	à moyen terme
M	52	nous envisageons une augmentation globale de nos affaires
M	53	nos capitaux fixes ont augmenté de . . . %
M	54	le capital emprunté
M	55	les valeurs disponibles ont augmenté de . . . %
M	56	la société a augmenté le capital-actions de . . .
M	57	le dividende payé a augmenté de . . . par action
M	58	les recettes
M	59	le bénéfice
M	60	le bénéfice net
M	61	le bénéfice après impôt
M	62	la société a augmenté ses bénéfices de . . . % durant le premier trimestre de l'exercice
M	63	le taux de croissance
M	64	la récession économique générale
M	65	a diminué la demande
M	66	au cours du second semestre de l'exercice, la demande a baissé
M	67	et nous avons éprouvé des difficultés dans le domaine des ventes
M	68	il y a eu une baisse dans la production
M	69	nous devons nous attendre à une légère baisse dans la production
M	70	et les exportations ont baissé
M	71	ceci a diminué nos possibilités de croissance
M	72	l'augmentation des prix de l'énergie et des autres matières premières
M	73	a eu un effet nuisible
M	74	la concurrence est devenue plus forte
M	75	dû à la concurrence d'autres sociétés dans ce secteur
M	76	notre compétitivité a été affaiblie
M	77	les frais de personnel étaient aussi très élevés

M 78   la société a subi une perte totale l'an dernier de . . .
M 79   nos pertes dans certains secteurs étaient particulièrement
         importantes

N — Utilisation du téléphone

N   1   je voudrais parler à M . . .
N   2   ne quittez pas
N   3   la ligne est occupée
N   4   je vous passe la communication
N   5   allô
N   6   au revoir
N   7   M . . . n'est pas là pour le moment
N   8   aimeriez-vous laisser un message?
N   9   pouvez-vous lui donner le message suivant?
N 10   ceci est un message enregistré
N 11   voulez-vous me passer le poste . . . s'il vous plaît
N 12   je vous téléphone d'une cabine
N 13   raccrochez et recomposez le numéro
N 14   une communication urbaine
N 15   une communication à longue distance
N 16   une communication internationale
N 17   une communication en PCV à
N 18   je voudrais téléphoner en PCV à
N 19   je voudrais faire une communication à préavis
N 20   l'annuaire
N 21   vous devrez chercher le numéro dans l'annuaire
N 22   renseignements
N 23   pouvez-vous me donner le numéro de la société . . . ?
N 24   pouvez-vous me donner l'indicatif pour Manchester?
N 25   la ligne est mauvaise
N 26   je vais devoir raccrocher
N 27   vous pouvez composer le numéro vous-même
N 28   je vais devoir recomposer le numéro
N 29   j'ai fait le mauvais numéro
N 30   j'ai un croisement de lignes
N 31   j'ai été coupé
N 32   la tonalité

N 33 la tonalité pas libre
N 34 ne faites pas le 0 quand vous composez le numéro
N 35 je vous téléphone d'Angleterre
N 36 je vous rappellerai

O — Banque et (bureau de) poste

O 1 j'aimerais ouvrir un compte d'épargne
O 2 un compte courant
O 3 un compte de dépôt
O 4 un compte joint
O 5 un compte a été ouvert à votre nom
O 6 quel est le taux d'intérêt actuel?
O 7 quels sont les frais de banque?
O 8 le chequier
O 9 le virement automatique
O 10 j'ai un compte à la banque . . .
O 11 le numéro de mon compte est . . .
O 12 j'ai un compte d'épargne à la poste
O 13 je veux virer . . . sur mon compte
O 14 je veux fermer mon compte
O 15 je veux retirer . . . de
O 16 les retraits d'une telle somme sont sujets à un court délai
O 17 je veux verser . . . à mon compte courant
O 18 votre compte est à découvert
O 19 et la limite de votre découvert est de . . .
O 20 vous avez maintenant dépassé cette somme
O 21 je voudrais encaisser ce chèque
O 22 puis-je encaisser ce chèque?
O 23 je voudrais verser ce chèque à mon compte
O 24 je voudrais un relevé
O 25 vous recevrez des relevés mensuellement
O 26 quel est le solde actuel de mon compte?
O 27 le crédit
O 28 le débit
O 29 un prêt à long terme
O 30 à court terme
O 31 le bénéficiaire

O 32   la caisse d'épargne
O 33   la société de crédit immobilier
O 34   la carte de crédit
O 35   la carte Eurochèque
O 36   cinq timbres à . . . , s'il vous plaît
O 37   je veux envoyer ce paquet en France
O 38   par avion
O 39   par voie de terre
O 40   par colis postal
O 41   en recommandé
O 42   par livraison exprès
O 43   vous devez remplir une déclaration de douane
O 44   je voudrais envoyer un télégramme à . . .
O 45   par télex
O 46   poste restante
O 47   je voudrais un mandat pour la somme de . . .
O 48   B.P. numéro
O 49   code postal

P — Assurance

P   1   je voudrais m'assurer
P   2   l'assurance personnelle
P   3   l'assurance immobilière
P   4   la compagnie d'assurances
P   5   l'assuré, M . . . , nous a demandé de . . .
P   6   j'ai remis votre lettre au service des sinistres
P   7   je joins à cette lettre votre police d'assurance provisoire
P   8   il me faut un formulaire de proposition
P   9   vous recevrez la police d'assurance dans un bref délai
P 10   la police d'assurance doit être établie par notre siège social
P 11   je joins à cette lettre les conditions de la police d'assurance
P 12   le numéro de votre police d'assurance est . . .
P 13   vous devez nous donner le nom de l'assuré
P 14   la durée de votre police d'assurance est de . . .
P 15   je voudrais renouveler ma police d'assurance
P 16   j'ai annulé la police d'assurance
P 17   la somme assurée est de . . .
P 18   la prime mensuelle est de . . .

P 19   l'assurance couvre . . .
P 20   la demande d'indemnité
P 21   les dégâts
P 22   force majeure
P 23   l'assurance-incendie
P 24   l'assurance-automobile
P 25   l'assurance au tiers
P 26   l'assurance tous risques
P 27   l'assurance-voyage
P 28   il vous faut une carte verte
P 29   vous devez signaler l'accident à notre siège social
P 30   vous devez obtenir les noms des témoins
P 31   l'assurance-accidents
P 32   l'assurance-bagages
P 33   l'assurance-maladie
P 34   le courtier d'assurances

Q — Terminologie de bureau et télématique

Q   1   le classeur vertical
Q   2   le fichier
Q   3   le dictaphone
Q   4   le bureau
Q   5   le télex
Q   6   la machine à écrire avec mémoire
Q   7   le micro-ordinateur
Q   8   l'écran de visualisation
Q   9   le système de traitement de texte
Q 10   le clavier
Q 11   la touche
Q 12   le terminal d'ordinateur
Q 13   la disquette
Q 14   le lecteur de disquettes
Q 15   la banque de données
Q 16   la mémoire
Q 17   la plaquette de silicon

Q 18 le microprocesseur
Q 19 la calculatrice de poche
Q 20 le correcteur
Q 21 le tampon-date
Q 22 le trombone
Q 23 l'agrafe
Q 24 l'agrafeuse
Q 25 le taille-crayon
Q 26 la machine à affranchir
Q 27 le bloc-notes
Q 28 le classeur
Q 29 l'imprimante
Q 30 le photocopieur
Q 31 la télématique
Q 32 le vidéotex
Q 33 le système conforme aux normes télé-informatiques internationales
Q 34 il est accessible par téléphone de votre bureau
Q 35 l'annuaire électronique est accessible du terminal
Q 36 un modem assure l'interface avec le réseau télécom
Q 37 la communication dans les deux sens entre ordinateurs
Q 38 le système autorise la messagerie et le courrier électronique
Q 39 ce modèle permet l'insertion de parties variables dans un texte
Q 40 le télétex
Q 41 le télécopieur (le fax)
Q 42 ce système vous permet de relier un ordinateur au réseau télex
Q 43 il autorise la réitération automatique des appels
Q 44 il envoie des messages aux heures demi-tarif
Q 45 la téléconférence
Q 46 en relation directe avec
Q 47 en temps réel
Q 48 la conception assistée par ordinateur (CAO)
Q 49 la fabrication assistée par ordinateur (FAO)
Q 50 l'enseignement assisté par ordinateur (EAO)
Q 51 la publication assistée par ordinateur (PAO)
Q 52 le système expert
Q 53 la base de données
Q 54 la base de données relationnelle
Q 55 l'information est mise à jour toutes les 24 heures
Q 56 le tableur

Q 57 les données sont stockées en forme de fichiers, qui sont gérés par le système

Q 58 les informations stockées sont organisées en pages numérotées

Q 59 le disque peut être lu par tout ordinateur compatible

Q 60 ce modèle est compatible IBM

Q 61 ce modèle fonctionne sous MS-DOS et n'est pas compatible PS–DOS

Q 62 le clone

Q 63 le système d'exploitation

Q 64 les messages erreur

Q 65 un octet

Q 66 un kilo-octet (Ko)

Q 67 un mega-octet (Mo)

Q 68 ce modèle a 512 Ko de RAM

Q 69 la capacité de disquette est de 1000 Ko

Q 70 le logiciel

Q 71 le progiciel (produit logiciel)

Q 72 le programme est fourni sur disquette

Q 73 la configuration peut être adaptée pour se conformer à vos besoins

Q 74 et est disponible en version italienne

Q 75 le programme a un curseur déroulant

Q 76 le déplacement du curseur peut s'effectuer par le moyen de la souris

Q 77 le crayon optique

Q 78 la disquette système

Q 79 la disquette archive

Q 80 double face

Q 81 double densité

Q 82 il est nécessaire de formater la disquette

Q 83 une disquette au format 3.5″

Q 84 le répertoire de disquette

Q 85 le sous-répertoire

Q 86 la disquette source

Q 87 la disquette cible

Q 88 la sauvegarde

Q 89 le fichier peut être copié de la disquette A sur la disquette B

Q 90 le programme est protégé

Q 91 déplacer un texte

Q 92 supprimer un texte

Q 93 ajouter un texte

Q 94 il y a un dictionnaire pour vérifier et corriger l'orthographe
Q 95 fusionner des fichiers
Q 96 le texte peut être envoyé directement à l'imprimante
Q 97 le matériel
Q 98 l'ordinateur personnel
Q 99 le mini-ordinateur
Q 100 le mainframe
Q 101 une disquette
Q 102 un disque dur
Q 103 le CD-ROM
Q 104 le vidéodisque
Q 105 les périphériques
Q 106 le moniteur monochrome
Q 107 le moniteur coleur
Q 108 le moniteur à cristaux liquides
Q 109 le moniteur à plasma
Q 110 l'écran affiche 25 lignes de 80 caractères
Q 111 l'imprimante parallèle
Q 112 l'imprimante série
Q 113 l'imprimante matricielle
Q 114 l'imprimante à marguerite
Q 115 l'imprimante laser
Q 116 la fonte
Q 117 la tête
Q 118 le chargeur
Q 119 le capot insonorisant
Q 120 le traceur
Q 121 le scanner
Q 122 de qualité courrier
Q 123 la cassette ruban est facile à changer
Q 124 un faible niveau de bruit
Q 125 le contrat de maintenance
Q 126 la maintenance préventive
Q 127 toute pièce usée ou défectueuse sera remplacée gratuitement
Q 128 le réglage
Q 129 pourvu qu'il y ait des visites régulières de contrôle
Q 130 le matériel ne peut être réparé sur le site
Q 131 le disque dur est endommagé
Q 132 la faute était due à une baisse de tension
Q 133 la panne était due à une faute de logiciel
Q 134 l'alimentation électrique
Q 135 le livret d'utilisation

Q 136 le composant
Q 137 le boîtier
Q 138 la mini-cassette n'était pas raccordée à l'ordinateur
Q 139 la touche de fonction ne marchait pas
Q 140 vous auriez dû obtenir un listing du répertoire de la disquette
Q 141 normalement ce télécopieur transmet des pages A4 en moins de 12 secondes
Q 142 le poste de travail ne fonctionne pas
Q 143 la faute réside dans le processeur 16 bits
Q 144 le processeur devrait supporter jusqu'à 8 postes de travail
Q 145 l'usager ignorait le fait que le service était payant
Q 146 la transmission de données par paquets

R — Noms de pays et de villes

R **1** Aix-la-Chapelle
R **2** Afrique
R **3** Alexandrie
R **4** Algérie
R **5** Alger
R **6** Amsterdam
R **7** Anvers
R **8** Argentine
R **9** Arnhem
R **10** Asie
R **11** Athènes
R **12** Australie
R **13** Autriche
R **14** Avignon
R **15** Baden-Baden
R **16** Bagdad
R **17** Bahreïn
R **18** Barcelone
R **19** Bâle
R **20** Bayreuth
R **21** Beyrouth
R **22** Belfast

R	23	Belgique
R	24	Belgrade
R	25	Berlin
R	26	Berne
R	27	Bilbao
R	28	Bochum
R	29	Bolivie
R	30	Bombay
R	31	Bonn
R	32	Bordeaux
R	33	Brasilia
R	34	Brésil
R	35	Bregenz
R	36	Brême
R	37	Bremerhaven
R	38	Brunswick
R	39	Bruxelles
R	40	Bucarest
R	41	Budapest
R	42	Bulgarie
R	43	Buenos-Aires
R	44	Cadiz
R	45	Le Caire
R	46	Canada
R	47	Les Canaries
R	48	Le Cap
R	49	Tchad
R	50	Chili
R	51	Chine
R	52	Cologne
R	53	Colombie
R	54	Constance
R	55	Copenhague
R	56	Cordoba
R	57	Corinthe
R	58	Costa-Rica
R	59	Cuba
R	60	Tchécoslovaquie
R	61	Damas
R	62	Delhi
R	63	Danemark
R	64	Dijon
R	65	Djakarta

R	**66**	Dortmund
R	**67**	Dresde
R	**68**	Dubai
R	**69**	Dublin
R	**70**	Dunkerque
R	**71**	Düsseldorf
R	**72**	Equateur (Ecuador)
R	**73**	Edimbourg
R	**74**	la CEE
R	**75**	Egypte
R	**76**	Eindhoven
R	**77**	Angleterre
R	**78**	Erfurt
R	**79**	Ethiopie
R	**80**	Europe
R	**81**	Les Malouines
R	**82**	Finlande
R	**83**	Florence
R	**84**	France
R	**85**	Francfort
R	**86**	Freiberg
R	**87**	Gdansk
R	**88**	Genève
R	**89**	Gênes
R	**90**	Côte d'Or
R	**91**	Giessen
R	**92**	Gotha
R	**93**	Göttingen
R	**94**	Graz
R	**95**	Grande-Bretagne
R	**96**	Grèce
R	**97**	Groningue
R	**98**	Guyane
R	**99**	La Haye
R	**100**	Halle
R	**101**	Hambourg
R	**102**	Hanovre
R	**103**	La Havane
R	**104**	Heidelberg
R	**105**	Helsinki
R	**106**	Hollande
R	**107**	Honduras
R	**108**	Hongrie

R 109	Islande
R 110	Inde
R 111	Indonésie
R 112	Innsbruck
R 113	Interlaken
R 114	Iran
R 115	Irak
R 116	Irelande
R 117	Israël
R 118	Istamboul
R 119	Italie
R 120	Côte d'Ivoire
R 121	Jamaïque
R 122	le Japon
R 123	Jena
R 124	Jérusalem
R 125	Jordanie
R 126	Kaiserslautern
R 127	Karl Marx Stadt (Chemnitz)
R 128	Karlsruhe
R 129	Kassel
R 130	Kiel
R 131	Kitzbühel
R 132	Klagenfurt
R 133	Coblence
R 134	Cracovie
R 135	Lausanne
R 136	Liban
R 137	Leipzig
R 138	Libye
R 139	Lille
R 140	Lima
R 141	Linz
R 142	Lisbonne
R 143	Ljubljana
R 144	Londres
R 145	Lübeck
R 146	Lucerne
R 147	Lugano
R 148	Luxembourg
R 149	Lyon
R 150	Maastricht
R 151	Magdebourg

R 152	Mayence
R 153	Malaysia
R 154	Malte
R 155	Mannheim
R 156	Marseille
R 157	La Mecque
R 158	Mexique
R 159	Mexico
R 160	Milan
R 161	Monaco
R 162	Montevideo
R 163	Montreux
R 164	Maroc
R 165	Moscou
R 166	Munich
R 167	Münster
R 168	Naples
R 169	les Pays-Bas
R 170	New Delhi
R 171	New York
R 172	Nouvelle-Zélande
R 173	Nicaragua
R 174	Nice
R 175	Irlande du Nord
R 176	Norvège
R 177	Nuremberg
R 178	Oslo
R 179	Ostende
R 180	Padoue
R 181	Panama
R 182	Paraguay
R 183	Paris
R 184	Passau
R 185	Pékin
R 186	Pérou
R 187	les Philippines
R 188	Le Pirée
R 189	Pologne
R 190	Portugal
R 191	Prague
R 192	Katar
R 193	Récife
R 194	Reykjavik

R 195	Riad
R 196	Rio de Janerio
R 197	Rome
R 198	Rostock
R 199	Rotterdam
R 200	Roumanie
R 201	Russie
R 202	Sarrebruck
R 203	Saint-Pétersbourg (Léningrad)
R 204	Salzbourg
R 205	Sardaigne
R 206	Arabie Saoudite
R 207	Ecosse
R 208	Séville
R 209	Sicile
R 210	Singapour
R 211	Afrique du Sud
R 212	Amérique du Sud
R 213	Corée du Sud
R 214	Espagne
R 215	Split
R 216	Steyr
R 217	Stockholm
R 218	Strasbourg
R 219	Stuttgart
R 220	Suède
R 221	Suisse
R 222	Syrie
R 223	Tanger
R 224	Téhéran
R 225	Tel Aviv
R 226	Thaïlande
R 227	La Haye
R 228	Thessalonique
R 229	Tokyo
R 230	Toronto
R 231	Toulon
R 232	Toulouse
R 233	Trèves
R 234	Tripoli
R 235	Tunis
R 236	Tunisie
R 237	Turin

R 238 Turquie
R 239 Ulm
R 240 Emirats Arabes Unis
R 241 Royaume-Uni
R 242 Etats-Unis
R 243 Utrecht
R 244 Vancouver
R 245 Vénézuela
R 246 Venise
R 247 Vienne
R 248 le Pays de Galles
R 249 Varsovie
R 250 Weimar
R 251 les Antilles
R 252 Wismar
R 253 Wolfsburg
R 254 Yougoslavie
R 255 Zagreb
R 256 Saragosse
R 257 Zurich
R 258 Zwickau

S — Abbréviations

S 1 cpte.
S 2 Frs.
S 3 Sté
S 4 a.b.s.
S 5 dz.
S 6 éd.
S 7 CE
S 8 p.ex.
S 9 P.J.
S 10 etc.
S 12 c.-à-d.
S 13 S.A.
S 14 p.pon
S 15 T.V.A.

Index

ITALIANO

Sommario

Prefazione

Il presente volume è stato creato per chi debba svolgere o capire la corrispondenza commerciale in inglese, francese, tedesco, italiano o spagnolo. Contiene frasi importanti in ognuna delle cinque lingue, ed è diviso in sezioni per facilitare l'uso. Contiene, inoltre, in ognuna delle lingue, il vocabolario necessario per l'uso del telefono, per le operazioni con la Banca e con l'Ufficio Postale, e elenchi di nomi di nazioni e di città.

Dovrebbe essere d'aiuto non solo a chi si occupa già di corrispondenza commerciale, ma anche a chi studia o insegna la materia. Gli autori hanno evitato di dare troppo peso a una lingua o all'altra, e il libro è impostato in modo tale da essere utile sia alla segretaria francese che desideri comporre lettere in inglese sia allo studente italiano che voglia capire le lettere scritte in tedesco. Ci sono dieci possibili combinazioni di lingue, che rendono questo libro particolarmente utile a tutte le aziende che si occupano di commercio con l'estero.

Come si adopera questo libro

Il libro è diviso in cinque parti, una per ogni lingua, e ogni parte è suddivisa in sezioni come per esempio: *Richieste di informazioni e offerte, Ordini,* ecc. Nelle varie sezioni, ogni frase è contrassegnata da una lettera chiave e da un numero (**A36, B45,** ecc.), che corrispondono esattamente alla stessa frase in ognuna delle altre lingue. Se si prende, per esempio, la frase inglese **B45** 'the samples must be returned within two weeks' si troverà sotto la stessa lettera e lo stesso numero nella parte italiana la frase 'i campioni dovranno essere restituiti entro 15 giorni', e nella parte tedesca 'die Muster müssen binne 2 Wochen zurückgeschickt werden', ecc.

Per facilitare la ricerca di una data parola o frase, per ogni lingua c'è un indice che rimanda direttamente alla lettera chiave e al numero corrispondente.

E' importante tenere presente che se non si trova una particolare frase, bisogna cercare di sostituirla con un'altra frase simile.

Le parole e le frasi messe fra parentesi quadre nella parte inglese appartengono all'inglese nordamericano.

A — Espressioni generali

A	1	Egregio Signore
A	2	Egregi Signori
A	3	Egregio Signor X
A	4	Gentilissima Signora (Gent.ma Sig.ra)
A	5	Gentilissima Signorina (Gent.ma Sig.na)
A	6	alla cortese attenzione di
A	7	confidenziale
A	8	oggetto
A	9	accusiamo ricevuta della Vs. lettera
A	10	Vi ringraziamo per la Vs. lettera
A	11	del 3 corrente
A	12	ci riferiamo alla Vs. lettera
A	13	Vs. riferimento (Vs. rif.)
A	14	ns. riferimento (ns. rif.)
A	15	il Vs. nominativo ci è stato segnalato da persone con cui siamo in relazioni d'affari
A	16	ci premuriamo di rispondere alla Vs. lettera del . . .
A	17	non abbiamo ancora ricevuto risposta alla ns. lettera del
A	18	a seguito della ns. conversazione telefonica del
A	19	sono lieto di apprendere che
A	20	il ns. rappresentante ci ha informati
A	21	dietro raccomandazione del ns. rappresentante
A	22	ci dispiace apprendere che
A	23	abbiamo ricevuto la Vs. lettera tramite
A	24	è interessante sapere che
A	25	la Vs. lettera sopra citata
A	26	la Vs. lettera sotto citata
A	27	Vi faremo sapere per telefono
A	28	Vi faremo sapere per telegramma
A	29	a seguito del ns. incontro del
A	30	abbiamo saputo da
A	31	ci dispiace comunicarVi
A	32	abbiamo il piacere di comunicarVi
A	33	è interessante sapere che
A	34	alleghiamo il ns. catalogo
A	35	con la presente confermiamo
A	36	Vi preghiamo comunicarci
A	37	Vi preghiamo di accertare la causa

A 38 l'informazione richiesta è per
A 39 non appena Vi sarà possibile
A 40 non appena riceveremo
A 41 a seguito della ns. lettera
A 42 a seguito della ns. telefonata
A 43 ci dispiace profondamente che
A 44 ci sorprende sapere che
A 45 Vi saremmo grati se voleste gentilmente inviarci
A 46 siamo certi che approverete queste misure
A 47 speriamo Vi sia possibile
A 48 ci dispiace non aver risposto prima
A 49 abbiamo avuto ora l'occasione di
A 50 alleghiamo
A 51 in plico a parte
A 52 con lo stesso invio
A 53 a giro di posta
A 54 Vi restituiamo
A 55 che ci avete mandato
A 56 ci permettiamo di suggerire che
A 57 Vi assicuriamo che
A 58 riferendoci alla ns. precedente corrispondenza
A 59 non Vi sorprenderà
A 60 saremo ben lieti di
A 61 nel caso non sia possibile
A 62 abbiamo appena saputo che
A 63 siamo certi che capirete che
A 64 fateci la cortesia di
A 65 come ben sapete
A 66 in risposta alla gentile Vostra
A 67 secondo i dati in ns. possesso
A 68 Vi ricordiamo che
A 69 ci dispiace doverVi ricordare che
A 70 come richiesto nella Vs. lettera del
A 71 avremo bisogno di informazioni dettagliate sui Vs. prodotti
A 72 saremmo grati di conoscere la Vs. opinione in materia
A 73 ci sembra sia importante che Voi
A 74 stiamo provvedendo ad inviarVi
A 75 a seguito del colloquio con il Vs. rappresentante
A 76 dato che stiamo iniziando le ns. relazioni commerciali
A 77 apprendiamo dalla Vs. lettera che
A 78 ci permettiamo segnalarVi che
A 79 gradirei avere un colloquio con X

A 80	dobbiamo disdire il ns. incontro del
A 81	di Vs. pieno gradimento
A 82	la ns. sede centrale è a
A 83	la ns. sede centrale si è trasferita a
A 84	faremo tutto il possibile per risolvere la questione
A 85	Vi elenchiamo qui in seguito i particolari
A 86	il ns. direttore è attualmente in viaggio di affari
A 87	fateci sapere non appena possibile
A 88	ci auguriamo che possiate capire il ns. punto di vista
A 89	siamo spiacenti per il disturbo recato Vi
A 90	non si è dato giusto peso a questo
A 91	Vi suggeriamo di rivedere
A 92	X ci ha/hanno fatto una ottima impressione
A 93	non possiamo accettare
A 94	troverete particolari di
A 95	se possiamo esserVi di aiuto in qualsiasi maniera
A 96	faremo del ns. meglio
A 97	ci rendiamo conto che
A 98	abbiamo già dato istruzioni affinché
A 99	non appena la merce sarà pronta
A 100	quando saprete la data
A 101	qualora decideste di farlo
A 102	nel caso che
A 103	se l'avessimo saputo
A 104	in un prossimo futuro
A 105	più in là
A 106	saremmo lieti di ricevere questa informazione
A 107	alleghiamo una busta affrancata per la risposta
A 108	alleghiamo un buono internazionale per la risposta
A 109	qualora ce ne fosse bisogno
A 110	in tempo
A 111	il Signor X ci ha consigliati di rivolgerci a Voi
A 112	a tutt'oggi non abbiamo avuto molto successo
A 113	per via ordinaria
A 114	per via aerea
A 115	per raccomandata
A 116	Vi preghiamo di prendere cura particolare
A 117	fra due settimane
A 118	i cui nominativi saremmo lieti di inviarVi
A 119	stando alle loro informazioni
A 120	saremmo disposti a
A 121	siamo convinti che
A 122	ci interesserebbe

A 123	contiamo su una pronta risposta
A 124	speriamo esserVi stati di aiuto
A 125	Vi siamo grati
A 126	speriamo continuerete a
A 127	Distinti saluti.
A 128	Con i ns. migliori saluti.
A 129	all./
A 130	firmato
A 131	per/p.p. (per procura)

B — Richieste di informazioni e offerte

B	1	abbiamo saputo che siete produttori di
B	2	siamo specializzati nella produzione di
B	3	siamo proprietari (titolari) di
B	4	siamo alla ricerca di un fornitore di fiducia
B	5	Vi preghiamo inviarci informazioni dettagliate su
B	6	ci interessano soprattutto i seguenti articoli:
B	7	Vi prego inviarmi tutte le informazioni che possano essermi utili
B	8	per permettermi di fare la scelta più idonea ai miei fini
B	9	parecchi nostri clienti si sono mostrati interessati a
B	10	Vi preghiamo inviarci opuscoli riguardanti i Vs. prodotti
B	11	Vi preghiamo inviarci il Vs. catalogo più recente
B	12	il Vs. ultimo opuscolo
B	13	il Vs. listino prezzi aggiornato
B	14	siamo venuti a conoscenza della Vs. società tramite la stampa specializzata
B	15	siamo Vs. clienti da molti anni
B	16	apprendiamo dalla Vs. pubblicità
B	17	la ns. scorta si sta esaurendo
B	18	la ns. scorta si è esaurita
B	19	Vi preghiamo comunicarci se avete in magazzino
B	20	abbiamo in magazzino
B	21	la Vs. gentile richiesta di informazioni sui ns. prodotti
B	22	abbiamo bisogno di ricevere la merce non oltre il 2 aprile

B	**23**	per permetterci di lanciare il Vs. prodotto sul mercato
B	**24**	siamo disposti a farVi un'offerta di favore
B	**25**	durante la mia recente visita alla Fiera
B	**26**	ho visto una campionatura dei Vs. prodotti
B	**27**	ci permettiamo di segnalarVi
B	**28**	a condizione che
B	**29**	Vi preghiamo inviarci una campionatura dei Vs. prodotti
B	**30**	prevediamo di poter ordinarVi questa merce regolarmente
B	**31**	in grossi quantitativi
B	**32**	Vi preghiamo informarci se è possibile ricevere una fornitura in prova
B	**33**	Vi preghiamo informarci per quanto tempo ci è possibile tenere questo prodotto in prova
B	**34**	restiamo in attesa della Vs. offerta
B	**35**	siamo interessati ai Vs. prodotti
B	**36**	la qualità dei prodotti è di primaria importanza
B	**37**	a condizione che i prezzi delle materie prime non subiscano variazioni
B	**38**	i ns. prodotti vengono accuratamente collaudati per garantirne la qualità
B	**39**	tutti i ns. prodotti sono coperti da 24 mesi di garanzia
B	**40**	siamo disposti a sostituire gratuitamente eventuali parti difettose
B	**41**	a causa di materiali o lavorazione difettosi
B	**42**	entro i primi tre mesi dalla consegna
B	**43**	accettiamo ordini per quantitativi minimi di
B	**44**	i campioni verranno forniti gratuitamente
B	**45**	i campioni dovranno essere restituiti entro 15 giorni
B	**46**	Vi fattureremo i campioni
B	**47**	insieme ai campioni
B	**48**	Vi preghiamo inviarci una campionatura dei Vs. prodotti
B	**49**	non possiamo fornirVi questo prodotto in prova
B	**50**	in conto vendita
B	**51**	in prova
B	**52**	intendiamo allargare la ns. attuale gamma di prodotti
B	**53**	entro 4 settimane dall'ordine
B	**54**	Vi preghiamo inviarci informazioni dettagliate sui Vs. prodotti
B	**55**	apprendiamo dal Vs. opuscolo
B	**56**	a causa di una forte richiesta da parte dei ns. clienti
B	**57**	abbiamo cessato la produzione di questi articoli
B	**58**	non produciamo più questi articoli su grande scala
B	**59**	Vi consigliamo di rivolgerVi a

B	60	10 motori modello . . .
B	61	nei seguenti quantitativi e misure
B	62	Vi preghiamo inviarci la Vs. migliore offerta per
B	63	gradiremmo vedere i Vs. modelli più recenti
B	64	particolari sui Vs. modelli più recenti
B	65	a condizione che qualità e prezzi siano soddisfacenti
B	66	pesi e misure sono elencati nel catalogo illustrato
B	67	per quantitativi superiori a
B	68	per ordinativi minimi di
B	69	nei seguenti colori
B	70	nei seguenti disegni
B	71	secondo il disegno allegato
B	72	Vi preghiamo comunicarci se il Vs. catalogo è disponibile in lingua francese
B	73	abbiamo visto il Vs. materiale pubblicitario
B	74	Vi preghiamo inviarci i Vs. prezzi all'ingrosso
B	75	prezzi al minuto
B	76	i ns. prezzi sono elencati nel listino allegato
B	77	i ns. prezzi sono segnati sul campione
B	78	i prezzi quotati sono prezzi pieni
B	79	questi sono i ns. prezzi più bassi
B	80	possiamo praticare uno sconto del . . . % sui prezzi di listino
B	81	possiamo offrire uno sconto introduttivo del . . . %
B	82	Vi preghiamo comunicarci se potete praticarci uno sconto speciale
B	83	sconto commercianti
B	84	Vi preghiamo indicare le condizioni di pagamento
B	85	i prezzi attuali resteranno in vigore fino all'8 maggio
B	86	i prezzi quotati dovrebbero includere la consegna all'indirizzo sopra indicato
B	87	Vi preghiamo fornirci i prezzi in Lire Sterline
B	88	i prezzi in vigore alla data di spedizione
B	89	i prezzi quotati nella Vs. lettera
B	90	i prezzi seguenti
B	91	se i Vs. prezzi sono competitivi
B	92	al prezzo di . . . cadauno
B	93	al prezzo speciale di . . .
B	94	Vi preghiamo indicarci i Vs. prezzi e tempi di consegna
B	95	questi prezzi sono i più bassi che possiamo offrire
B	96	possiamo praticare uno sconto per l'esportazione del . . . %
B	97	i ns. prezzi sono comprensivi di assicurazione

B 98	i ns. prezzi sono inferiori a quelli della concorrenza
B 99	cadauno
B 100	franco fabbrica
B 101	franco magazzino
B 102	i ns. prezzi si intendono franco a bordo (F.O.B.) Londra
B 103	l'imballaggio è incluso
B 104	l'imballaggio è escluso
B 105	franco Madrid
B 106	franco frontiera
B 107	porto franco frontiera
B 108	costo e nolo (C.&F.)
B 109	franco stazione ferroviaria (F.O.R.)
B 110	costo assicurazione e nolo (C.I.F.)
B 111	franco lungo bordo (F.A.S.)
B 112	franco domicilio
B 113	franco banchina
B 114	franco magazzino
B 115	ci pregiamo sottoporVi le seguenti quotazioni:
B 116	Vi preghiamo informarci se possiamo effettuare il pagamento a 20 giorni
B 117	lavoriamo a margine ridotto
B 118	per grossi quantitativi
B 119	l'offerta è valida per 5 giorni
B 120	l'offerta è valida purché accettata entro il 5 marzo
B 121	a condizione che la merce non sia stata venduta
B 122	ci riserviamo il diritto di cambiare i prezzi
B 123	Vi ringraziamo della Vs. richiesta di informazioni sui ns. prodotti
B 124	se la qualità dei prodotti sarà soddisfacente
B 125	Vi inoltreremo un ordine di prova
B 126	se la merce sarà soddisfacente
B 127	Vi inoltreremo ordini più consistenti
B 128	per i primi ordini
B 129	per gli ordini successivi
B 130	finché dureranno le scorte
B 131	il Vs. ordine sarà evaso secondo le Vs. esigenze
B 132	le ns. condizioni di vendita sono le seguenti:
B 133	la pronta ed accurata evasione del Vs. ordine
B 134	ci pregiamo sottoporVi i seguenti prodotti da Voi richiesti
B 135	se i prezzi Vi sono accettabili
B 136	alle seguenti condizioni

C — Ordini

C   1   abbiamo esaminato la Vs. offerta
C   2   abbiamo esaminato attentamente i Vs. campioni
C   3   gli articoli del Vs. catalogo soddisfano le ns. esigenze
C   4   se saremo soddisfatti della Vs. prima consegna
C   5   vorremmo ordinare, in base ai campioni inviatici
C   6   Vi trasmettiamo il seguente ordine
C   7   l'ordine dovrà essere evaso immediatamente
C   8   siamo disposti a trasmetterVi un ordine programmato
C   9   l'ordine si basa sui Vs. prezzi di listino
C 10   vorremmo ordinare 5 pezzi di ognuno dei seguenti articoli
C 11   alleghiamo il ns. ordine n. 8765 di . . .
C 12   Vi preghiamo inviarci immediatamente i seguenti articoli
C 13   Vi facciamo presente che la merce deve esserci fornita
        dalle Vs. scorte
C 14   abbiamo bisogno di ricevere la merce entro 10 giorni
C 15   se non Vi è possibile effettuare la consegna entro questa
        data
C 16   ci riferiamo al ns. ordine del 5 maggio
C 17   ci riferiamo al ns. ordine n. 9675
C 18   i Vs. prezzi ci sembrano piuttosto elevati
C 19   se Vi fosse possibile ridurre del . . . % la Vs. offerta
C 20   saremmo disposti a trasmetterVi il seguente ordine
C 21   i Vs. prezzi sono più alti di quelli del ns. fornitore
        precedente
C 22   possiamo ottenere questa merce da un altro fornitore ad
        un prezzo più favorevole
C 23   siamo impegnati con un altro fornitore
C 24   abbiamo già coperto il ns. fabbisogno
C 25   abbiamo ricevuto la Vs. offerta troppo tardi
C 26   la qualità del Vs. campione non è soddisfacente
C 27   se potete fornire la merce migliorandone la qualità
C 28   se potete fornire la merce in quantitativi minori
C 29   Vi preghiamo comunicarci il quantitativo massimo che
        potete fornire immediatamente
C 30   dobbiamo modificare leggermente il Vs. ordine
C 31   speriamo che questa modifica Vi sia accettabile
C 32   l'articolo n. 487 non è attualmente disponibile
C 33   a causa di contrattempi con il ns. fornitore

C 34   per uno sciopero
C 35   per scarsa disponibilità di materie prime
C 36   per mancanza di personale
C 37   siamo indietro con la produzione
C 38   perciò non possiamo garantire la consegna per il 4 marzo
C 39   siamo disposti a cambiare gli articoli
C 40   ci riserviamo il diritto di respingere la consegna
C 41   vorremmo portare il quantitativo a . . .
C 42   non possiamo avvalerci della Vs. offerta
C 43   non possiamo accettare i Vs. condizioni di pagamento
C 44   non possiamo accettare i Vs. termini di consegna
C 45   non possiamo prendere in considerazione la Vs. offerta
C 46   non abbiamo bisogno attualmente di questi articoli
C 47   non abbiamo spazio libero in magazzino
C 48   in questo momento non possiamo accettare il Vs. ordine
C 49   il ns. programma di commesse è al completo
C 50   non possiamo iniziare la produzione fino ad agosto
C 51   vogliamo disdire il ns. ordine
C 52   abbiamo disdetto telegraficamente il ns. ordine
C 53   Vi preghiamo eliminare i seguenti articoli dal ns. ordine
C 54   ci riserviamo il diritto di disdire l'ordine
C 55   abbiamo ricevuto oggi il Vs. ordine
C 56   confermiamo il Vs. ordine del 12 maggio
C 57   provvederemo ad evadere il Vs. ordine il più presto
         possibile
C 58   il Vs. ordine è pronto per la consegna
C 59   il Vs. ordine è pronto e a Vs. disposizione
C 60   restiamo in attesa di ulteriori istruzioni
C 61   Vi preghiamo provvedere al ritiro della merce
C 62   abbiamo iniziato la produzione della merce
C 63   Vi preghiamo confermare il suddetto ordine il più presto
         possibile
C 64   avremo bisogno di una decina di giorni per completare il
         Vs. ordine

D — Consegna, trasporto, dogana

D	1	confermiamo la data di consegna richiesta nella Vs. lettera
D	2	attendiamo le Vs. istruzioni riguardanti la consegna
D	3	dobbiamo insistere sulla consegna immediata
D	4	il ritardo nella consegna è dovuto a
D	5	possiamo consegnare la merce immediatamente
D	6	richiediamo la consegna il più presto possibile
D	7	il ritardo nella consegna ci ha causato contrattempi notevoli
D	8	Vi preghiamo comunicarci la data di consegna
D	9	la prima data di consegna possibile sarà fra un mese
D	10	faremo del ns. meglio per rispettare la data di consegna
D	11	siamo in grado di consegnare la merce prima della data confermata
D	12	il ns. spedizioniere è
D	13	la merce sarà pronta per la spedizione ai primi di maggio
D	14	la merce è pronta e a Vs. disposizione
D	15	non appena riceveremo il Vs. ordine spediremo la merce
D	16	possiamo spedire la merce in container
D	17	la consegna sarà a 120 giorni
D	18	Vi preghiamo comunicarci se Vi sarà possibile consegnare la merce per questa data
D	19	il tempo di consegna è di 120 giorni
D	20	la merce dovrà essere consegnata non oltre la fine del mese prossimo
D	21	le date di consegna richieste nella ns. lettera dovranno essere rispettate
D	22	la consegna dovrà essere puntuale
D	23	non potremo accettare la merce se la data di consegna sarà scaduta
D	24	non sarà possibile consegnare la merce entro la prevista scadenza di 60 giorni
D	25	potremo effettuare la consegna entro il 5 agosto
D	26	non abbiamo ancora ricevuto la merce
D	27	Vi preghiamo comunicarci la causa di questo ritardo
D	28	franco di porto
D	29	la partita consiste di
D	30	la partita è stata caricata sulla nave Berlin
D	31	l'arrivo della merce a Dover è previsto per il 21 luglio

D 32 speriamo che la merce Vi giunga in buone condizioni

D 33 non abbiamo ancora ricevuto la merce speditaci il 15 marzo

D 34 la partita che avete promesso di consegnarci il 13 febbraio

D 35 Vi spediremo tutta la merce in un'unica partita

D 36 la partita consiste di due casse di 50 Kg. cadauna

D 37 la spedizione della merce

D 38 la merce Vi è stata spedita oggi

D 39 la merce è pronta per la spedizione

D 40 abbiamo trasmesso alla ns. banca i documenti di spedizione

D 41 la merce sarà spedita il 9 giugno

D 42 le casse sono state ritirate dal corriere

D 43 non appena riceveremo le Vs. istruzioni, Vi invieremo il ns. avviso di spedizione

D 44 abbiamo consegnato al ns. corriere la merce da Voi ordinata

D 45 il Vs. ordine non precisa con quale mezzo la merce deve essere spedita

D 46 come spedizione aerea

D 47 trasporto merci per via aerea

D 48 per ferrovia

D 49 per via aerea

D 50 per via mare

D 51 per via camion

D 52 merce in transito

D 53 franco di nolo

D 54 escluso il nolo

D 55 incluso il nolo

D 56 spese di nolo

D 57 porto di imbarco

D 58 porto di destino

D 59 per ridurre al minimo i danni di trasporto

D 60 polizza di carico

D 61 bolla di nolo

D 62 fattura consolare

D 63 documenti di spedizione

D 64 bolla di spedizione aerea

D 65 certificato di valore

D 66 il certificato di origine non era in regola

D 67 non possiamo imballare la merce nella maniera da Voi richiesta

D 68 è indispensabile un imballaggio accurato

D 69 l'imballaggio dovrà essere robusto
D 70 l'imballaggio non è conforme alle ns. norme
D 71 Vi preghiamo comunicarci se disponete di un imballaggio diverso
D 72 il Vs. imballaggio è scadente
D 73 Vi preghiamo imballare accuratamente
D 74 non possiamo accettare le Vs. lamentele sulla difettosità dell'imballaggio
D 75 le casse d'imballo non dovranno essere rese
D 76 le casse saranno numerate consecutivamente
D 77 non possiamo accettare richieste di imballaggio speciale
D 78 Vi precisiamo che la merce dovrà essere imballata in
D 79 carta da imballo
D 80 cartone ondulato
D 81 trucioli di legno
D 82 rivestito di
D 83 containers
D 84 fusti
D 85 balle
D 86 gabbie
D 87 casse
D 88 barattoli
D 89 vasi
D 90 palette
D 91 barili
D 92 gabbie di legno
D 93 sacchi
D 94 i cartoni non sono da rendere
D 95 le gabbie dovranno essere marcate come segue
D 96 antiurto
D 97 impermeabile
D 98 a prova di danni
D 99 tenere al secco
D 100 tenere al fresco
D 101 alto
D 102 alto
D 103 basso
D 104 maneggiare con cura
D 105 lato da aprire
D 106 sollevare
D 107 fragile
D 108 attenzione!
D 109 infiammabile

D 110 peso netto
D 111 peso lordo
D 112 peso morto
D 113 carico
D 114 scarico
D 115 pesi e misure
D 116 il peso lordo è indicato su ogni gabbia
D 117 diritti doganali a carico dell'acquirente
D 118 franco sdoganato Londra
D 119 soggetto a diritti doganali
D 120 abbiamo dovuto pagare diritti doganali di . . . su questi articoli
D 121 su questa merce dovrete pagare diritti doganali
D 122 diritti doganali a carico del destinatario
D 123 il valore doganale della merce
D 124 dichiarazione doganale
D 125 spese di sdoganamento
D 126 sdoganamento
D 127 abbiamo ricevuto la fattura doganale
D 128 la dogana di Aquisgrana ha imposto una soprattassa sulla partita
D 129 abbiamo bisogno della ricevuta doganale
D 130 le autorità doganali di Dover hanno bloccato la spedizione
D 131 sono entrati in vigore nuovi regolamenti doganali
D 132 provvederemo alle formalità doganali
D 133 soprattassa doganale
D 134 magazzino doganale
D 135 deposito franco
D 136 in deposito franco
D 137 immagazzinaggio
D 138 deterioramento
D 139 furto
D 140 tasse aeroportuali
D 141 tasse portuali
D 142 spese di facchinaggio
D 143 tariffe doganali
D 144 le spese di sdoganamento saranno a ns. carico

E — Fatture, pagamenti e solleciti

E 1   accusiamo ricevuta della spedizione

E 2   la spedizione è arrivata ieri alla ns. fabbrica

E 3   la merce è arrivata in buone condizioni

E 4   la merce ci è pervenuta senza danni

E 5   la merce da noi ordinata il 4 aprile è arrivata puntualmente

E 6   Vi rimettiamo in allegato la ns. fattura n°

E 7   Vi rimettiamo in allegato la ns. fattura riguardante la merce consegnataVi il 3 maggio

E 8   la fattura allegata riguarda la merce consegnataVi contro il Vs. ordine n°

E 9   Vi preghiamo provvedere puntualmente al saldo della ns. fattura

E 10 Vi preghiamo provvedere al saldo della ns. fattura entro il 12 maggio

E 11 Vi preghiamo effettuare il pagamento della fattura sul conto n°

E 12 Vi preghiamo provvedere al pagamento della fattura a giro di posta

E 13 rimettiamo in allegato il ns. estratto conto

E 14 l'importo complessivo da pagare è di . . .

E 15 la cifra è da intendersi netta di sconto

E 16 lo sconto è già stato defalcato

E 17 sconto già defalcato del . . . %

E 18 abbiamo defalcato dalla fattura lo sconto abituale del . . . %

E 19 Vi segnaliamo un errore nella Vs. fattura

E 20 avete commesso un errore nel conteggio totale della Vs. fattura n.

E 21 Vi preghiamo inviarci una fattura rettificata

E 22 Vi preghiamo rettificare la fattura

E 23 Vi preghiamo rettificare l'estratto conto

E 24 notiamo che sulla Vs. fattura ci praticate uno sconto commercianti solamente del . . . %

E 25 abbiamo defalcato dalla fattura la somma di . . .

E 26 lo sbaglio è dovuto a un errore di battitura

E 27 uno sbaglio del ns. ufficio contabilità

E 28 una svista

E 29 Vi confermiamo di aver rettificato il saldo, che è di . . .

E	30	Vi inviamo in allegato la ns. nota di accredito
E	31	la nota di addebito
E	32	Vi preghiamo provvedere al saldo immediato
E	33	contiamo di ricevere il Vs. pagamento entro la settimana prossima
E	34	Vi preghiamo rimetterci l'importo dovuto nei prossimi giorni
E	35	Vi facciamo presente che le ns. condizioni di pagamento sono
E	36	ci permettiamo ricordarVi le ns. condizioni di pagamento
E	37	documenti contro accettazione
E	38	pagamento alla consegna (C.O.D.)
E	39	documenti contro pagamento
E	40	pagamento anticipato
E	41	la lettera di credito documentaria
E	42	una lettera di credito documentaria a Vs. favore
E	43	la cambiale documentaria
E	44	revocabile
E	45	irrevocabile
E	46	confermato/a
E	47	non confermato/a
E	48	la tratta documentaria
E	49	la cambiale a vista
E	50	la cambiale con scadenza a vista
E	51	la cambiale a data fissa
E	52	pagamento a ricevimento merce
E	53	al cambio attuale
E	54	in contanti
E	55	banconote
E	56	monete
E	57	moneta di corso legale
E	58	il versamento su conto corrente postale
E	59	il beneficiario
E	60	il creditore
E	61	il debitore
E	62	il pagherò
E	63	il credito commerciale
E	64	pagabile presso la Banca . . .
E	65	una tratta a 60 giorni
E	66	un credito di . . . da aprirsi presso la Banca . . .
E	67	abbiamo dato disposizioni alla ns. banca di rimetterVi l'importo dovuto
E	68	abbiamo versato sul Vs. conto l'importo di . . .

E	69	abbiamo accreditato questo importo sul Vs. conto
E	70	abbiamo dato disposizioni alla ns. banca di versare l'importo sul Vs. conto
E	71	abbiamo trasferito sul Vs. conto l'importo di . . .
E	72	a saldo del Vs. conto
E	73	il ns. conto presso la Banca . . .
E	74	Vi rimettiamo in allegato il ns. assegno di . . .
E	75	un assegno sbarrato
E	76	un assegno non sbarrato
E	77	un vaglia postale
E	78	l'assegno è stato incassato
E	79	un assegno del Vs. conto
E	80	Vi rimettiamo in allegato il ns. assegno di . . . a saldo della Vs. fattura
E	81	£600, meno £45 per l'imballaggio
E	82	rimettiamo in allegato il ns. assegno per la metà dell'importo
E	83	il trasferimento bancario
E	84	l'assegno bancario
E	85	l'importo è stato accredidato sul Vs. conto
E	86	Vi preghiamo inviarci una ricevuta il più presto possibile
E	87	accusiamo ricevuta del Vs. pagamento
E	88	Vi ringraziamo della Vs. rimessa
E	89	abbiamo accettato la Vs. tratta
E	90	la Vs. rimessa di . . . è stata ricevuta dalla ns. banca
E	91	Vi ringraziamo della Vs. sollecitudine nel saldare la ns. fattura
E	92	abbiamo ricevuto il Vs. avviso di pagamento
E	93	siete in ritardo di più di 30 giorni con i pagamenti
E	94	la ns. fattura è tuttora scoperta
E	95	restiamo in attesa della Vs. rimessa
E	96	sul Vs. conto c'è un saldo a ns. favore di . . .
E	97	le fatture scoperte devono essere saldate entro la fine del mese
E	98	non abbiamo ancora ricevuto il saldo del ns. estratto conto del mese di settembre
E	99	nel caso non abbiate ricevuto il ns. estratto conto Ve ne alleghiamo una copia
E	100	Vi preghiamo comunicarci il motivo del ritardo nel pagamento
E	101	poiché questa somma ci è dovuta da parecchio tempo
E	102	non abbiamo ancora ricevuto risposta al ns. sollecito di pagamento

E 103	Vi preghiamo provvedere immediatamente a quanto sopra
E 104	nonostante i ns. vari solleciti di pagamento
E 105	al fine di recuperare la somma dovutaci
E 106	non avete risposto ai ns. solleciti
E 107	d'ora in poi le ns. fatture dovranno essere saldate immediatamente
E 108	dovete ancora rimetterci l'importo di . . .
E 109	è nostra prassi per gli ordini iniziali richiedere il pagamento a 15 giorni
E 110	Vi facciamo presente che il termine di pagamento è scaduto il 4 luglio
E 111	questo è il ns. ultimo sollecito di pagamento
E 112	dobbiamo esigere ora il pagamento immediato
E 113	se non riceveremo la Vs. rimessa entro i primi del mese prossimo
E 114	il ritardo nei Vs. pagamenti è del tutto inaccettabile
E 115	la fattura è andata smarrita
E 116	saremo costretti a trasmettere la pratica al ns. legale
E 117	il ns. legale avrà l'incarico di recuperare l'importo dovutoci
E 118	la somma dovutaci sarà recuperata dal ns. legale
E 119	prenderemo le misure necessarie per il recupero della somma dovutaci
E 120	per via legale
E 121	abbiamo rimesso la pratica nelle mani dei ns. legali
E 122	Vi concediamo altri 12 giorni per provvedere al pagamento
E 123	potete effettuare un pagamento in acconto
E 124	ci avete richiesto una dilazione
E 125	speriamo possiate capire il ns. punto di vista
E 126	siamo disposti ad accordarVi una dilazione

F — Reclami

| F | 1 | la merce consegnataci il 3 corrente non corrisponde al ns. ordine |
| F | 2 | ci dispiace dover fare un reclamo riguardante la Vs. partita n° |

F	3	ci permettiamo segnalarVi uno sbaglio nella partita che abbiamo ricevuto ieri
F	4	il colore degli articoli è sbagliato
F	5	le misure sono sbagliate
F	6	gli articoli non corrispondono ai disegni che Vi abbiamo trasmesso
F	7	la qualità della merce non soddisfa le ns. esigenze
F	8	non siamo soddisfatti della qualità della merce
F	9	per questi motivi non possiamo accettare la merce
F	10	gli articoli sono difettosi
F	11	ci avete spedito 500...anziché 250 come ordinato
F	12	c'è stato uno sbaglio nell'evasione del ns. ordine
F	13	il contenuto delle gabbie non corrisponde alla bolla di consegna
F	14	dalla partita manca l'articolo n.
F	15	la merce non è conforme ai campioni
F	16	i prodotti sembrano essere di lavorazione diversa
F	17	le gabbie sono state rotte
F	18	la merce è stata danneggiata dal fuoco
F	19	la merce non è stata maneggiata con cura ed ha subito dei danni
F	20	la merce è arrivata danneggiata
F	21	gravemente danneggiata
F	22	parecchi articoli sono graffiati
F	23	rotti
F	24	leggermente danneggiati
F	25	danneggiati dal caldo
F	26	danneggiati dall'acqua
F	27	la merce deve essere stata danneggiata in transito
F	28	la merce deve essere stata male imballata
F	29	l'imballaggio è di qualità scadente
F	30	le gabbie dovevano essere rinforzate con striscie di metallo
F	31	le gabbie sono state costruite male
F	32	gli articoli sono arrugginiti
F	33	i danni si sono verificati tra la dogana britannica e la ns. fabbrica
F	34	i danni si sono verificati prima dell'arrivo della merce a Dover
F	35	Vi preghiamo provvedere alla sostituzione il più presto possibile
F	36	questo ci ha causato notevoli difficoltà in quanto avevamo urgente bisogno della merce
F	37	abbiamo urgente bisogno degli articoli rimanenti

F 38	ci dispiace informarVi che tutti gli articoli dovranno essere sostituiti
F 39	siamo disposti a tenere la merce
F 40	al prezzo ridotto di . . . cadauno
F 41	Vi rendiamo l'intera partita
F 42	Vi rendiamo una parte della partita
F 43	Vi rendiamo tutti gli articoli danneggiati in transito
F 44	siamo costretti a disdire l'ordine
F 45	possiamo accettare la merce danneggiata se siete disposti a farci uno sconto del . . . %
F 46	potremo vendere la merce danneggiata solo a un prezzo molto ridotto
F 47	tutti gli articoli dovranno essere sostituiti
F 48	speriamo che in futuro eviterete simili errori
F 49	questo ci ha causato notevoli inconvenienti con numerosi clienti
F 50	ci permettiamo suggerirVi di contattare il Vs. spedizioniere
F 51	la compagnia di navigazione
F 52	la società ferroviaria
F 53	la compagnia aerea
F 54	a ns. avviso ulteriori indagini sono di Vs. competenza
F 55	siamo costretti a chiederVi il risarcimento dei danni
F 56	siamo costretti ad esigere il risarcimento dei danni
F 57	Vi preghiamo accreditarci il valore della merce danneggiata
F 58	per future ordinazioni saremo costretti a rivedere la ns. posizione
F 59	abbiamo esaminato il Vs. reclamo
F 60	poiché i danni si sono verificati in transito
F 61	Vi consigliamo di rivolgerVi a . . .
F 62	è la prima volta che ci serviamo di questo spedizioniere
F 63	i difetti da Voi elencati sono coperti dalla ns. assicurazione
F 64	questi danni sono coperti dalla ns. garanzia
F 65	secondo i termini della ns. garanzia
F 66	potete chiedere il rimborso dell'importo pagato
F 67	Vi preghiamo accettare le ns. scuse per l'errore commesso
F 68	siamo disposti a sostituire gli articoli con altri di qualità simile
F 69	alleghiamo un assegno di . . . a titolo di rimborso
F 70	sostituiremo la merce a ns. spese
F 71	ci dispiace sapere che la ns. partita non è all'altezza delle Vs. aspettative

F	72	siamo disposti ad offrirVi uno sconto del . . . %
F	73	abbiamo defalcato dal Vs. conto il . . . %
F	74	abbiamo controllato accuratamente la merce
F	75	non riscontriamo difetti nella merce
F	76	non possiamo accettare la responsabilità del danno
F	77	come potete verificare dai termini del contratto
F	78	ci dispiace non poter accettare la restituzione della merce
F	79	Vi consigliamo di denunciare il fatto alla compagnia di assicurazione
F	80	Vi segnaliamo che il periodo di garanzia è scaduto
F	81	Vi consigliamo chiedere alla compagnia di navigazione di verificare i danni
F	82	abbiamo bisogno della relazione dello spedizioniere con l'elenco dei danni
F	83	date le circostanze non possiamo accettare il Vs. reclamo

G — Rappresentanze

G	1	stiamo cercando un rappresentante cui affidare la vendita all'estero dei ns. prodotti
G	2	abbiamo bisogno di un rappresentante cui affidare la vendita dei ns. prodotti
G	3	stiamo cercando un rappresentante per la ns. filiale di . . .
G	4	il rappresentante dovrà lavorare esclusivamente per noi
G	5	dovrà impegnarsi a non collaborare con i ns. concorrenti
G	6	e dovrà limitare le sue attività a questa zona
G	7	suo compito principale sarebbe di sottoporre i ns. cataloghi e campioni alla clientela
G	8	per questa posizione si richiede la conoscenza del settore
G	9	abbiamo bisogno di un rappresentante specializzato
G	10	non è indispensabile la conoscenza del settore
G	11	provvediamo noi stessi all'addestramento dei nostri rappresentanti
G	12	siamo una piccola azienda produttrice di . . .
G	13	questi articoli hanno ottime possibilità di vendita
G	14	sappiamo che Lei ha una buona esperienza nella vendita di questo tipo di prodotto
G	15	vorremmo sapere se è in grado di introdurre questi articoli sul mercato italiano

G 16	desideriamo lanciare questo prodotto sul mercato tedesco
G 17	secondo noi esiste all'estero una richiesta notevole di tali prodotti
G 18	Lei rappresenta già diverse aziende britanniche
G 19	sarebbe compito Suo sviluppare per noi questo mercato
G 20	saremmo disposti a spendere in media . . . all'anno per la pubblicità
G 21	dovrà esporre nel Suo salone la gamma completa dei ns. prodotti
G 22	il rappresentante riceverà gratuitamente materiale pubblicitario
G 23	siamo agenti esclusivi
G 24	rappresentanza esclusiva
G 25	siamo rappresentanti a provvigione
G 26	abbiamo bisogno di un ufficio vendite in Spagna
G 27	siamo concessionari
G 28	agenti commissionari
G 29	agenti a tempo pieno
G 30	agenti a tempo parziale
G 31	intermediario
G 32	consegnatario
G 33	giacenza merce in conto deposito
G 34	merce in conto deposito
G 35	agente per l'esportazione
G 36	agente per gli acquisti
G 37	il committente
G 38	siamo certi che la Vs. merce troverà sbocco immediato in questo paese
G 39	abbiamo saputo che cercate un rappresentante per la Francia
G 40	abbiamo una buona esperienza di questo tipo di lavoro
G 41	Vi sottoponiamo il ns. nominativo per questa rappresentanza
G 42	abbiamo rappresentato con successo numerose aziende simili
G 43	siamo ben introdotti nei grandi magazzini londinesi
G 44	intendiamo lavorare intensivamente sul mercato tedesco
G 45	siamo disposti ad assumere la responsabilità del servizio dopo vendita
G 46	non abbiamo impegni con altre aziende in questo paese
G 47	ci impegniamo a non rappresentare alcuno dei Vs. concorrenti

G 48   saremmo disposti anche ad offrire la ns. consulenza sul marketing e sulla pubblicità dei prodotti

G 49   abbiamo una vasta rete di contatti in Francia

G 50   siamo disposti a concederVi la rappresentanza

G 51   inizialmente il contratto sarà limitato ad un periodo di . . . anni

G 52   il contratto potrà essere rinnovato per un ulteriore periodo di 12 mesi

G 53   il contratto potrà essere disdetto da entrambe le parti

G 54   con un preavviso di . . . mesi

G 55   è previsto un periodo di prova di . . . mesi

G 56   l'accordo di rappresentanza sarà soggetto ad un periodo di prova

G 57   Le concederemo i diritti esclusivi di vendita

G 58   potremo mettere una macchina a Sua disposizione

G 59   La preghiamo di farci sapere entro . . . settimane se queste condizioni Le sono accettabili

G 60   abbiamo già concluso un accordo di rappresentanza con un'altra società

G 61   possiamo concederLe la rappresentanza dei ns. prodotti per la Francia

G 62   Le invieremo ampie informazioni su tutti i ns. prodotti

G 63   i ns. opuscoli dovranno essere tradotti in francese e in inglese

G 64   siamo certi potrà provvedere alla traduzione di questi documenti

G 65   se preferisce possiamo provvedere noi stessi a farli tradurre

G 66   il materiale pubblicitario sarà fornito da noi

G 67   a ns. spese

G 68   le spese saranno a carico della ns. società

G 69   le spese saranno a carico del rappresentante

G 70   zona di rappresentanza

G 71   forniremo opuscoli in lingua francese

G 72   intraprenderemo una intensa campagna pubblicitaria

G 73   siamo disposti ad assumerci parte delle spese

G 74   tutte le vendite concluse dal rappresentante

G 75   la merce viene venduta a provvigione

G 76   i ns. rappresentanti lavorano a provvigione

G 77   offriamo uno stipendio base di . . . più una provvigione del . . . %

G 78   non è nostra prassi offrire uno stipendio base

G 79 la ns. provvigione normale per i rappresentanti esteri è del
. . . %

G 80 questa provvigione sarà pagata su tutti gli ordini trasmessi
tramite Lei o i Suoi intermediari

G 81 la provvigione sarà pagata su tutti gli ordini provenienti
dalla Sua zona

G 82 la provvigione sarà pagata a saldo avvenuto delle fatture

G 83 la provvigione include Sue eventuali spese

G 84 a condizione che ci trasmetta un dettagliato conto spese

G 85 provvederemo al rimborso spese dietro presentazione di
ricevute

G 86 verranno rimborsate le spese da Lei sostenute per
l'accoglienza dei clienti

G 87 la provvigione sarà il . . . % del fatturato

G 88 offriamo una provvigione del . . . % su tutte le vendite da
Lei effettuate

G 89 provvigione di vendita

G 90 la provvigione sarà versata ogni tre mesi

G 91 la provvigione sarà pagata su tutti gli ordini

G 92 preferiamo liquidare la provvigione alla fine di ogni
trimestre

G 93 preferiamo un estratto conto mensile

H — Referenze

H 1 il Sig. X ha sottoposto la sua candidatura per la posizione
di . . . presso la ns. azienda

H 2 ci ha fornito il Vs. nominativo a titolo di referenza

H 3 Vi saremmo grati se voleste darci informazioni riguardanti
il Sig. X

H 4 informazioni sul suo carattere e sulle sue capacità

H 5 se è una persona su cui fare affidamento

H 6 Vi preghiamo informarci se siete stati soddisfatti delle sue
prestazioni

H 7 per questa posizione si richiede una persona della massima
serietà

H 8 la posizione è molto impegnativa

H	9	abbiamo bisogno di una persona capace di adattarsi alle varie circostanze di lavoro
H	10	ogni informazione verrà trattata con la massima riservatezza
H	11	lavora presso la ns. azienda da 5 anni
H	12	lavora presso la ns. azienda da poco tempo
H	13	lavora presso la ns. azienda da quando ha finito gli studi
H	14	ha seguito con noi un corso di addestramento per la posizione di . . .
H	15	ha lavorato presso di noi dal giugno del 19 . . . all'agosto del 19 . . .
H	16	ha lasciato la ns. azienda dopo 3 anni per andare a lavorare all'estero
H	17	svolgeva le mansioni di . . .
H	18	è stato licenziato 4 anni fa
H	19	è stato licenziato per riduzione di personale nell'aprile del 19 . . .
H	20	è una persona efficiente
H	21	è una persona su cui fare affidamento
H	22	onesto e lavoratore
H	23	puntuale
H	24	possiede un carattere piacevole
H	25	è specializzato in . . .
H	26	è ambizioso
H	27	è senza dubbio per questo motivo che si è candidato per questa posizione
H	28	nella ns. azienda le possibilità di carriera sono attualmente limitate
H	29	ha un buono spirito di iniziativa nel lavoro
H	30	ha sempre goduto di buona salute
H	31	non è stato un buon lavoratore
H	32	non era una persona su cui fare affidamento
H	33	era spesso assente dal lavoro
H	34	era spesso in ritardo
H	35	non era molto puntuale
H	36	il suo lavoro era spesso poco accurato
H	37	per motivi di salute
H	38	era di salute delicata
H	39	e il suo lavoro ne ha risentito
H	40	è per questo motivo che ho delle riserve nel raccomandarVelo
H	41	ha dimostrato scarso spirito d'iniziativa ed è lento nello svolgimento del suo lavoro

H	42	è una persona su cui non fare affidamento
H	43	il suo lavoro era in generale soddisfacente
H	44	il suo lavoro era sempre di altissima qualità
H	45	il suo lavoro era sempre di qualità eccezionale
H	46	siamo sempre stati soddisfatti del modo in cui svolgeva le sue mansioni
H	47	lo raccomandiamo senza alcuna riserva
H	48	il suo lavoro era spesso mediocre
H	49	non siamo in grado di fornirVi informazioni su questo candidato
H	50	lo conosciamo da poco tempo
H	51	lo conosciamo da 10 anni
H	52	e siamo lieti di fornire le sue referenze
H	53	quindi Le consigliamo di rivolgersi a . . .
H	54	dovrebbero essere in grado di fornirLe più ampie informazioni
H	55	la ditta . . . ci ha appena trasmesso un ordine importante
H	56	ci hanno chiesto un credito di . . .
H	57	ci hanno fornito il Vs. nominativo come referenza
H	58	poiché è la prima volta che trattiamo con questa azienda
H	59	Le saremmo grati per ogni informazione sulla loro situazione finanziaria
H	60	e sulle loro prospettive a lungo termine
H	61	a medio termine
H	62	a breve scadenza
H	63	sulla loro competitività nel mercato interno
H	64	sul mercato estero
H	65	Vi preghiamo informarci se godono di buona fama sia sul mercato interno sia all'estero
H	66	informazioni sul credito di cui godono e sulla loro solvibilità
H	67	Le saremmo grati per ogni informazione sull'azienda
H	68	ci è stato riferito che Lei conosce l'azienda da tempo
H	69	a Suo parere ci conviene concedere un credito di . . . ?
H	70	senza garanzie
H	71	Le assicuriamo la più completa discrezione
H	72	tratteremo le Sue informazioni con la massima discrezione
H	73	saremo lieti di controcambiare il favore
H	74	conosciamo questa azienda da 6 anni
H	75	siamo in relazioni d'affari con l'azienda da 5 anni
H	76	sono ns. clienti fissi
H	77	sono in relazioni d'affari con noi da molti anni
H	78	l'azienda gode di un'ottima fama

H	79	si trova in una buona situazione finanziaria
H	80	l'azienda dispone di buone risorse finanziarie
H	81	su questa azienda si può fare ampio affidamento
H	82	l'azienda ha sempre mantenuto puntualmente i propri impegni
H	83	siamo certi che Lei può concedere questo credito senza esitazioni
H	84	abbiamo dovuto inviare ripetuti solleciti a questa azienda nei mesi scorsi
H	85	ci devono ancora . . .
H	86	non hanno ancora saldato le ns. fatture dell'anno scorso
H	87	si trovano in difficoltà finanziarie
H	88	non dispongono di capitali sufficienti
H	89	non sarebbe consigliabile concedere un credito a questa azienda
H	90	Le consigliamo di agire con cautela
H	91	non possiamo accettare responsabilità alcuna per queste informazioni
H	92	poiché non conosciamo questa azienda
H	93	disponiamo di scarse informazioni su questa azienda
H	94	ci sembra che l'azienda sia stata fondata di recente
H	95	purtroppo non siamo in grado di darLe consigli in merito
H	96	purtroppo non siamo in grado di fornirLe le informazioni richieste
H	97	non conosciamo sufficientemente l'azienda
H	98	Le consigliamo quindi di rivolgersi a . . .

I — Domande d'impiego e inserzioni

I	1	siamo un'azienda ben avviata con sede nell'Inghilterra meridionale
I	2	cerchiamo . . .
I	3	abbiamo bisogno di . . .
I	4	abbiamo bisogno di assumere . . .
I	5	a partire dall'8 ottobre
I	6	per sostituire uno dei ns. rappresentanti
I	7	per sostituire il ns. direttore all'esportazione

I	8	si richiede esperienza nel campo dell'esportazione
I	9	si richiede un venditore con esperienza del settore
I	10	cerchiamo una persona di età compresa tra 25 – 35 anni
I	11	e si richiede una esperienza minima di 5 anni nel campo di . . .
I	12	è preferibile la conoscenza della lingua inglese
I	13	è indispensabile la conoscenza di lingue estere
I	14	la persona prescelta dovrà saper svolgere un lavoro d'équipe
I	15	deve essere in grado di adattarsi alle diverse esigenze della clientela
I	16	e di delegare responsabilità
I	17	abbiamo bisogno di una persona che possa adattarsi alle varie circostanze di lavoro
I	18	alla direzione del ns. ufficio estero
I	19	la posizione comporta una autovettura ad uso personale
I	20	siamo disposti ad offrire uno stipendio minimo di . . .
I	21	lo stipendio sarà commisurato all'età ed all'esperienza
I	22	stipendio trattabile
I	23	stipendio minimo di . . . annue
I	24	mensili
I	25	lo stipendio è di . . . nette
I	26	lo stipendio lordo è di . . .
I	27	esiste anche una gratifica
I	28	ritenute fiscali di circa il . . . %
I	29	per i contributi
I	30	lo stipendio è esente da tasse
I	31	la ditta provvederà gratuitamente all'alloggio
I	32	6 settimane di ferie all'anno
I	33	le ferie pagate
I	34	settimana lavorativa di 35 ore
I	35	settimana lavorativa di 6 giorni
I	36	è in vigore un orario di lavoro flessibile
I	37	i candidati dovranno essere disposti a svolgere lavoro straordinario
I	38	c'è un fondo pensioni aziendale
I	39	La preghiamo fornirci i nominativi di due persone come referenze
I	40	uno dei nominativi dovrebbe essere quello del Suo attuale datore di lavoro
I	41	abbiamo bisogno anche di una referenza della Sua Banca
I	42	dalla Vs. inserzione sul . . . ho saputo
I	43	ho saputo tramite persone con cui sono in relazioni d'affari

I	44	ho letto la Vs. inserzione sul . . . della settimana scorsa
I	45	vorrei sottoporre la mia candidatura per questa posizione
I	46	Vi prego inviarmi ulteriori ragguagli su questa posizione
I	47	insieme a un modulo da compilare
I	48	come potrete constatare dall'allegato curriculum
I	49	possiedo una notevole esperienza di questo tipo di lavoro
I	50	ho anche partecipato a vari convegni in materia
I	51	sono certo di possedere i requisiti necessari per questa posizione
I	52	sono attualmente impiegato presso un'azienda di esportazioni
I	53	sto cercando un posto simile
I	54	desidero ora cambiare impiego
I	55	vorrei lavorare per una organizzazione più vasta
I	56	con collegamenti internazionali
I	57	al fine di migliorare le mie possibilità di carriera
I	58	per motivi personali
I	59	cerco un posto che possa offrirmi più vaste responsabilità
I	60	vorrei lavorare all'estero
I	61	vorrei migliorare le mie possibilità di carriera
I	62	vorrei trovare un posto che mi offra migliori prospettive
I	63	vorrei poter sfruttare la mia conoscenza delle lingue
I	64	parlo correntemente il francese e il tedesco
I	65	possiedo una conoscenza scolastica dell'inglese
I	66	sono qualificato in . . .
I	67	sono diplomato in . . .
I	68	sono laureato in . . .
I	69	in dattilografia ho raggiunto . . . battute al minuto
I	70	in stenografia ho raggiunto . . . parole al minuto
I	71	possiedo una certa esperienza nel campo dei microelaboratori
I	72	sono in grado di usare gli elaboratori di testi
I	73	sono nato a . . .
I	74	ho studiato a . . .
I	75	dove ho conseguito . . .
I	76	nelle seguenti materie
I	77	ho frequentato l'Università di . . .
I	78	dove ho studiato . . . come materia principale
I	79	e . . . come materia secondaria
I	80	e mi sono laureato in . . .
I	81	ho superato l'esame di stato
I	82	con lode
I	83	non ho superato i seguenti esami

I 84   in seguito ho lavorato presso un'azienda di esportazioni
I 85   ho passato 3 anni all'estero
I 86   nel 19 . . . sono stato nominato capo ufficio
I 87   nel 19 . . . sono stato licenziato per riduzione di personale
I 88   e da allora sono disoccupato
I 89   ho seguito dei corsi serali di . . .
I 90   ho seguito un corso di segretariato bilingue
I 91   qualora voleste convocarmi per un colloquio
I 92   sono libero per un eventuale colloquio in qualsiasi momento
I 93   sono libero per un eventuale colloquio solo il venerdì
I 94   Vi prego di rimandare la data del mio colloquio
I 95   sarò disponibile a partire dal 16 giugno
I 96   nella speranza vogliate prendere in considerazione la mia candidatura
I 97   allego una referenza del mio precedente datore di lavoro
I 98   allego copie delle referenze dei miei due ultimi datori di lavoro
I 99   e copie dei miei diplomi
I 100   elenco i nominativi di due persone alle quali potrete chiedere mie referenze
I 101   le seguenti persone sono disposte a fornire referenze sul mio conto
I 102   Vi pregherei di non rivolgerVi al mio attuale datore di lavoro
I 103   prima del colloquio
I 104   senza il mio consenso
I 105   allego una busta affrancata per la risposta
I 106   allego un buono internazionale per la risposta
I 107   sarò lieto di fornirVi tutte le informazioni a Voi necessarie
I 108   ho fatto domanda per la posizione di . . .
I 109   e Le sarei grato qualora fosse disposto a fornire le mie referenze

J — Cambiamento di indirizzo, ecc.

J	1	la ns. sede centrale non è più a Londra
J	2	la ns. sede centrale è stata trasferita a Francoforte
J	3	abbiamo aperto una nuova filiale a Madrid
J	4	a causa del costante aumento dei ns. affari
J	5	ci siamo trasferiti in una nuova sede più grande a Bordeaux
J	6	potremo quindi offrire un servizio migliore alla ns. clientela
J	7	Vi assicuriamo che manterremo l'alto livello del ns. servizio
J	8	abbiamo cambiato indirizzo
J	9	il nuovo indirizzo è il seguente
J	10	Vi preghiamo inoltrare la corrispondenza a questo indirizzo
J	11	Vi preghiamo comunicare al Vs. uffico spedizioni il nuovo indirizzo
J	12	abbiamo cambiato numero telefonico
J	13	e il ns. nuovo numero telefonico è. . .
J	14	abbiamo cambiato ragione sociale
J	15	la nuova ragione sociale è . . .
J	16	la ns. azienda si è fusa con la . . .
J	17	a partire dal 14 maggio opereremo sotto il nuovo nome di . . .
J	18	non ci occupiamo più di questo settore
J	19	non fabbrichiamo più questi prodotti
J	20	abbiamo cessato la produzione di questi articoli 3 anni fa
J	21	ci specializziamo ora soltanto nella produzione di . . .
J	22	la produzione di questi articoli è stata rilevata dalla . . .
J	23	il ns. stabilimento di Torino verrà demolito a marzo
J	24	e trasferiremo la produzione a Zurigo
J	25	abbiamo dovuto chiudere il ns. stabilimento di Birmingham
J	26	abbiamo chiuso il ns. ufficio estero
J	27	Vi consigliamo di metterVi in contatto con la ns. casa madre
J	28	la ns. consociata di Parigi
J	29	la ns. azienda è stata rilevata dalla . . .

J	30	la . . . ha acquistato il . . . % del pacchetto azionario della ns. azienda
J	31	la società si è sciolta
J	32	abbiamo cessato le attività 6 mesi fa
J	33	l'azienda è fallita
J	34	l'azienda è in mano al curatore
J	35	il Sig . . . è stato promosso
J	36	è ora vicedirettore
J	37	dirige il ns. nuovo ufficio esportazione di Vienna
J	38	è stato nominato al consiglio di amministrazione
J	39	è stato trasferito ad un'altra filiale
J	40	il Sig . . . non lavora più presso di noi
J	41	è impiegato presso un'altra azienda
J	42	è andato in pensione in agosto
J	43	il ns. direttore generale Sig . . . è deceduto 5 mesi fa
J	44	al suo posto è stato nominato il Sig . . .
J	45	le sue mansioni sono state assunte dal Sig. X

K — Viaggi e prenotazioni albergo

K	1	vorrei prenotare un posto sul treno Parigi-Heidelberg
K	2	in partenza da Parigi alle 13.45, in arrivo a Heidelberg alle 19.55
K	3	il rapido
K	4	il TEE
K	5	è un treno a prenotazione obbligatoria?
K	6	la prenotazione dei posti è obbligatoria su tutti i rapidi
K	7	questo treno non fa servizio nei giorni festivi
K	8	il treno fa servizio solo nei giorni feriali
K	9	il treno locale
K	10	il treno speciale
K	11	il treno straordinario
K	12	il treno parte dal binario n. 6
K	13	un posto vicino al finestrino
K	14	in uno scompartimento non fumatori
K	15	la cuccetta
K	16	il vagone letto

K	17	il vagone ristorante
K	18	il vagone con servizio di buffet
K	19	controllo passaporti in treno
K	20	desidera viaggiare in prima?
K	21	un posto in uno scompartimento di prima classe
K	22	a che ora arriva il treno a . . . ?
K	23	allego una copia del mio itinerario
K	24	un biglietto di andata
K	25	un biglietto di andata e ritorno in giornata
K	26	un biglietto di andata e ritorno
K	27	il biglietto di ingresso ai marciapiedi
K	28	bisogna pagare un supplemento per questo treno?
K	29	c'è deposito bagagli in stazione?
K	30	dove si trova il deposito bagagli automatico?
K	31	dove si trova l'ufficio oggetti smarriti?
K	32	questo biglietto è valido per tutti i percorsi?
K	33	il biglietto non è trasferibile
K	34	posso fare l'abbonamento mensile per l'autobus?
K	35	tessera per più corse
K	36	a che ora parte la nave da Calais?
K	37	il traghetto
K	38	Vi prego inviarmi informazioni sui traghetti
K	39	l'hovercraft
K	40	una cabina per due persone
K	41	una cabina di prima classe
K	42	vorrei fare una prenotazione per un'automobile più due passeggeri
K	43	praticate sconti per una comitiva di 20 persone?
K	44	sul traghetto Dover-Calais
K	45	a che ora parte il volo n. . . . per . . . ?
K	46	il volo charter
K	47	il volo di linea
K	48	vorrei prenotare 3 posti sul primo volo in partenza per . . .
K	49	da quale terminal parte l'aereo?
K	50	vengono serviti i pasti durante il volo?
K	51	classe economica
K	52	classe affari
K	53	siete pregati di confermare la prenotazione 24 ore prima della partenza
K	54	le tasse aeroportuali sono incluse nel prezzo?
K	55	il bagaglio a mano
K	56	l'assistente di volo
K	57	l'assistente di volo

K	58	si servono bevande durante il volo
K	59	i passeggeri sono pregati di registrare i bagagli almeno 45 minuti prima della partenza
K	60	cerco una camera di prezzo medio
K	61	vorrei prenotare una camera singola con bagno
K	62	una camera doppia
K	63	una camera a due letti
K	64	con doccia
K	65	con gabinetto e doccia
K	66	Vi prego di farmi sapere il prezzo di una camera singola
K	67	nell'alta stagione
K	68	nella bassa stagione
K	69	nella bassa stagione
K	70	dal 19 al 30 aprile
K	71	accettate prenotazioni per comitive?
K	72	vorrei organizzare la riunione dei ns. rappresentanti in ottobre
K	73	e cerco un albergo adatto vicino all'aeroporto
K	74	vorremmo che un autobus ci venisse a prendere all'aeroporto
K	75	vorremmo che un autobus ci portasse in albergo
K	76	il prezzo di una camera doppia per 3 notti è di . . .
K	77	questi sono prezzi tutto compreso
K	78	compresa la prima colazione
K	79	la mezza pensione
K	80	la pensione completa
K	81	servizio e I.V.A. compresi
K	82	la mancia
K	83	Vi preghiamo comunicarci i prezzi tutto compreso
K	84	riscaldamento centrale in tutte le camere
K	85	acqua corrente calda e fredda in tutte le camere
K	86	la prima colazione viene servita fino alle 10.00
K	87	l'albergo ha un parcheggio privato
K	88	il parcheggio sotterraneo
K	89	il parcheggio a più livelli
K	90	c'è un parcheggio nelle vicinanze
K	91	l'albergo è situato in una posizione tranquilla
K	92	è attrezzato per convegni
K	93	ha una sala convegni con una capienza di 100 persone
K	94	è situato vicino al centro della città
K	95	quanto dista l'albergo dall'aeroporto?
K	96	c'è un servizio d'autobus per l'aeroporto?
K	97	si trova solo a pochi minuti dal centro

K	98	si trova in una parte tranquilla della periferia
K	99	sul fiume
K	100	c'è l'ascensore
K	101	il portiere di notte
K	102	c'è un ufficio cambio
K	103	la presente per confermarVi la mia prenotazione
K	104	Vi prego inviarmi una copia del menù e la lista dei vini
K	105	Vi prego comunicarmi se è necessario versare un acconto
K	106	Vi prego inoltrare il conto alla mia azienda, la . . .
K	107	purtroppo sono costretto a cambiare la data della mia partenza
K	108	arriverò a . . . solo il 21 luglio
K	109	sono costretto a disdire la mia prenotazione presso il Vs. albergo

L — Immobili: vendita e affitto

L	1	vendesi casa
L	2	affittasi casa
L	3	l'appartamento
L	4	l'appartamento
L	5	il superattico
L	6	la villa
L	7	la villetta/il villino
L	8	il 'bungalow'
L	9	una unità di una villetta bifamiliare
L	10	la casa a schiera
L	11	2 camere da letto, soggiorno, cucina, servizi, garage, giardino
L	12	vorremmo affittare una casa per 18 mesi circa
L	13	Vi preghiamo comunicarci quanto costa affittare un appartamento simile
L	14	l'affitto è di . . . mensili
L	15	all'anno
L	16	se è disposto ad affittare l'appartamento per due anni
L	17	possiamo offrirLe uno sconto del . . . %
L	18	stiamo cercando dei locali ad uso ufficio nel centro della città

L 19 vorremmo acquistare un immobile nel centro della città
L 20 siamo disposti a pagare una cifra massima di . . .
L 21 in una posizione amena
L 22 in una zona residenziale
L 23 nella zona verde
L 24 per ulteriori informazioni rivolgersi a . . .
L 25 possibilità di mutuo
L 26 possibilità di prestito
L 27 al . . . % di interessi
L 28 senza interessi
L 29 per un affitto mensile di . . .
L 30 al prezzo di . . . al metro quadro
L 31 possiamo occuparci noi del mutuo
L 32 possiamo ottenere un prestito tramite la ns. compagnia di assicurazioni
L 33 abbiamo parecchie case-vacanze da vendere nella Francia meridionale
L 34 voli gratuiti per ispezionare le proprietà
L 35 la multiproprietà

M — Relazioni finanziarie

M 1 la riunione si terrà presso la sede principale della società
M 2 l'assemblea generale annuale
M 3 la ns. assemblea generale si terrà quest'anno il 3 luglio
M 4 l'assemblea ordinaria
M 5 è stata convocata una assemblea straordinaria
M 6 l'ordine del giorno dell'assemblea generale
M 7 eventuali discussioni sul verbale
M 8 varie ed eventuali
M 9 alla riunione erano presenti:
M 10 il direttore generale
M 11 il presidente
M 12 il direttore alle vendite
M 13 il direttore all'esportazione
M 14 il rappresentante estero
M 15 il direttore del personale
M 16 i rappresentanti degli operai

M	17	i membri del sindacato
M	18	gli azionisti
M	19	il consiglio di amministrazione
M	20	il verbale è stato redatto da . . .
M	21	il presidente ha dato il benvenuto agli azionisti
M	22	ed ha presentato la relazione sul bilancio dell'esercizio chiuso al . . .
M	23	ed ha presentato il verbale della riunione precedente
M	24	abbiamo aumentato la produzione
M	25	la produzione è aumentata
M	26	abbiamo aumentato la produzione del . . . % rispetto all'anno scorso
M	27	e creato nuovi posti di lavoro
M	28	il ns. fatturato è aumentato del . . . %
M	29	l'aumento del fatturato
M	30	abbiamo aumentato le esportazioni del . . . %
M	31	a seguito di un aumento degli investimenti
M	32	abbiamo fatto investimenti rilevanti nei ns. stabilimenti
M	33	abbiamo aumentato la ns. quota di mercato
M	34	i ns. prodotti hanno trovato facile sbocco in altri paesi europei
M	35	al fine di consolidare la ns. posizione sul mercato
M	36	dobbiamo sviluppare la ns. posizione sul mercato
M	37	il mercato estero
M	38	il mercato interno
M	39	i ns. maggiori mercati sono la Francia e l'Italia
M	40	c'è stata una svolta favorevole nelle ns. vendite in Germania
M	41	con vendite interne di . . .
M	42	le ns. vendite complessive sono aumentate da . . . a . . .
M	43	le ns. vendite complessive sono calate da . . . a . . .
M	44	prevediamo delle buone possibilità di vendita a lungo termine
M	45	abbiamo sfruttato in pieno la ns. capacità produttiva
M	46	dobbiamo mantenere il ns. primato in questo settore
M	47	il ns. programma di investimenti a lungo termine
M	48	ci permetterà di migliorare la qualità dei ns. prodotti
M	49	il ns. programma di sviluppo
M	50	a breve scadenza
M	51	a medio termine
M	52	prevediamo un incremento in tutti i settori della ns. attività
M	53	il ns. capitale fisso è aumentato del . . . %

M 54   il capitale preso a prestito
M 55   le ns. disponibilità liquide sono aumentate del . . . %
M 56   il capitale azionario dell'azienda è stato portato a . . .
M 57   il dividendo su ogni azione è stato portato a . . .
M 58   il ricavo
M 59   l'utile
M 60   l'utile netto
M 61   l'utile al netto di tasse
M 62   l'azienda ha aumentato i propri utili del . . . % nel primo trimestre
M 63   il tasso di incremento
M 64   la recessione economica generale
M 65   ha ridotto la richiesta
M 66   nel secondo semestre la richiesta è calata
M 67   e abbiamo avuto difficoltà nelle vendite
M 68   c'è stato un calo nella produzione
M 69   dobbiamo far fronte a un lieve calo della produzione
M 70   e le esportazioni sono diminuite
M 71   questo ha ridotto le ns. possibilità di incremento
M 72   l'aumento del costo dell'energia e delle materie prime
M 73   ha avuto un effetto negativo
M 74   è aumentata anche la concorrenza
M 75   a causa della concorrenza da parte di altre aziende del settore
M 76   la ns. competitività è diminuita
M 77   anche i costi del lavoro sono stati elevatissimi
M 78   l'azienda ha chiuso l'esercizio con una perdita complessiva di . . .
M 79   in alcuni settori le ns. perdite sono state particolarmente forti

N — Uso del telefono

N 1   vorrei parlare con il Sig . . .
N 2   rimanga in linea
N 3   la linea è occupata
N 4   Le passo la comunicazione
N 5   pronto

N 6 arrivederci
N 7 il Sig . . . non c'è in questo momento
N 8 vuole lasciare un messaggio?
N 9 può trasmettergli questo messaggio?
N 10 qui parla la segreteria telefonica
N 11 mi passi l'interno . . . per favore
N 12 chiamo da un telefono pubblico
N 13 riattacchi e rifaccia il numero
N 14 la chiamata urbana
N 15 la chiamata interurbana
N 16 la chiamata internazionale
N 17 la chiamata da addebitare al destinatario
N 18 vorrei fare una chiamata a . . . da addebitare al destinatario
N 19 vorrei fare una chiamata personale
N 20 l'elenco telefonico
N 21 dovrà cercare il numero sull'elenco
N 22 il servizio informazioni abbonati
N 23 vorrei sapere il numero della ditta . . .
N 24 vorrei sapere il prefisso di Manchester
N 25 la linea è disturbata
N 26 dovrò riattaccare
N 27 può chiamare direttamente
N 28 dovrò rifare il numero
N 29 ho fatto il numero sbagliato
N 30 ho un'interferenza con un'altra linea
N 31 è caduta la linea
N 32 il segnale di centrale
N 33 il segnale di occupato
N 34 deve tralasciare lo zero quando compone il numero
N 35 telefono dall'Inghilterra
N 36 richiamerò più tardi

O — Banca e ufficio postale

O 1 vorrei aprire un conto di risparmio
O 2 un conto corrente
O 3 un conto di deposito

O 4   un conto a più firme
O 5   è stato aperto un conto a Suo nome
O 6   qual è il tasso di interesse attuale?
O 7   a quanto ammontano le spese bancarie?
O 8   il libretto di assegni
O 9   l'ordine bancario
O 10   il mio conto è presso . . .
O 11   il numero del mio conto è . . .
O 12   ho un conto corrente postale
O 13   vorrei trasferire . . . sul mio conto
O 14   voglio chiudere il mio conto
O 15   voglio prelevare . . .
O 16   i prelevamenti di questa portata sono soggetti a un lieve ritardo
O 17   voglio versare . . . sul mio conto corrente
O 18   il Suo conto è scoperto
O 19   e il limite del Suo fido è di . . .
O 20   Lei ha superato ora questo limite
O 21   voglio incassare questo assegno
O 22   posso cambiare qui questi travellers' cheques?
O 23   vorrei versare questo assegno sul mio conto
O 24   vorrei un estratto conto
O 25   l'estratto conto viene inviato mensilmente
O 26   qual è il mio saldo attuale?
O 27   l'accredito
O 28   l'addebito
O 29   un prestito a lunga scadenza
O 30   a breve scadenza
O 31   l'intestatario
O 32   la cassa di risparmio
O 33   la società di credito edilizio
O 34   la carta di credito
O 35   la carta Eurocheque
O 36   cinque francobolli da . . . pence per favore
O 37   voglio spedire questo pacco in Francia
O 38   per via aerea
O 39   per via ordinaria
O 40   come pacco postale
O 41   per raccomandata
O 42   per espresso
O 43   deve compilare una dichiarazione doganale
O 44   vorrei inviare un telegramma a . . .
O 45   per telex

O 46 fermo posta
O 47 vorrei un vaglia postale da . . . sterline
O 48 Casella Postale numero . . .
O 49 Codice di Avviamento Postale

P — Assicurazioni

P 1 vorrei stipulare un contratto di assicurazione
P 2 l'assicurazione di persone
P 3 l'assicurazione immobiliare
P 4 la compagnia di assicurazioni
P 5 l'assicurato, il Sig . . . , ci ha pregato di . . .
P 6 ho inoltrato la Sua lettera all'ufficio risarcimenti
P 7 allego un certificato di copertura provvisoria
P 8 vorrei un modulo di proposta di assicurazione
P 9 riceverà la polizza fra poco
P 10 la polizza dovrà essere emessa dalla ns. sede centrale
P 11 trasmettiamo in allegato le condizioni di polizza
P 12 il numero della polizza è . . .
P 13 deve comunicarci il nominativo dell'assicurato
P 14 la durata della polizza è di . . .
P 15 vorrei rinnovare la mia polizza
P 16 ho disdetto la polizza
P 17 la somma assicurata è di . . .
P 18 il premio mensile è di . . .
P 19 l'assicurazione copre . . .
P 20 la richiesta di risarcimento
P 21 i danni
P 22 il caso fortuito
P 23 l'assicurazione contro gli incendi
P 24 l'assicurazione auto
P 25 l'assicurazione contro terzi
P 26 l'assicurazione contro tutti i rischi
P 27 l'assicurazione di viaggi
P 28 deve avere la carta verde
P 29 deve denunciare l'incidente alla ns. sede centrale
P 30 deve ottenere i nominativi dei testimoni
P 31 l'assicurazione contro gli infortuni

P 32 l'assicurazione bagagli
P 33 l'assicurazione malattie
P 34 il broker di assicurazione/il mediatore di assicurazione

Q — Terminologia d'ufficio e informatica

Q 1 il classificatore
Q 2 lo schedario
Q 3 il dittafono
Q 4 la scrivania
Q 5 la telescrivente
Q 6 la macchina per scrivere a memoria elettronica
Q 7 il microcomputer
Q 8 il video
Q 9 l'elaboratore di testi
Q 10 la tastiera
Q 11 il tasto
Q 12 il terminale
Q 13 il floppy disc / il dischetto
Q 14 il disc drive unit / l'unità di pilotaggio dei dischi
Q 15 la banca dei dati
Q 16 la memoria
Q 17 il microcircuito integrato
Q 18 il microprocessore
Q 19 il calcolatore tascabile
Q 20 il correttore fluido
Q 21 il datario
Q 22 il fermaglio
Q 23 il punto
Q 24 la cucitrice
Q 25 il temperamatite
Q 26 l'affrancatrice
Q 27 il blocco per appunti
Q 28 il raccoglitore
Q 29 la stampante
Q 30 la copiatrice

Q 31 l'informatica / la tecnologia dell'informazione

Q 32 il viewdata / la videoinformazione

Q 33 il sistema è conforme alle norme internazionali sulle telecomunicazioni

Q 34 vi si può accedere per telefono dal vostro ufficio

Q 35 si può accedere all'elenco telefonico elettronico dal terminale

Q 36 un modem fornisce l'interfaccia con la rete di telecomunicazioni

Q 37 la comunicazione a due vie fra elaboratori

Q 38 il sistema comprende funzioni di messaggi e posta elettronici

Q 39 questo modello consente la fusione della posta elettronica

Q 40 il teletex

Q 41 il fax (l'apparecchio facsimile)

Q 42 questo sistema consente di collegare un elaboratore alla rete Telex

Q 43 comprende la funzione di chiamata e di risposta automatica

Q 44 trasmette messaggi fuori delle ore di punta

Q 45 la teleconferenza

Q 46 in linea

Q 47 (in) tempo reale

Q 48 Computer Aided Design (CAD) / la progettazione computerizzata

Q 49 Computer Aided Manufacture (CAM) / la produzione computerizzata

Q 50 Computer Aided Learning (CAL) / l'insegnamento computerizzato

Q 51 il sistema di editoria personale computerizzata

Q 52 il sistema esperto

Q 53 la banca dati

Q 54 la banca dati relazionale

Q 55 le informazioni vengono aggiornate quotidianamente

Q 56 il foglio elettronico

Q 57 i dati sono memorizzati sotto forma di archivi gestiti dal sistema

Q 58 i dati memorizzati sono organizzati in pagine numerate

Q 59 il disco può essere letto da qualsiasi elaboratore compatibile

Q 60 questo modello è IBM compatibile / compatibile con i modelli IBM

Q 61   questo modello utilizza il sistema MS-DOS e non è
       compatibile con il sistema PC-DOS
Q 62   compatibile
Q 63   il sistema operativo
Q 64   i messaggi di errore
Q 65   il byte
Q 66   il kilobyte
Q 67   il megabyte
Q 68   questo modello ha 512K di memoria RAM
Q 69   la capacità del disco è di 1000K
Q 70   il software
Q 71   il pacchetto software
Q 72   questo pacchetto viene fornito su disco
Q 73   la configurazione può essere adattata alle vostre esigenze
Q 74   ed è disponibile una versione italiana
Q 75   il programma ha un menù comandato dal cursore
Q 76   il cursore può essere spostato utilizzando il mouse
Q 77   la penna elettronica
Q 78   il disco del sistema
Q 79   il disco di lavoro
Q 80   a doppia faccia
Q 81   a doppia densità
Q 82   è necessario formattare il disco
Q 83   un disco da 3,5 pollici
Q 84   l'indice del disco
Q 85   il sotto-indice
Q 86   il disco sorgente
Q 87   il disco destinazione
Q 88   la copia di riserva
Q 89   l'archivio può essere copiato dal disco A al disco B
Q 90   il programma è protetto
Q 91   spostare testo
Q 92   cancellare testo
Q 93   aggiungere testo
Q 94   esiste un dizionario per la verifica e la correzione
       dell'ortografia
Q 95   fondere archivi
Q 96   il testo può essere inviato direttamente alla stampante
Q 97   l'hardware
Q 98   il personal computer
Q 99   il minicomputer
Q 100 il mainframe / il processore centrale
Q 101 il floppy disk / il dischetto

Q 102	il disco rigido
Q 103	CD ROM
Q 104	il videodisco
Q 105	le periferiche
Q 106	il monitor monocromatico
Q 107	il monitor a colori
Q 108	il monitor a cristalli liquidi
Q 109	il monitor al plasma
Q 110	lo schermo visualizza 25 righe di 80 caratteri
Q 111	la stampante parallela
Q 112	la stampante seriale
Q 113	la stampante ad aghi
Q 114	la stampante a margherita
Q 115	la stampante a laser
Q 116	la serie di caratteri
Q 117	la testina di stampa
Q 118	il caricatore di carta
Q 119	il coperchio per stampante insonorizzato
Q 120	un plotter / un tracer / uno strumento per tracciare disegni grafici
Q 121	uno scanner / un lettore a scansione
Q 122	di qualità lettera
Q 123	il nastro è facile da cambiare
Q 124	un basso livello di rumore
Q 125	il contratto di manutenzione
Q 126	la manutenzione preventiva
Q 127	eventuali parti logore o difettose saranno sostituite gratuitamente
Q 128	la regolazione
Q 129	a condizione che la macchina sia ispezionata regolarmente
Q 130	l'hardware non può essere riparato sul posto
Q 131	il disco rigido è danneggiato
Q 132	il guasto è stato causato da un abbassamento della tensione
Q 133	l'avaria è stata causata da un difetto software
Q 134	l'alimentazione elettrica
Q 135	il manuale per l'utente
Q 136	il componente
Q 137	l'involucro
Q 138	il registratore a cassetta non era collegato all'elaboratore
Q 139	il tasto funzione era fuori uso
Q 140	avreste dovuto elencare il contenuto del disco

Q 141 questo apparecchio fax trasmette normalmente una pagina
formato A4 in meno di 12 secondi
Q 142 la stazione di lavoro è guasta
Q 143 il guasto è nel processore a 16 bits
Q 144 il processore dovrebbe pilotare fino a 8 stazioni di lavoro
Q 145 l'utente non sapeva che il servizio non era gratuito
Q 146 la commutazione di pacchetti

R — Nomi di nazioni e città

R   1   Aquisgrana
R   2   Africa
R   3   Alessandria d'Egitto
R   4   Algeria
R   5   Algeri
R   6   Amsterdam
R   7   Anversa
R   8   Argentina
R   9   Arnhem
R 10   Asia
R 11   Atene
R 12   Australia
R 13   Austria
R 14   Avignone
R 15   Baden–Baden
R 16   Baghdad
R 17   Bahrein
R 18   Barcellona
R 19   Basilea
R 20   Bayreuth
R 21   Beirut
R 22   Belfast
R 23   Belgio
R 24   Belgrado
R 25   Berlino
R 26   Berna
R 27   Bilbao
R 28   Bochum

R	29	Bolivia
R	30	Bombay
R	31	Bonn
R	32	Bordeaux
R	33	Brasilia
R	34	Brasile
R	35	Bregenz
R	36	Brema
R	37	Bremerhaven
R	38	Brunswick
R	39	Bruxelles
R	40	Bucarest
R	41	Budapest
R	42	Bulgaria
R	43	Buenos Aires
R	44	Cadice
R	45	Il Cairo
R	46	Canada
R	47	Isole Canarie
R	48	Città del Capo
R	49	Ciad
R	50	Cile
R	51	Cina
R	52	Colonia
R	53	Colombia
R	54	Costanza
R	55	Copenaghen
R	56	Cordoba
R	57	Corinto
R	58	Costa Rica
R	59	Cuba
R	60	Cecoslovacchia
R	61	Damasco
R	62	Delhi
R	63	Danimarca
R	64	Digione
R	65	Giacarta
R	66	Dortmund
R	67	Dresda
R	68	Dubai
R	69	Dublino
R	70	Dunkerque
R	71	Düsseldorf

R	**72**	Ecuador
R	**73**	Edimburgo
R	**74**	C.E.E.
R	**75**	Egitto
R	**76**	Eindhoven
R	**77**	Inghilterra
R	**78**	Erfurt
R	**79**	Etiopia
R	**80**	Europa
R	**81**	Isole Falkland
R	**82**	Finlandia
R	**83**	Firenze
R	**84**	Francia
R	**85**	Francoforte
R	**86**	Friburgo
R	**87**	Danzica
R	**88**	Ginevra
R	**89**	Genova
R	**90**	Ghana
R	**91**	Giessen
R	**92**	Gotha
R	**93**	Gottinga
R	**94**	Graz
R	**95**	Gran Bretagna
R	**96**	Grecia
R	**97**	Groninga
R	**98**	Guyana
R	**99**	L'Aia
R	**100**	Halle
R	**101**	Amburgo
R	**102**	Hannover
R	**103**	L'Avana
R	**104**	Heidelberg
R	**105**	Helsinki
R	**106**	Olanda
R	**107**	Honduras
R	**108**	Ungheria
R	**109**	Islanda
R	**110**	India
R	**111**	Indonesia
R	**112**	Innsbruck
R	**113**	Interlaken
R	**114**	Iran

R 115	Iraq
R 116	Irlanda
R 117	Israele
R 118	Istanbul
R 119	Italia
R 120	Costa d'Avorio
R 121	Giamaica
R 122	Giappone
R 123	Jena
R 124	Gerusalemme
R 125	Giordania
R 126	Kaiserslautern
R 127	Karl-Marx-Stadt (Chemnitz)
R 128	Karlsruhe
R 129	Kassel
R 130	Kiel
R 131	Kitzbühel
R 132	Klagenfurt
R 133	Coblenza
R 134	Cracovia
R 135	Losanna
R 136	Libano
R 137	Lipsia
R 138	Libia
R 139	Lilla
R 140	Lima
R 141	Linz
R 142	Lisbona
R 143	Lubiana
R 144	Londra
R 145	Lubecca
R 146	Lucerna
R 147	Lugano
R 148	Lussemburgo
R 149	Lione
R 150	Maastricht
R 151	Magdeburg
R 152	Magonza
R 153	Malaysia
R 154	Malta
R 155	Mannheim
R 156	Marsiglia
R 157	La Mecca

R 158	Messico
R 159	Città del Messico
R 160	Milano
R 161	Monaco
R 162	Montevideo
R 163	Montreux
R 164	Marocco
R 165	Mosca
R 166	Monaco
R 167	Münster
R 168	Napoli
R 169	Paesi Bassi
R 170	Nuova Delhi
R 171	New York
R 172	Nuova Zelanda
R 173	Nicaragua
R 174	Nizza
R 175	Irlanda del Nord
R 176	Norvegia
R 177	Norimberga
R 178	Oslo
R 179	Ostenda
R 180	Padova
R 181	Panama
R 182	Paraguay
R 183	Parigi
R 184	Passavia
R 185	Pechino
R 186	Perù
R 187	Filippine
R 188	Il Pireo
R 189	Polonia
R 190	Portogallo
R 191	Praga
R 192	Qatar
R 193	Recife
R 194	Reykjavik
R 195	Riyadh
R 196	Rio de Janeiro
R 197	Roma
R 198	Rostock
R 199	Rotterdam
R 200	Romania

R 201	Russia
R 202	Saarbrücken
R 203	San Petersburgo (Leningrado)
R 204	Salisburgo
R 205	Sardegna
R 206	Arabia Saudita
R 207	Scozia
R 208	Siviglia
R 209	Sicilia
R 210	Singapore
R 211	Sudafrica
R 212	America Meridionale
R 213	Corea del Sud
R 214	Spagna
R 215	Spalato
R 216	Steyr
R 217	Stoccolma
R 218	Strasburgo
R 219	Stoccarda
R 220	Svezia
R 221	Svizzera
R 222	Siria
R 223	Tangeri
R 224	Teheran
R 225	Tel Aviv
R 226	Thailandia
R 227	L'Aia
R 228	Salonicco
R 229	Tokyo
R 230	Toronto
R 231	Tolone
R 232	Tolosa
R 233	Treviri
R 234	Tripoli
R 235	Tunisi
R 236	Tunisia
R 237	Torino
R 238	Turchia
R 239	Ulma
R 240	Emirati Arabi Uniti
R 241	Regno Unito
R 242	Stati Uniti d'America
R 243	Utrecht

R 244 Vancouver
R 245 Venezuela
R 246 Venezia
R 247 Vienna
R 248 Galles
R 249 Varsavia
R 250 Weimar
R 251 Antille
R 252 Wismar
R 253 Wolfsburg
R 254 Iugoslavia
R 255 Zagrabia
R 256 Saragozza
R 257 Zurigo
R 258 Zwickau

S — Abbreviazioni

S   **1**   conto
S   **2**   F.lli
S   **3**   C.ia
S   **4**   presso
S   **5**   dozz.
S   **6**   ed.
S   **7**   E.E.
S   **8**   p.e.
S   **9**   all.
S   **10**   ecc.
S   **11**   cioè
S   **12**   c.m.
S   **13**   S.r.l.
S   **14**   p.p.
S   **15**   I.V.A.

Indice